TOTAL
COMMUNICATION

A Signed Speech Program for Nonverbal Children

Benson Schaeffer
Arlene Musil
George Kollinzas

RESEARCH PRESS
2612 North Mattis Avenue
Champaign, Illinois 61820

Benson Schaeffer dedicates this book to his mother, Gilda; his father, Charles; and his brother, Morton.

Arlene Musil dedicates this book to her father, William, who greatly inspired her; her mother, Mary, who continually supports her; and her brother, Bill, who provides her with scholarly encouragement.

George Kollinzas dedicates this book to his family: his parents, Jeanne and Dean, and the rest of the crew, Maria, Margaret, Peter, Paul, Elaine, and Kathy.

Contents

Introduction   ix

1 Overview of Total Communication: The Signed Speech Program   1

       SIGN LANGUAGE   11

2 The First Sign: A Request Expressing a Desire   13

    I. Components of a sign   13
    II. The initial sign   14
    III. Two examples: Tommy learns "popcorn";
       Sam learns "game"   15
    IV. Prompts   18
    V. Errors   22
    VI. Reinforcement   23
    VII. Mastery criterion   23

3 The Second Sign: Part Request and Part Description   25

    I. The second sign   26
    II. Example: Tim learns to request and describe "drink"   27
    III. Errors   29
    IV. Focusing on the object   30
    V. Focusing on relevant characteristics   31
    VI. Building a vocabulary   32

4 The First Multisign Request: "(Child) want x"   35

    I. The multisign request: "(Child) want x"   36
    II. Errors   38
    III. Building a vocabulary   39
    IV. Mastery criterion   39

5 The Signs "No," "Help," "Potty," and "Yes"   41

I. Conversion of natural movements into signs 42
II. The refusal "no" 42
III. The requests "help" and "potty" 45
IV. Teaching strategies 49
V. Mastery criterion 50
VI. The affirmation "yes" 50

SPEECH PRODUCTION 53

6 Initial Speech Sounds: Verbal Imitation Training 55

I. Components of a sound: Vowels and consonants, voicing, articulation 56
II. The first sound 57
III. The second and later sounds 58
IV. Example: Lance's initial sounds 59
V. Prompts 67
VI. Errors 73
VII. Reinforcement 73
VIII. Mastery criterion 73

7 Combinations of Sounds: Syllables and Words 75

I. Teaching strategies 76
II. Example: Joe learns the syllable "pem" 80
III. Building a vocabulary 81
IV. Two sample vocabularies 83
V. Imitation after the teacher 85
VI. Continued development and refinement 87
VII. Continued instructional support 91

SIGNED SPEECH 93

8 Signed Speech: Integration of Signs and Words 95

I. Critical speech skills: Imitation and pronunciation 96
II. Facilitating the initiation of Signed Speech 97
III. Teaching strategies 97
IV. Stuttering errors 104
V. Building a vocabulary 106
VI. Duration of Signed Speech instruction 106

9 Verbal Language: Fading Signs from Signed Speech 107

I. Facilitating the fading of signs 107

vi

II. Teaching strategies 108
III. Complicated utterances and new concepts 113

LINGUISTIC FUNCTIONS 115

10 Reference: A New Linguistic Function 117

I. The Reference function 118
II. Single-sign reference: Answering "What is this?" 118
III. Example: Jimmy learns single-sign reference 120
IV. The reference statement: "This x" 122
V. Example: John learns the reference statement 124
VI. Encouraging initiated reference 125
VII. Example: Jimmy initiates reference 126
VIII. Teaching strategies 127
IX. Mastery criteria 129

11 Person Concepts I: Names of People and Possession 131

I. Names of people: "Who is this?" 132
II. Possession: "Whose x is this?" 138
III. Discrimination between names as labels
and as possessive terms 144
IV. Person concepts in order of difficulty 145
V. Errors 146
VI. Teaching strategies 147
VII. Mastery criteria 149

12 Person Concepts II: Actions, Emotions, Social Greetings,
Direct Address, and Calling 151

I. Actions 151
II. Emotions: Happy, sad, angry, tired 155
III. Social greetings: "Hi" and "Bye-bye" 158
IV. Direct address 159
V. Calling a person by name 159
VI. Teaching strategies 160

13 Inquiry I: Language-guided Search for Hidden Objects 163

I. Searching for hidden objects on command 163
II. Mastery criteria 168

14 Inquiry II: Answering and Asking Questions about Location 169

I. Question-answering: "In" and "on" 169

  II. Question-asking: "Where is x?" and "What is this?"   174
  III. Lesson variety   176
  IV. Mastery criteria   176

15 Abstraction I: "I," "My," "Your," "No," and "Yes"   179

  I. The personal subject: "I"   180
  II. Personal possessives: "My" and "your"   180
  III. Affirmations and denials: "Yes" and "no"   182

16 Abstraction II: Initial Sight-Reading and Number Skills   185

  I. Initial sight reading   185
  II. Initial number skills   189

CLASSROOM MANAGEMENT   193

17 Classroom Management I: Eye Contact, Sitting Still,
Problem Behaviors, and Activity Labels   195

  I. Eye contact   195
  II. Sitting still   199
  III. Problem behaviors   200
  IV. Special issues in punishment   206
  V. Activity labels   210

18 Classroom Management II: Daily Schedule, Data Collection,
and Staff and Parent Training   213

  I. Daily schedule: Language lessons   213
  II. Daily schedule: Nonlanguage lessons   216
  III. Data collection   220
  IV. Staff and parent training   229

19 Sign Glossary   233

About the Authors   262

Introduction

Total Communication: The Signed Speech Program for Nonverbal Children is designed to promote the development of spontaneous sign language, spontaneous Signed Speech, and spontaneous verbal language. The terms *Signed Speech* and *Total Communication* refer to the simultaneous use of signs and words and to the teaching techniques associated with their production. "Signed Speech" is the simultaneous production of signs and words by nonverbal children *or* their teachers; "Total Communication" typically means the simultaneous production of signs and words by teachers. The instructional procedures specified here are designed to foster spontaneous communication: to help nonverbal children to use language as freely and creatively as possible. We say "foster" rather than "teach" because spontaneity cannot be taught. Although this program presents methods for systematic, rigorous, and intensive instruction, it is directed at more than mere mastery of some preestablished criterion. The Signed Speech Program is geared to develop maximally spontaneous language that will allow the children to communicate what, when, where, how, why, and to whom they wish.

We understand that a steady focus on spontaneity is difficult to maintain, especially given the pressures on the teacher that the need for a well-organized and smoothly running classroom imposes. We feel, however, that maintenance of spontaneous communication is absolutely necessary. Many verbal concepts and skills, even quite complex ones, can be taught to nonverbal children if broken into small enough parts and taught separately, then slowly integrated. The major problem is that the children typically use these verbal concepts and skills only in a rote, mechanical fashion and tend not to generalize them to new situations. For them to learn a more spontaneous use of language, they must be shown that language is personally meaningful, that it is their own personal tool for communication and expression.

The Signed Speech Program maximizes spontaneity through instruction in sign language and speech and through careful sequencing of linguistic content. Signing promotes spontaneity: nonverbal children who are taught sign language will use it spontaneously for much the same purposes that normal children use speech. Some children later add words or word approximations to their signs, and some of them move from simultaneous signs and words to words alone. (Because of differing abilities and histories, of course, not every child achieves the goal of spontaneous verbal language.) The Signed Speech Program first fosters spontaneous sign language, then spontaneous Signed Speech, and finally spontaneous verbal language. It follows a developmental sequence which roughly parallels the linguistic development of normal children.

In the chapters which follow, we present in detail the instructional methods and content sequences of the Signed Speech Program. If you follow these guidelines, the nonverbal child with whom you work will begin communicating spontaneously, first in signs, and later, perhaps, in Signed Speech and words. It is important to remember to always adapt the program to the child, not the child to the program. Only by following each child's interests and the particular developmental paths he takes will you be able to promote maximally spontaneous communication of personal value to him.

1

Overview of Total Communication: The Signed Speech Program

The Signed Speech Program is a sign language and verbal language acquisition program for nonverbal children that focuses on and promotes spontaneous communication. It is appropriate for profoundly retarded, severely retarded, trainable retarded, autistic, emotionally disturbed, severely and moderately language delayed, preschool developmentally delayed, and aphasic nonverbal children. Depending on the capability of the child, the intensity of instruction, and the setting, the program can be used for a 2- to 6-year language education. It has been field tested with approximately forty-five children from the categories just mentioned (Schaeffer, Musil, Kollinzas, & McDowell, 1977; Kollinzas & Musil, 1978). The program is designed, first, to maximize sign spontaneity; second, to maximize the probability that a child will move from spontaneous signing to spontaneous Signed Speech (that is, simultaneously produced signs and words), and then to spontaneous verbal language; and finally, to capitalize on the similarity between the spontaneous signing of nonverbal children and the spontaneous speech of normal children.

The goal of Signed Speech instruction is spontaneous spoken language, spontaneous Signed Speech, or spontaneous sign language. The program specifies teaching techniques, lesson content, and sequential structure. Children are taught sign language and verbal imitation (speech) as independent skills at the beginning of training and then gradually learn to use their sign language spontaneously. They have learned spontaneity when they sign unbidden, sign in new situations, sign egocentrically to themselves, sign completely novel, untaught utterances, and learn new signs incidentally. Like normal children, these children spontaneously request objects and activities in sign, describe aspects of their world, initiate social interactions, and occasionally carry on conversations, ask questions, and use signs in symbolic play (Schaeffer, 1978).

After several months of spontaneous signing, many children on their own begin to add verbal approximations to their signs. They are then taught to sign and speak simultaneously—that is, to use Signed Speech—and they soon learn to sign and speak at the same time even more spontaneously than they had previously signed without speaking. Over a period of months, the spontaneity of their signs transfers to and becomes so much a part of their speech that they begin occasionally to speak without signing. At this point, their teachers begin instruction in speaking without signing, and the children continue on their own to extend and refine their verbal language. Figure 1 presents a visual overview of the Signed Speech Program in terms of both utterance modes and linguistic functions.

In the remainder of this chapter, we describe the guidelines on which the Signed Speech Program is based and the linguistic functions it teaches (Figure 2 presents an outline of the Program). The guidelines are general rules for teaching spontaneous language: they broadly specify technique, content, and sequence. We also present a hierarchic view of the language concepts and skills the program teaches.

To maximize the spontaneity that sign instruction fosters, the Signed Speech Program follows eight guidelines.

1. Begin with the expression of desires. Teach the child to express his desires for objects and activities. This promotes spontaneity in a number of important ways. First, it focuses on the child's personal desires, interests, and knowledge; second, it teaches the child that through language he can achieve his own personal ends; third, it teaches the child an early and very basic linguistic function, the expression of desires; and fourth, it helps the teacher individualize instruction.

2. Deemphasize imitation and receptive language. In so doing, you keep the child from being constrained by the compliance and nonuse of language that such instruction may foster. An overemphasis on imitation may teach him to mimic the teacher rather than act on his own, to imitate language rather than try to understand it: this may inhibit spontaneous communication. We recommend that signs be taught by molding (or shaping) before imitative prompts (modeled signs) are introduced, and that complete imitative prompts (completely modeled signs) be reduced to partial imitative prompts as soon as possible. Partial prompts involve the child actively by forcing him to reconstruct the complete sign. Finally, since instruction in expressive language is necessarily also instruction in receptive language, we suggest teaching only expressive language until more complex linguistic functions such as Person Concepts and Inquiry are introduced.

3. Use structured waiting. After teaching the child to sign for desired objects and activities through molding, you should remove

Figure 1 The Signed Speech Program

TIME	UTTERANCE MODE		LINGUISTIC
	Verbal	Sign	FUNCTION
	Imitation	Language	*Expression of Desires*

Expression of Desires
Requesting desired objects and activities: "What do you want?" "Tommy want x."
No as rejection: "Do you want x?" "No."

Reference
Labeling objects: "What is this?" "This x."

Person Concepts
Names: "Who is this?" "This Benson."
Possession: "Whose x is this?" "This Benson x."
Actions: "What is Tommy doing?" "Tommy walking."
Emotions: "How does Arlene feel?" "Arlene happy."
Social greetings: "Hi George"; "Bye-bye Pete."

Signed Speech

Inquiry
Language and search: "Where is x?" "In cup." "What is in the cup?" "X in cup."
Question-answering and -asking: "Who is walking?" "George walking." "What is this?" asked by the child.

[fade signs]
Speech

Abstraction
Personal pronouns: "I want x" replaces "Tommy want x"; "Whose x is this?" "This (my/your) x."
Truth-value: "Is this an x?" "(Yes/No)."
Sight reading
Number skills

3

molding cues one by one and wait for the child to produce an increasingly more complete sign on his own. Molding provides the child with rote information, and waiting frustrates him into producing the complete sign by himself.

4. Foster self-correction. The child's rephrasing of utterances and changing of topics in midstream constitutes self-correction. Fostering this habit teaches him an important aspect of spontaneity.

5. Avoid associating communication with punishment. Punishment for communication errors conditions fear of language, disorganizes the processing of complex linguistic concepts and constructions, and thus lowers a child's language potential.

6. Provide indirect information. In other words, use the Grant's Tomb technique: "Who is buried in Grant's tomb?" For example, a child who cannot answer the question "What do you want?" can be given indirect information by the question "Do you want the x?" Providing indirect information to guide the child's answer facilitates the incidental learning of language.

7. Reward spontaneity and include it in the mastery criteria. Since the goal of instruction is spontaneous communication, it is important to reward the child for signing spontaneously and to explicitly include spontaneity in the criteria for mastery. Rewards increase the probability that the child will continue to sign spontaneously.

Signs are not considered mastered until the child uses them in situations away from the original teaching situation and in the absence of the objects or activities to which they refer. From this point of view, manipulative signing to escape a difficult situation and overgeneralization of a sign to an inappropriate object or activity are considered forms of spontaneity and deserve an occasional reward.

8. Teach Signed English using Total Communication. Signed English is a system of signing that mirrors spoken English. It has the same word order and specifies one sign for every word. We recommend basing instruction on *Signing Exact English* (with supplements) by Gustason, Pfetzing, and Zawalkow (1980) and *The Signed English Dictionary* by Bornstein, Hamilton, Saulnier, and Roy (1975). The sign glossary in this book (Chapter 19) is drawn from these versions of Signed English.

The teacher's use of Total Communication facilitates the transition from signs to Signed Speech to speech by teaching the child the associations between signs and words. To maximize the probability that the child will learn to communicate in spontaneous Signed Speech, the Signed Speech Program follows six guidelines (Schaeffer, 1980).

1. Teach Signed English using Total Communication. Instruction in Signed English through Total Communication (the simultaneous use of signs and words by teachers) helps the child move from spontaneous sign language to spontaneous Signed Speech. Signed English has the same syntax as spoken English; Total Communication teaches the child to associate signs and words and models the simultaneous production of signs and words.

2. **Teach both sign language and speech production.** At the beginning, teach sign language and speech production as separate skills in separate verbal imitation and sign language sessions. A child is more likely to add speech to his signs if he is taught speech production as well as sign language, but these should be taught as independent skills so he can integrate them on his own when he is ready. Early attempts to teach simultaneous production would confuse and frustrate him.

Because speaking is harder for the typical nonverbal child than signing, the major determinant of whether or not he will move from sign language to Signed Speech is the strength, flexibility, and creativity of his speech skills. It is therefore important to teach him speech through verbal imitation before he initiates Signed Speech and to continue speech instruction both while he is learning, and after he has mastered, Signed Speech.

3. **Teach the child to imitate your speech sounds after you complete them and to pronounce sign words.** The child's ability to imitate the teacher's sounds *after* the teacher completes them, rather than echo the teacher *while* he speaks, is a crucial factor in the initiation of Signed Speech.

4. **Prompt Signed Speech by speaking as the child signs and by maintaining syllable-sign-movement correspondences.** Speak the corresponding word as the child produces a sign. This helps the child learn the associations between signs and words and encourages him to begin speaking as he signs. When doing this, it is important to maintain syllable-sign-movement correspondences, that is, to say one syllable with each of the child's sign movements and to teach the child to produce exactly as many movements as there are syllables in the word. This will emphasize the connection between signs and words.

5. **Wait for the child to initiate Signed Speech.** The child is the best judge of when he is ready to add words to his signs. The teacher should wait for him to initiate Signed Speech before beginning to teach it.

6. **Place gradually increasing pressure on the spoken words of Signed Speech, lagging a little behind the child.** The preceding five guidelines are general rules for increasing the likelihood that the child will initiate Signed Speech. This guideline describes how to teach Signed Speech after the child initiates it. It is important to increase instructional pressure on the spoken words of the child's Signed Speech gradually. Speaking is difficult for the child to learn—much more dif-

ficult than signing—and is easily disrupted. Therefore, the instructor should always lag a little bit behind the pupil. The child's own initiation of improvement in his Signed Speech is the best indicator that he is ready for an increase in instructional pressure.

This guideline suggests a natural instructional sequence. The teacher first differentially reinforces Signed Speech with larger rewards than for signs alone. Then he prompts the child to speak while signing—without, however, introducing negative reinforcement for not speaking. After this he uses structured waiting to prompt the child into Signed Speech: that is, he does not reward the child until he speaks as he signs. The instructor then introduces explicit say-and-sign Signed Speech lessons. Lastly, but only after the child is consistently producing relatively clearly articulated Signed Speech, the instructor interrupts ongoing Signed Speech to teach the child to pronounce the words more clearly and to maintain tighter syllable-sign-movement correspondences.

After children have used Signed Speech for several months, many begin fading the signs from their Signed Speech and begin speaking without signing. To maximize the probability that this will happen, the Signed Speech Program follows three guidelines.

1. **Strengthen the speech skills necessary for verbal language by teaching the child to speak loudly and quickly.** When a child begins speaking without signing, he occasionally speaks more softly and slowly than he did when he also signed and loses his train of thought. He is more reserved because he no longer has his signs as speech supports. The teacher can help the child overcome his speaking difficulties by teaching him to speak more loudly and quickly.

2. **Wait for the child to initiate verbal language.** As with Signed Speech, it is important to wait for the child to initiate spoken language before teaching it.

3. **Gradually increase the instructional pressure on spoken language, lagging a little behind the child.** First remove the signing requirement, and then tell the child not to sign and prevent him from signing. Again, always lag a little behind the child.

The Signed Speech Program capitalizes on the similarity between the spontaneous language of previously nonverbal children and the spontaneous language of normal children by sequencing linguistic functions for instruction in approximately the same order that normal children acquire those functions. Thus, we now outline the order in which normal children acquire linguistic functions and the order in which the Signed Speech Program teaches them. We also discuss the relationships between the two orders, although a full treatment of the correspondence between the language of nonverbal mentally handi-

capped and normal children and the implications for language programs is beyond the scope of this overview (see Schaeffer, unpublished manuscript).

According to Halliday (1975) normal infants acquire linguistic functions in the following approximate order:

1. Instrumental ("I want that object.")
2. Regulatory ("I want that activity.")
3. Interactional ("Hi, you and me together.")
4. Personal (egocentric speech)
5. Reference (simple naming)
6. Heuristic ("What is that?")
7. Imaginative (pretend-play)
8. Conversation

The first four functions do not appear to emerge in a particular order. During months twelve to fifteen, normal children express the Reference function in their first actual spoken words by simply naming objects, and around age two they acquire the last three functions.

The linguistic functions in the Signed Speech Program and the order in which they are taught are as follows:

1. Expression of Desires (requesting objects and activities)
2. Reference (labeling, naming, describing)
3. Person Concepts (using names of people, expressing emotions, using direct address)
4. Inquiry (asking and answering search-related questions)
5. Abstraction (learning pronouns, yes-no truth values, sight reading, and number skills)

Expression of Desires refers to instruction of the nonverbal child in requesting desired objects (corresponding to the Instrumental function) and in requesting desired activities (corresponding to the Regulatory function).

Reference (or labeling) corresponds to the normal child's use of his first words. The Signed Speech Program teaches the nonverbal child labeling second because normal children learn to name with words only after learning to request with gestures and gesture-sound combinations.

Person Concepts include the use of people's names, people's names as possessive terms, human actions, emotions, and direct address by name. Instruction in Person Concepts teaches the nonverbal child the most important concepts and skills of the Interactional function (which includes more concepts and skills than can be completely taught). The Signed Speech Program teaches Person Concepts third because the social interactions demanded by these concepts are actually inhibited by early instruction and also because the nonverbal child needs to know about naming (or Reference) before he can use Person Concepts. Inquiry includes language-guided search for objects, answering questions related to location of objects, and asking search-related questions. It teaches the nonverbal child important parts of the Heuristic function (which is itself too broad to be completely taught). Abstraction refers to using language about language. The abstractions the Signed Speech Program teaches include personal pronouns, yes and no as answers to truth-value questions, initial sight reading, and initial number skills. The use of abstractions underlies the Imaginative and Conversation functions.

In summary, Figure 2 presents a detailed hierarchic outline of actual language concepts and skills taught in the Signed Speech Program. The chapters which follow detail instructional procedures for teaching most of the concepts and skills listed, and the sign glossary at the end of the book describes the signs used in the Signed Speech Program and those in the initial sign vocabulary suggested in Chapter 18.

REFERENCES

Bornstein, H., Hamilton, L. B., Saulnier, K. L., & Roy, H. L. (Eds.). *The Signed English dictionary: For preschool and elementary levels.* Washington, DC: Gallaudet College Press, 1975.

Gustason, G., Pfetzing, D., & Zawalkow, E. *Signing exact English: Revised and enlarged.* Rossmoor, CA: Modern Signs Press, 1980.

Halliday, M. A. K. *Learning how to mean.* London: Edward Arnold, 1975.

Kollinzas, G., & Musil, A. *Signed Speech curriculum guide.* Unpublished manuscript, 1978. (Available from Beaverton Schools, Dist. #48, P.O. Box 200, Beaverton, OR.)

Schaeffer, B. Teaching spontaneous sign language to nonverbal children: Theory and method. *Sign Language Studies*, 1978, *21*, 317-352.

Schaeffer, B. Teaching Signed Speech to nonverbal children: Theory and method. *Sign Language Studies*, 1980, *26*, 29-63.

Schaeffer, B. *Linguistic functions and language intervention.* Unpublished manuscript (Available from Neurological Sciences Center, Good Samaritan Hospital, 1015 N.W. 22nd Avenue, Portland, OR 97210.)

Schaeffer, B., Musil, A., Kollinzas, G., & McDowell, P. Spontaneous verbal language for autistic children through signed speech. *Sign Language Studies*, 1977, *17*, 287-328.

Sign Language

The sign language component of the Signed Speech Program specifies procedures for teaching the child to sign spontaneously requests which express his desires. The program begins with the Expression of Desires because this function relates to the child's personal interests and is hence the easiest to learn, and also because its use strongly fosters spontaneous communication. Chapter 2 describes methods for teaching the first sign; Chapter 3, methods for teaching the second and later signs; Chapter 4, methods for teaching the first multisign utterance; and Chapter 5, methods for teaching the signs "no," "help," "potty," and "yes." All initial signs are taught as requests which express desires. As the child learns these signs, he also learns his first linguistic function, and as he expresses his desires, he learns that language is a useful personal tool.

2

The First Sign: A Request Expressing a Desire

I. Components of a sign

II. The initial sign

III. Two examples: Tommy learns "popcorn" Sam learns "game"

IV. Prompts

V. Errors

VI. Reinforcement

VII. Mastery criterion

The initial sign you teach enables the child to express a desire by making a request. Therefore, it should stand for a strongly desired food, activity, toy, or other object. Signs for foods and activities are often easiest to teach. In choosing the sign, first ask the child's parents what foods he likes to eat, what simple games he likes to play, what activities he likes to engage in, what toys he likes to play with, and what objects he is interested in. Or you may see what the child prefers by offering him various foods and play activities and seeing which ones he chooses.

I. COMPONENTS OF A SIGN. The three components of a sign are position, hand shape, and final movement. The production of a sign begins with placing the hand(s) in the correct position in relation to the body (such as in front of the mouth) and then forming the shape of the sign. It ends with the final movement of the hands. Each component is stressed at a different stage.

13

A. **Final movement.** This is typically stressed first: the teacher places the child's hands in the proper position and teaches the child to produce the final movement.

B. **Position of the hands in relation to the body.** This is typically stressed only after the child is able to produce the final movement spontaneously.

C. **Hand shape.** This is usually stressed last; precision of hand shape in sign, analogous to clarity of articulation in speech, is best taught after an imprecise but spontaneous sign has been established. We describe the signs to which we refer in this and other chapters in the sign glossary (Chapter 19).

II. **THE INITIAL SIGN.**

A. **Molding.** This is the best technique with which to start teaching the child the initial sign(s). To mold, grasp the child's hands and form them into and through the sign. Teach the child to sign with his dominant hand, the hand with which he most often reaches for desired objects, pushes away undesired objects, and touches people.

Present the desired object or activity. When the child reaches for it, leans forward, opens his mouth in anticipation, or otherwise indicates his desire, mold his hands into and through the sign as you verbalize the corresponding word. Praise the child with the signed and spoken statement "Good signing" and give him what he has "requested."

B. **Fading assistance.** As the child gradually begins signing spontaneously, fade your assistance, or molding—first from the final movement, then from hand positioning, and finally from hand shaping.

1. *Final movement.* Place the child's hands in position, shape them, and mold the child through the final movement. Then position and shape his hands and wait for him to produce the final movement by himself.

2. *Position of the hands in relation to the body.* After you have positioned the child's hands for him many times, wait for him to position them by himself.

3. *Hand shape.* Finally, work on the precision (or clarity) of the hand shape. Prompt increasingly more accurate versions of the original spontaneous, but crude, approxima-

tions to the sign. Use prompts generously while initially teaching the child to shape his hands, and then, as the child improves, gradually fade them.

III. **TWO EXAMPLES: TOMMY LEARNS "POPCORN"; SAM LEARNS "GAME."** When you teach the initial sign, you should capitalize on the child's desires, base your instruction on the child's natural reaching movements, and accept approximations. To give you a more concrete impression of what takes place as the first sign is taught and to stress the importance of the child's desires, natural reaching movements, and sign approximations, we present the following examples.

A. **"Popcorn": Tommy's first sign.** Tommy and his teacher, Arlene, sat on chairs facing one another: Tommy's chair was taller than Arlene's so that their eyes were on the same level; Arlene held him between her knees to keep him in his chair. She began instruction by showing Tommy a piece of popcorn. He looked at it, opened his mouth in anticipation, and reached for it with his hand. As he began to reach, Arlene molded his hand through the sign for popcorn. She thus converted the natural reaching movement that expressed his desire into a sign.

The sign for popcorn that Arlene helped Tommy produce consisted of his rotating the horizontally outstretched index finger of his right hand in the space between his upper lip and his nose. As Arlene repeatedly molded him through the sign, two phenomena became evident. First, there was some resistance: Tommy occasionally resisted Arlene's efforts to move his hand. Second, there was anticipation: over the course of many trials Tommy began to anticipate and cooperate with Arlene's molding. He began to place his hands in the proper places for her to mold him through the successive sign components.

At this point, Arlene began teaching Tommy to produce the final movement spontaneously—in this case to rotate his index finger on his own. She showed him the popcorn. When he reached for it, she positioned his hand in the space above his upper lip and shaped his hand into an outstretched index finger and fist. She did not mold him through the final movement of turning the index finger; rather, she waited for him to rotate his finger on his own. Her waiting frustrated his desire to obtain the popcorn he expected, and his frustration prompted him to produce the final movement spontaneously. We call this "structured waiting." Structured waiting is the technique of helping a child form part of the sign and then waiting for his frustration to prompt him to produce the rest of it spontaneously. This technique is useful with both simple and complex concepts, for it prompts problem solving, an important component of spontaneity.

After Tommy regularly produced the final movement of the "popcorn" sign spontaneously, Arlene used structured waiting to teach him to put his hands into the proper position for signing by himself: she gradually stopped moving his hand all the way up to the space in front of his upper lip. She began fading her assistance by first lifting his hand only as far as his chin and then waiting for him to move it the rest of the way and produce the final movement. Then she lifted his hand only as far as his chest, and, finally, she did not lift his hand at all. When she first completely removed her assistance (by sitting on her hands), Tommy tried hard to pull her hands toward him. He seemed to want her to move his hand up to his chest before he completed the positioning and produced the final movement. He tired of his efforts to gain assistance when he found that she would not give him her hands, and he finally produced the entire sign by himself: position, hand shape, and final movement, in sequence.

It is important to note the imprecision of Tommy's hand shape and his production of sign approximations. Tommy's hand shape was imprecise even after he began signing spontaneously: his index finger was often crooked rather than straight, and he often stuck out two fingers instead of just one. Arlene helped him refine his hand shape by adding and fading various prompts after he began signing spontaneously. The "popcorn" sign Tommy learned is called a baby sign. In the adult sign the rotation of the index finger is preceded by a slap on the opposite fist at chest level by the hand whose index finger produces the final movement. Many of Tommy's attempts at signing resulted only in approximations to even the simplified baby sign.

Early in training, approximations to adult signs or baby signs can be accepted and even explicitly taught, since the nonverbal child learning to sign, like the normal child learning to talk, must be allowed to determine some of the form of his spontaneous and appropriate communication patterns. Overly strict adherence to adult criteria will inhibit him and

interfere with the development of spontaneity.

B. "Game": Sam's first sign. Sam enjoyed playing "Ten Little Indians." His teacher, Benson, played the game with him by singing the song as he counted Sam's fingers. Because Sam liked to play the game, Benson decided to teach him to request it with the sign for "game." He taught Sam a simplified sign rather than the complex adult sign (the coordinated swiveling of two hands, each forming the letter "G").

Benson began instruction by playing "Ten Little Indians" with Sam several times in succession. After Sam became involved in the game and expected play to continue, Benson ceased initiating play and waited for Sam to express his own desire for it. Instead of taking Sam's hands in his, Benson waited for Sam to grasp his hands. When Sam reached for them, Benson converted this natural movement into the arbitrary sign chosen to represent "game": a downward turn of the right hand from the wrist. Benson chose the one-handed downward turn rather than a two-handed downward turn that would more closely approximate the adult sign because Sam usually reached for play with both hands. Benson felt that if Sam were taught a two-handed sign, he might be unable to differentiate his natural two-handed reaching motion from the sign.

Benson converted Sam's natural reaching movements into a one-handed turn. Initially, Sam reached for Benson's right hand with two hands. Benson encouraged the right hand by grasping it and discouraged the left hand by placing it on Sam's left knee. Gradually Sam learned to reach with only his right hand. Benson discouraged extraneous movements, both deliberate and random, by the gentle use of minimal tactile prompts.

After Sam learned to reach with his right hand for Benson's left hand (at about chest level), Benson began raising his own left hand higher and higher toward his own left shoulder. Sam, therefore, had to reach higher and higher to grasp it. In this way, Sam gradually learned to reach out toward Benson's shoulder rather than to grasp Benson's hand reflexively. When Sam was regularly reaching toward Benson's shoulder, Benson started to place his hand on Sam's when Sam had completed the reach and to press Sam's hand down onto Benson's knee. His aim was to convert Sam's upward reach into an upward-then-downward

movement that could be foreshortened into a wrist turn, that is, into the sign itself. At first, Sam depended on Benson's light tap at the high point of the upward reach and on the feel of Benson's knee at the low point of the downward reach. Benson gradually faded these prompts, however, and Sam soon learned to reach up and down as Benson reached up and down in front of Sam without touching him. Then, as Benson faded his mirror reach, Sam gradually foreshortened his movement. Finally he began requesting "Ten Little Indians" with a spontaneous right-handed downward turn of his wrist. Fluctuations in Sam's performance necessitated the occasional reintroduction and subsequent fading of prompts that had been introduced and faded earlier.

IV. **PROMPTS.** Now that you have an idea of what a sign is and how the first sign is taught, we can consider in greater detail the tactile, visual, and verbal prompts you will use to teach signs.

A. **Tactile prompts.** These are the first prompts you will use because you will begin instruction by molding the child through the sign. As you do so, you will notice that the child comes to anticipate your assistance by beginning to move his hands into a position that makes it easier for you to help him through the sign. At this point, you can begin fading your tactile assistance by touching his hands more and more lightly and by letting him produce more and more of the sign on his own. You will find that you can shift from firm and complete physical assistance, to gentler but still complete assistance, to very light touches at transition points (between positioning, hand shaping, and final movement) and, lastly, to short gestures at transition points which do not actually touch the child. Thus, you will gradually fade your tactile prompts into visual prompts, and the child will come to look for your guidance rather than reach for it. (When the child's performance worsens, as it occasionally will, you will need to shift temporarily back to tactile prompts.)

B. **Visual prompts.** There are many visual prompts you will find useful as you teach signs: short gestures which tell the child what movements to make, imitative prompts (fully or partially modeled signs), referent prompts (presentation of part or all of the desired object for which the child is signing), and combined prompts (imitative and referent

prompts combined). We have already mentioned the short gestures deriving from tactile prompts and shall only consider here imitative, referent, and combined prompts.

1. *Imitative prompts.* As you teach the child a sign, you will have occasion to prompt appropriate signing by modeling the correct sign, or part of it, for the child.

The point to note is that modeled signs can be more powerful imitative prompts than you would like them to be. The goal of instruction is spontaneous communicative signing. Imitative prompts may interfere with the development of spontaneity by only teaching the child to mimic and comply—to rely on his teacher rather than on himself. Therefore, do not introduce imitative prompts until after the child has learned through molding to sign spontaneously for his first object or activity, and do not use them too often. As you teach more and more signs, you will find that the child will learn to imitate your movements and modeled signs on his own. You will not have to teach him to imitate signs and, because imitation can hinder spontaneous signing, you should not.

After the child learns on his own to imitate your signs, you need not worry about occasionally modeling signs for him. Imitative prompts are excellent teaching aids when they are not overused. As you model more and more signs for the child, you will find that he will become capable of responding on the basis of partial, as opposed to full or complete, imitative prompts. You may switch to the use of partial imitative prompts as soon as the child is ready for them. Partially modeled signs are more effective than fully modeled signs for promoting spontaneity because they prompt the child to reconstruct the whole sign on his own.

2. *Referent prompts.* The sight of the referent, that is, the desired object whose sign you are teaching, is the visual prompt that will eventually cue spontaneous signing. The obviousness of this fact should not blind you to the possibilities for manipulating the referent prompt. If you are teaching the sign for a food, you can enhance the salience of the food and stimulate the child's desire by moving the food toward and away from his mouth as you show it to him. You can also pique his desire by gradually bringing the food, part by part, out from

behind a screen or down off a shelf that hides it from sight. This will tantalize the child and teach him to actively reconstruct remembered information which he can use as a prompt for signing. The ability to use remembered, rather than sensorily present, information is a crucial aspect of spontaneity.

3. *Combined prompts.* Sometimes you will want to present part of the sign combined with the sight of the desired object as a prompt, that is, to combine an imitative and a referent prompt. For example, the sign for candy is formed by rubbing the palm of the flattened right or left hand, fingers outstretched and touching, up and then down against the right or left cheek. You can present a combined prompt for candy by holding a piece of candy against your flattened right hand with your thumb and by moving both your hand (palm in) and the candy up and then down parallel to your right cheek but a few inches away from it. Your partially modeled sign combined with the sight of the object is a powerful prompt for the child.

C. **Verbal prompts.** There are three types of verbal prompts (besides the words in Signed Speech) that you can use as you teach signs: whole words, parts of words, and phrases.

1. *Whole words.*

a. *With spontaneous signs*—Each time the child spontaneously produces a complete sign or a sign approximation, say the corresponding word. The word you utter teaches him the association between the sign and the word and will, after he learns to imitate sounds, prompt him to speak as he signs, that is, to initiate Signed Speech.

b. *During molding and modeling*—Whenever you mold the child through a sign or model one for him, you should utter the corresponding word. This will also help teach the child the association between the sign and the word.

c. *With partial prompts*—The words you say as you provide partial tactile and visual prompts help the child produce the sign you are attempting to cue. For example, saying the word "candy" as you present an incomplete model of the candy sign or an incomplete view of a piece of candy makes it easier for the child to sign "candy" in response.

2. *Parts of words.* You can use parts of words as prompts for signs and also for the purpose of further refining the child's signs.

   a. *Partial words as sign prompts*—You can use parts of words to prompt a sign—for example, "pop" or "p" to prompt the popcorn sign and "gai" or "g" to prompt the game sign.

   b. *Partial words for refining signs*—It is important for you to teach the child to produce one final hand movement to correspond to each syllable in the word. The closer the correspondence between signs and words, the easier it will be for the child to learn the associations between them and the sooner he will initiate Signed Speech. Partial words are useful for teaching the one-movement-per-syllable rule. For example, the final movement of the popcorn sign consists of two components, one turn of the index finger forward for "pop" and one turn backward for "corn." Suppose the child turns his finger forward but does not follow with a backward turn. You can utter the partial word "pop" as he turns his finger forward, wait until he turns it backward before you say "corn," and then give the child the popcorn. If, on the other hand, the child turns his finger quickly forward and backward many times, you can either slow your verbalization of "p-o-p-c-o-r-n" or utter a short, burstlike "popcorn" to help the child turn his finger less frequently.

3. *Phrases.*

   a. *"What do you want?"*—As you teach a sign, you will hold out the desired object and wait for the child to produce the sign. Occasionally, however, you will want to say and sign "What do you want?" as you hold out the object. The reason for occasionally asking the question as you present the object is to teach the child to respond to a question and to familiarize him with the concept "want," which he will learn later as part of the request "(Child) want x."

   b. *"Do you want the x?"*—It is a good idea to occasionally provide the child with the completely modeled sign and word as part of the utterance "Do you want the x?" As you provide this "indirect" information, the child learns to pick up and use incidental information about signs: this ability will facilitate his spontaneous communication.

V. ERRORS. As the child learns his first sign, he will make many errors. He will often produce the sign with components which are very imprecisely articulated or simply wrong. After he knows more than one sign, he will often confuse signs. Correct the child's errors either by providing the prompts he needs or by allowing him to correct himself, that is, by fostering self-correction skills.

A. Providing prompts. Early in training it is a good idea to provide the child with the prompts he needs to sign accurately so that he will be successful most of the time. Success builds his confidence in his signing ability. It is also a good idea, however, to provide no more help than the child needs. In this way he does not learn to overrely on your assistance. The child who relies too heavily on his teacher's help will not sign as spontaneously as the child who relies on himself.

B. Fostering self-correction. Self-correction is a component of spontaneous communication and a form of self-reliance. To foster it, occasionally wait for the child to repeat an incorrect sign without attempting to help him, to see whether or not he can correct himself. When he is not rewarded, he will tend to repeat a sign, and the repeated sign will occasionally be executed correctly. Reward signs corrected through repetition lavishly, with the desired object, praise, and physical affection. In this way you strengthen the child's self-correction skills.

If you have previously rewarded his self-corrections, the child will almost automatically repeat a sign you do not reward. Some repetitions will be obvious attempts at self-correction, others will not. The child's repetitions provide you with many opportunities for promoting self-correction. In addition, they allow you to develop a very useful general tool: the simultaneously signed and spoken command "Again." You can easily teach the child to repeat poorly executed signs by signing and saying "Again." His ability to respond to this command will allow you to encourage repetition and to explicitly foster self-correction.

VI. REINFORCEMENT. We have considered methods for teaching the child to produce a sign. Now we discuss what to do after the child produces the sign, that is, how to reinforce the child for making the sign.

A. **Complete signs.** After the child produces a complete sign, give him the desired object he has requested, some affectionate physical contact, and sign and say "Good signing." After you reward the child and sign and say "Good signing," you may model the sign and say the corresponding word to increase the effect of your reward. Do not model the sign after every correct sign, however, or the child may begin imitating you and end by repeating signs too often, that is, he may begin "stuttering" in sign. Sign stuttering interferes with instruction and spontaneity. In addition, you should not model the correct sign before you have given the child the object and signed and said "Good signing." Signs modeled prior to reinforcement prompt unwanted repetitions even more than do signs modeled after. Furthermore, if you sign and say "Good signing" before you give the child the desired object he may begin inappropriately imitating the signs "Good" and "signing." You should feel free to use a variety of phrases in addition to "Good signing" to reinforce the child. An occasional "Good boy (girl)," "Good work," "Very nice," or "Great" will introduce variety and make the lesson more interesting.

B. **Sign approximations.** When the child spontaneously produces approximations to the correct sign, perhaps during sign lessons when the object is not present or perhaps during other parts of the school day, you should praise him. Then prompt him through, and reward him for, a more accurate version of the sign. It is very important to support strongly and to extend with much care the child's early spontaneous signing.

VII. MASTERY CRITERION. The child's first spontaneous sign is a request for a desired object or activity and only inadvertently a description of that object or activity. (Only after the child learns to discriminate among a number of spontaneous signs will he begin to separate the use of signs to request desired objects and activities from the use of signs to describe.) The criterion for mastery of the first spontaneous sign is that the child consistently (that is, on 90 percent of the trials) produce the correct sign on his own to request the desired object you present and that he do so in the absence of any prompt, command, or question from you related to the object.

The number of trials, sessions, or days of consistent, accurate, and unprompted signing you will need to require of the child before you can conclude that he has mastered his first sign will vary from child to child. Some children learn their first sign during the first 45-minute sign language lesson; these children can be said to have mastered the sign if they use it consistently and accurately during their second lesson. Others take two weeks or more to learn their first sign, and these children can probably only be said to have mastered their first sign after they have used it consistently for one or two weeks. Other children, of course, fall in between, or even beyond, these two extremes.

The child's spontaneous and appropriate expression of a desire with a request is what allows you to assert that he has mastered his first spontaneous sign. You will probably become convinced that the child knows the sign only when he produces the sign spontaneously in the absence of the object. He may produce the sign, for example, during play periods and during lunch. The child's use of his first sign in nonclassroom settings in the absence of the object shows that he has grasped the idea that to sign is to make a request.

3

The Second Sign: Part Request and Part Description

I. The second sign

II. Example: Tim learns to request and describe "drink"

III. Errors

IV. Focusing on the object

V. Focusing on relevant characteristics

VI. Building a vocabulary

The child's second sign is both a request and a description. The child learns to sign for a desired object and to discriminate his second sign from his first by using it to request only the object to which it refers. Because the new sign will function as a request, you should choose a sign that refers to an object of high interest, usually a food or a toy. Since the child will have to learn to discriminate it from his first sign it is also best to choose a sign that is dissimilar to the first one. Optimally, it will differ from the first sign in terms of (1) sign components (position, hand shape, and final movement), (2) perceptual and conceptual properties (the way the object to which it refers looks, feels, tastes, and is used) and (3) corresponding word (sound elements and number of syllables in the word corresponding to it).

The differences between Tim's first sign, "cookie," and his second sign, "drink," are a good illustration. Tim's "cookie" sign consisted of two taps of the closed right fist on the upturned palm of the left hand at about lap level. (The two taps corresponded to the two syllables of the word "cookie.") His "drink" sign consisted of one backward rotation of the right hand toward the back of his head. The hand was shaped to accommodate an imaginary cup, with the tip of the extended right thumb resting against the right cheek as if to tilt and empty the cup. "Cookie" is thus a two-handed, two-movement, hand-touching-hand sign which is produced near the waist with closed fingers, and "drink" is a one-handed, one-movement, hand-touching-face sign which is produced near the head with the thumb separated from the other fingers. "Cookies" are sweet, chewable, smallish, solid, directly graspable foods, and "drinks" are flowing, immediately swallowable, not directly graspable masses usually consumed out of cups and glasses. Last, the word "cookie" has two syllables and different sound elements from the one-syllable word "drink."

I. **THE SECOND SIGN.** The child learns his second sign much as he learns his first one. After he masters this sign, he can then learn to discriminate between the second and first sign, that is, to request with the appropriate sign each of the desired objects.

A. **The second sign in isolation.** Begin by presenting only the desired object on successive trials and provide the child with the prompts he needs to produce the sign correctly most of the time. As before, mold him through the sign, then gradually fade your prompts to allow the child to learn to sign on his own.

B. **Discrimination between the first and second sign.** This step is best taught by first using blocked trials and then following these with random trials.

1. *Blocked trials.* After the child is consistently producing his second sign on his own, you may switch back to and reteach him his first sign. Then you can begin alternating between blocks of trials on the two signs. Present the object to which his second sign refers on successive consecutive trials and reteach the child to produce his second sign consistently on his own, then switch back to his first sign, and so forth. You will find that the number of trials per block that the child requires to relearn and switch to the alternate sign will decrease over successive blocks of trials.

2. *Random trials.* When the child can switch to the alternate sign in three to five trials after you switch to the alternate object, you may begin presenting the two ob-

jects in random order. The child will gradually learn to respond appropriately to your random presentations, that is, to discriminate between his two signs for the purpose of making requests.

II. **EXAMPLE: TIM LEARNS TO REQUEST AND DESCRIBE "DRINK."** To give you an impression of what you may experience as you teach the child to use his second sign, we describe what transpired as Tim's teacher, Benson, taught Tim the sign "drink" and then the discrimination between "drink" and his first sign, "cookie."

A. **The second sign, "drink."** Benson taught Tim his second sign, "drink," much as he had earlier taught him "cookie." However, when he first held out a drink—some fruit juice in a cup—Tim tried to sign "cookie." Benson then quickly grasped Tim's hands and molded them through the sign for "drink." As he guided Tim's right hand through the new sign, he also held Tim's left palm with his right hand, thus preventing Tim from forming the upturned "cookie" palm with the left hand while signing for "drink" with the right. The typical child tries to produce his first, old sign when the second, new sign is introduced. By quickly molding the child through the new sign before he can produce the old one, you can easily eliminate such errors.

Benson taught Tim the sign "drink" in several stages: he molded Tim through the sign completely. Then with his own analogously shaped right hand, he guided Tim's right hand lightly through a backward face-level, thumb-touching-cheek rotation, as if to tilt an imaginary cup. Next Benson lifted his own right hand from his lap slightly, forming it into the shape of an imaginary cup analogous to Tim's and rotating it slightly backward. Finally, he merely held the juice out and waited for Tim to sign "drink." Benson thus gradually moved from molding, to tactile and visual prompts, to visual prompts, to the referent alone. At the same time, he shifted his stress from the final movement of the "drink" sign, to hand position, to hand shape. He used structured waiting to prompt spontaneous production of the final movement and the position. Benson spoke the word "drink" while molding Tim through the sign and while Tim produced all or part of the sign on his own, and provided Tim with enough prompts to keep his level of accuracy high and build his confidence. Assistance was faded gradually to allow Tim to control the pace of learning to sign "drink."

B. Discrimination between the first and second sign.

    1. *Blocked trials.* After Tim learned to sign "drink" in the absence of any command when shown the cup of juice, Benson switched back to and retaught him his first sign, "cookie," in a block of "cookie" trials. As he retaught "cookie," Benson moved from molding to tactile and visual prompts, to visual prompts, to the referent alone. Tim had to relearn to use two hands as he relearned the sign "cookie" and to keep his hands from his face as he signed. He accomplished these tasks easily with the help of Benson's prompts. He relearned his first sign, "cookie," with much less molding and prompting and in many fewer trials than he had originally.

    After Tim was consistently signing "cookie" on his own when shown a cookie, Benson switched back to a block of "drink" trials and retaught him the "drink" sign. Then he switched back to "cookie," and so forth. As block followed block, Tim began relearning the alternate sign in fewer trials, and Benson faded from molding to providing him with minimal tactile and visual prompts.

    2. *Random trials.* After Tim was switching to the alternate sign in an average of three to five trials and molding was no longer necessary, Benson began presenting either a cookie or a drink of juice in random order. At first, he presented the cookie to Tim at lap level and the drink at mouth level, in order to provide Tim with position prompts. (Benson had occasionally used these position prompts when first teaching Tim the two signs.) Gradually, however, he faded these prompts and began presenting the cookie and the drink at the same intermediate mid-chest level. The use of distinctive position prompts early in random-trial training helps the child discriminate between his first and second signs. These position prompts can be easily faded later.

    By the time Benson initiated random trials, Tim had begun learning to use imitative prompts, that is, to produce the sign "cookie" or "drink" when Benson showed him part of that sign. Therefore, during random trials, Benson used partial imitative prompts, such as the upturned left "cookie" palm without the right "cookie" fist, and the curved "drink" right hand without the extended thumb and not lifted to face level, to help Tim learn to use the two signs as discriminative requests. He used partial imitative prompts frequently at the start of random trials and then faded them. (Benson's partial imitative prompts did not interfere with Tim's spontaneous communication because they required Tim to reconstruct the whole sign on the basis of information about a part, not merely to mimic Benson.)

Whenever the quality of Tim's performance temporarily worsened, Benson moved from random trials back to blocked trials. The quality of almost all children's performance fluctuates enough to require the teacher to backtrack occasionally. Over the course of many trials, however, Tim learned to sign "cookie" when Benson presented a cookie and "drink" when Benson presented a drink. In other words, he learned to use the signs as discriminative requests.

III. **ERRORS.** Signing errors are to be expected at all stages of instruction. They fall into two classes: within-sign and between-sign. A within-sign error involves the production of a low-quality appropriate sign, that is, a sign in which one or more components are imprecisely formed or simply absent. A between-sign error involves the production of a high-quality but inappropriate sign, that is, a precisely formed sign that designates an object other than the one presented.

A. **Within-sign errors.** These errors occur during all phases of instruction but are especially frequent during early training. Prompting is the preferred correction procedure at this time because it keeps the child's success rate high and develops her confidence. After the child masters the final movement and the position, self-correction should be encouraged.

B. **Between-sign errors.** These errors also occur during all phases of instruction, though they are more frequent during the blocked or random trials. You can expect the child who knows more than one sign to produce between-sign errors, and you can correct such errors with prompts. Between-sign errors are best used, however, to foster self-correction. The child who can correct her own errors will be able to sign more spontaneously and learn new signs more easily than will the child who cannot. The three basic techniques for fostering self-correction are encouraging repetition, providing negative information, and rewarding precompletion switching. If you use all three techniques, the child will acquire more productive self-correction skills than if you use one.

1. *Encouraging repetition.* To do this, you ignore the child's inappropriate sign and wait for her to produce the correct one. After she does so, you then ask her to repeat the correct sign by signing and saying "Again" before giving the reward. As the child repeats the correct sign, she will learn that it is a particular sign and not just a different one. You do not want to teach her merely to switch to a different sign when she is not rewarded, but to switch to the correct one. Such explicit self-correction becomes more important as the child learns more signs.

2. *Providing negative information.* To do this, you say and sign "No" after the child produces an incorrect sign, wait for her to produce the correct sign, have her repeat it, and then give her the object she has requested. The child will gradually learn that "No" means that she has produced an inappropriate sign and will come to use your "No" as a signal to self-correct.

3. *Rewarding precompletion switching.* Occasionally the child will begin an inappropriate sign, stop in mid-sign, and switch to the appropriate sign, especially after she develops the habit of self-corrective sign switching. These precompletion switches tell you that the child is beginning to learn when and how to correct herself before she completes an incorrect sign. It is important to reward her immediately with the object she requests.

IV. **FOCUSING ON THE OBJECT.** After the child knows two or more signs, it is necessary for him to fully attend to the object you present in order to sign for it appropriately. (Not all children have problems paying attention, but most do.) Make sure, therefore, that the child sees the object before you allow him to sign for it. To help him look before he signs, you can hold his hands in his lap until he looks at the object. Less restrictively, you can shake the object before his eyes or, if he is facing away from the object, turn his head in its direction. The Signed Speech commands "Look-at-the x" and "Pay-attention" are also useful aids for maintaining the child's attention (see Chapter 17 for a discussion of how to use these commands to promote eye contact and attention to objects).

V. **FOCUSING ON RELEVANT CHARACTERISTICS.** The child's appropriate use of signs as discriminative requests depends on her understanding that a sign stands for a class of objects. Teaching the child to discriminate between occasions appropriate to the use of each of her two signs will not, by itself, develop this understanding. It will also be necessary to teach her to ignore those characteristics of the two objects that do not give information about the sign to produce. For most nonverbal children, position is a potent irrelevant characteristic. Therefore, you should teach the child to ignore the position of the object. Though you may have taught her about the irrelevance of position during random trials, when you introduced and faded it as a prompt, the child may need more instruction. To make it easier for her to ignore position and other irrelevant cues, you should train her to produce the sign when the object appears in any position and in any container. The child must also learn to produce the sign for any member of the object class, to sign for the object in a variety of settings, and to understand that she may sign with either hand (in the case of one-handed signs).

A. **Ignoring position.** Teach the child to ignore position after she learns to sign consistently for each of her two desired objects presented randomly in the same position. As you will have already introduced and faded position as a prompt during random trials, she will be ready to learn more about the irrelevance of position. You may present her with objects in a wide variety of positions: close to your body, close to the child's body, on your left side, on your right, above your head, at lap level, in your right hand, in your left, alone or with like objects, and in several different containers. The child will learn that position is irrelevant to the two signs.

B. **The object as a member of an object class.** Whenever possible, you should present the child with several different members of the object's class. As you show her a wide variety of cookies, for example, she will learn that the sign "cookie" stands for any member of this class.

C. **The object in a wide variety of settings.** You may occasionally present the child with desired objects in settings other than the lesson room, and you may have others do so as well. In addition, when the child signs in the absence of the desired objects (during verbal imitation lessons, during play periods, or during lunch), you should now and then give her the objects she is requesting.

D. **Signing with either hand.** The child will usually sign one-handed signs with her dominant hand and two-handed signs with her dominant hand always in the same role, as you taught her. Occasionally, however, she will produce a one-handed sign with her nondominant hand or reverse hand roles in forming two-handed signs. When she does so, give her the object she requests to teach her that signs are not hand specific. After the child knows the sign, you can then allow her to reach for the object with one hand and sign with the other. This will teach her that the signs are not reach-specific.

VI. **BUILDING A VOCABULARY.** We have thus far considered only the child's first and second signs. In this section we present guidelines relevant to the teaching of all the child's initial signs.

A. **The third and later signs.** You may teach the child the third through tenth (or twelfth) signs in the same manner as you taught the first two signs. Introduce each new sign after the child consistently uses his other signs correctly. Teach the sign by itself first, then in alternating blocks on the new sign and blocks on all of the old signs, and, lastly, in randomly ordered trials on the new and all of the old signs. The child will require less prompting and fewer training trials to learn each suceeding new sign, because he will learn more and more about learning to sign. He will gradually become capable of imitating new signs on his first attempts and of using partial imitative prompts. Finally, he will gain in dexterity and so have less trouble with hand shape.

B. **Learning rate.** Different children learn signs at different rates, and the quality of a given child's performance fluctuates widely. Low-functioning slow learners require more prompts and more training trials and have greater difficulties with irrelevant characteristics than do fast learners. In addition, they have more difficulty making the transition from signing for desired foods to signing for desired objects. Almost all children learn to sign more readily for food than for objects; for slow learners, however, the transition from one to the other can be troublesome.

C. **Using signs in new ways.** Be sure to reward the child for using signs in new situations and for new purposes. The more you respond to the child's new uses of signs, the more spontaneous he will be. You may find him using his initial ten to twelve signs in the following new ways.

1. *To request an object whose sign-label he does not know.* For example, Jimmy signed "swing" to request a piggyback ride because he knew the sign "swing" but not the sign "ride."

2. *To discontinue an undesired activity.* For example, Jimmy signed "swing" when his teacher tried to engage him in ball-rolling because he did not like ball-rolling.

3. *In combination with other communicative gestures.* The child may grasp your hand and sign, point to an object and sign, touch your face to gain your attention and sign, or reject what you are offering him and sign for something else.

D. **Activity signs.** You may teach activity signs during play periods at the same time as you teach object signs during sign language lessons without teaching the child to discriminate between activity signs and object signs. Most children do not confuse activity signs such as "swing" and "ride" with object signs such as "candy" and "ball." One reason is probably that they experience activities and objects very differently. Children typically experience a more prolonged physical interaction with the teacher after he grants a request for an activity than after he grants a request for an object, and they are prompted to produce activity and object requests in different ways. The teacher produces the activity sign at the same time that he asks the child to request an activity (with "Does Tommy want to swing?" for example), but only needs to show the child the object to obtain a request for it.

E. **The multisign request.** It is best to delay teaching the multisign request "(Child) want x" until the child uses and discriminates correctly among ten to twelve single-sign requests. If you teach him the multisign request before he can consistently determine which occasions are appropriate to the ten to twelve signs he can produce, you will only confuse him and interfere with the growth of spontaneity.

4

The First Multisign Request: "(Child) want x"

I. The multisign request: "(Child) want x"

II. Errors

III. Building a vocabulary

IV. Mastery criterion

The first multisign utterance to teach the child is the multisign request "(Child) want x," where (Child) denotes the child's name and x denotes the object or activity he desires. The first sign you taught the child functioned as a single-sign request; the second through tenth (or twelfth), as discriminative single-sign requests. Now you want to extend his communicative capacities. You teach him to produce multisign requests that express the same desires as did his single-sign requests. In other words, you extend his requests of the form "x" to the lengthened form "(Child) want x." This will give them a syntactic form to correspond with their linguistic function and will prepare the child to learn other multisign utterances.

You teach "(Child) want x," where "(Child)" denotes the child's name, rather than "I want x," because "(Child)" can be given a concrete meaning more easily than can "I." When you begin teaching the multisign request "(Child) want x," "(Child)" will probably be an arbitrary sign to him. It will become meaningful only later when you teach him his own and other people's names during instruction in Person Concepts (Chapters 11 and 12).

With the help of his parents, create for the child a name sign that meaningfully represents him. This is formed with the first letter of the person's name and touches the person's body in such a way as to characterize a positive personal aspect, either a physical characteristic or a personal quality. For example, a girl named Pat with piercing eyes might sign her name by touching the manual letter "P" to her face next to one of her eyes: a boy named Martin who laughs a lot might sign his name by touching the manual letter "M" to one side of his mouth. Name signs, like other signs, have as many movements as there are syllables in the person's spoken name. Thus "Pat" would be signed with one "P" motion and Martin with two "M" motions. You should choose a name sign for the child which he will be able to discriminate easily from the "want" in "(Child) want x." Since the "want" sign is formed near the chest, a name sign in which the child touches another part of his body will be the best choice.

We might mention here that the sign "want" in "(Child) want x" tends to be naturally meaningful for a nonverbal child. To make this sign, the child extends and then draws toward his chest his parallel outstretched arms and semigrasping hands. The motion he produces resembles reaching for and grasping an imaginary desired object, and so is easy for him to learn.

I. **THE MULTISIGN REQUEST: "(CHILD) WANT X."** The basic technique for teaching this request and other multisign utterances is backward chaining: the last sign first, then the next to the last sign, and so forth. You taught the child to sign "x" when he wanted an x. To extend this backwards to the multisign request, you now teach him to sign first "Want x," then to sign "(Child) want x."

A. **"Want x."** You begin instruction on "Want x" by presenting an x and molding the child through the sign "Want" before he can form the sign "x." Mold him through the sign "Want" and wait for him to sign "x" on his own, but prompt him to sign "x" if he hesitates. The typical child quickly learns to sign "x" on his own after he is molded through "Want." When he is doing this regularly, you can then fade your molding, moving from complete molding with a verbal prompt (the "W" of "Want"), to light taps and a verbal prompt, to a verbal prompt alone, to an unvoiced mouth-shape prompt, and, finally, to the absence of any prompt. As you gradually remove prompts for "Want," the child will begin signing "Want x" on his own. When he is doing this regularly, you may then introduce another desired object, y, whose sign, "y," he produces spontaneously and appropriately, and teach him to sign "Want y." After he is signing this on his own, you can begin alternating between blocks of "Want x" and "Want y" trials. Then, when he is switching from "Want x" to "Want y" blocks in three to five trials, you may begin presenting "Want x" and "Want y" trials in random order. He will soon learn to sign "Want x" and "Want y" on his own as two-sign discriminative requests in the same way that he previously signed "x" and "y" alone. After he masters the two-sign request with two objects, you may introduce other objects using the same teaching format.

The instructor should note that the format for teaching the two-sign request "Want x" is analogous to that for teaching single-sign requests. First, a particular two-sign request such as "Want x" is taught by itself; next, blocks of "Want x" and "Want y" trials are alternated; and finally, single "Want x" and "Want y" trials are randomly presented. When other two-sign requests are later introduced, each is first taught alone, then in alternating blocks on the new two-sign request and all previously mastered two-sign requests, and finally, in a random sequence of the new and all old two-sign requests. Therefore, you should use the methods you used with single-sign requests when you teach two-sign requests of the form "Want x."

1. *Speak as the child signs.* This means saying "Want" as the child signs "Want" and "x" as he signs "x" during all phases of instruction and also when he signs spontaneously. Your words will teach the child word-sign-object associations and thereby prompt him to speak as he signs.

2. *Use referent prompts.* You should not hesitate to present and withdraw the x in order to tempt the child to sign "Want x."

3. *Use partial imitative prompts.* You should also not hesitate to use partial "Want" and partial "x" signs as prompts to help the child make his request.

4. *Give indirect information.* To give the child indirect information about the "Want" sign, you can say, "What do you WANT?" with a particularly loud "WANT?" (as you sign, "What do you want?") immediately before presenting the object you would like him to request. Your vocal emphasis of "WANT" will act as a prompt for this sign.

B. **"(Child) want x."** After the child is signing "Want x" on his own for three to five days to request any of the desired objects whose signs he knows, you may begin teaching him to make the three-sign request "(Child) want x." You teach this by backward chaining and by using the same instructional format you employed with "Want x": a single three-sign request in isolation, then another, then alternating blocks on the two three-sign requests, then randomly ordered trials on the two three-sign requests, then a third three-sign request in isolation, and so forth. As you continue instruction, the child will learn to request all desired objects and activities whose signs he knows by using the three-sign request "(Child) want x."

II. **ERRORS.** The child who knows a multisign utterance can produce more errors than can the child who knows only single-sign utterances: she can misorder signs, leave out a sign, or "stutter" in sign, that is, repeat a given sign more than once. Misordering and leaving out signs are usually easy to correct with prompts (manual, verbal, and imitative). Stuttering in sign, that is, the unwanted repetition of signs, tends to be a more difficult error to correct. The child who signs "(Child) (Child) (Child) (Child) . . ." instead of "(Child) want x," or "(Child) want want want . . . ," or any of the other stuttering errors possible, may become frustrated and compound her stuttering errors out of fear. The following techniques are useful for the elimination of such errors.

A. **Mold the child through a complete utterance.** Sometimes this will provide her with the information she needs to produce the utterance on her own. To prevent her from learning to overrely on molding, you should not reward the child for utterances you mold her through, but require her to produce the complete utterance on her own *after* you mold her through it.

B. **Slow the signing of the child.** Children stutter partly because they do not take enough time to form their signs. For this reason, slowing the signing will often eliminate the problem. You may use two techniques: holding the sign and talking slowly as the child signs.
   1. *Holding the sign.* To do this, you can hold the child's hands in the sign configuration for five to ten seconds

after she completes the stuttered sign. This both slows the child down and prevents the stutter. After you hold her in sign, you then have her produce the multisign phrase containing it on her own before giving her the object she requests.

2. *Talking slowly as the child signs.* The child relies on your voice as a prompt to sign and therefore you can use it partly to control how fast she signs. When you lengthen the words you utter and the pauses between words, the child will probably respond by signing more slowly. You should reward her for the slow signing which accompanies your slow talk. Because you talk as the child signs even when she signs well, she will not come to overrely on your slow talk.

III. **BUILDING A VOCABULARY.** It is important to not introduce new single-sign requests while you are teaching the two-sign and the three-sign request. The child will readily learn new signs within the three-sign request format after he has mastered the three-sign request with the objects and activities whose signs he knows. While he is in the process of learning the three-sign request, however, a new single-sign request, or a new sign in the three-sign request, will only be confusing.

Should the child take a sudden, intense interest in an object or activity while you are teaching three-sign requests, however, you may make an exception to this guideline and teach the sign as a single-sign request. Learning signs related to the child's own intense interests typically does not interfere with other new learning. We wish we could tell you how to judge whether or not an interest is sudden and intense, but we cannot; you will have to trust your own judgment.

IV. **MASTERY CRITERION.** The criterion for mastery of the three-sign request, like that for single-sign requests, has two aspects: production and spontaneity. The child must be able to produce the appropriate three-sign request when you hold out a desired object whose sign she knows and ask her what she wants. In addition, however, because your goal is spontaneous language, the child must use the three-sign requests spontaneously, just as she previously used single-sign requests. Spontaneous use can be manipulative—as when, for example, the child asks for an absent food during play time, for a play activity during lunch time, or for a hug when you are scolding her.

Or, the child may overgeneralize, using a three-sign request containing the known sign "B" to ask for the desired object A whose sign she does not know. You should practice three-sign requests and wait until the child begins using them spontaneously before beginning instruction in the next linguistic function, Reference.

5

The Signs "No," "Help," "Potty," and "Yes"

I. Conversion of natural movements into signs

II. The refusal "no"

III. The requests "help" and "potty"

IV. Teaching strategies

V. Mastery criterion

VI. The affirmation "yes"

After the child masters the multisign request "(Child) want x," he is ready to learn the following signs: "no," to indicate his refusal of an object or activity offered; "help," to express his desire for assistance in carrying out an activity; and "potty," (or "toilet"), to convey his need to eliminate. The child will use these signs to express his desires, much as he uses his other signs. Thus, he will extend his language to new areas of his life, possibly insert the new signs into his old three-sign request form on his own, and probably begin to understand the difference between general requests such as "help" and specific requests such as "potty" and "(Child) want x."

In addition to "no," "help," and "potty," we describe instruction in the use of "yes" to affirm a desire. We include it in this chapter because it is related to "no," but we consider it separately at the end because you will be teaching it only after the child uses "no" and "(Child) want x" spontaneously.

I. CONVERSION OF NATURAL MOVEMENTS INTO SIGNS. When initially teaching "no," "help," and "potty," you should attend to the child's spontaneous nonverbal messages, that is, the motor activities and gestures which express object refusal, desire for assistance, and need to eliminate. You teach the signs "no, " "help," and "potty" by converting each of these nonsymbolic forms of expression into signs.

   A. "No." When you present an object or the opportunity for an activity to a nonverbal child, he may communicate that he does not want the object or activity offered by moving away from it, pushing it away, or crying, whining, screaming, or displaying other signs of distress. You can transform these activities into the sign "no."

   B. "Help." When you ask a nonverbal child to perform an action or sequence of actions he is unable to execute (such as opening a tightly closed cookie jar), he may use a motor activity or gesture to request, or to convey his need for, your assistance. He might push or pull your hands toward the object or activity presenting difficulty, struggle with the object or activity and then stop when unsuccessful, or he might use previously acquired language to convey his request for help. For example, the child might sign, "John want shoe" to you when he wants your help with tying his shoes. You can then convert his spontaneous motor activity or gesture into the sign "help."

   C. "Potty." A nonverbal child may convey his need to eliminate through such motor activities as moving toward a potty chair (or toilet), squirming, or squatting. Whenever he engages in a motor activity which indicates the need to eliminate, you can shape his hand into the sign "potty" (or "toilet") and take him to the toilet (or potty chair).

II. THE REFUSAL "NO." To demonstrate how you might teach a nonverbal child the sign "no," and how you can transform the child's spontaneous, nonsymbolic messages into this sign, we present the following instructional formats and examples.

   A. Teaching "no."
      1. *Select disliked objects and activities.* You should select a group of objects or activities that the child is likely to

refuse when each is offered to him.

2. *Molding "no" after refusal.* To do this, you present an undesired object or the opportunity for an undesired activity to the child and ask, "Do you want (this/a) x?" When he begins to refuse through some spontaneous nonverbal form of expression such as moving away or pushing the object away, you then mold his pushing hand into and through the sign "no." You form the child's pushing hand into a palm-down fist, then move his fist from left to right several times, about six to twelve inches in front of his chest. As you mold him through the sign, you simultaneously say the word "no." Then you immediately remove the undesired object or activity and praise the child with the Signed Speech statement "Good signing."

3. *Fade prompts for "no."* When the child begins to anticipate molding, you should begin gradually fading your prompts, using the fading procedures delineated in Chapter 2. For example, you might begin fading your assistance by shaping and positioning the child's right fist in front of his chest and waiting for him to produce the side-to-side movement by himself. If he produces only a partial movement, you could vocalize the "n" in "no" (a partial-word verbal prompt) to prompt the complete side-to-side movement. As you fade your prompts, the child will learn to sign "no" on his own when you present him with the undesired object or activity.

4. *Offer a variety of undesired objects.* You may offer the child foods which he refuses to eat, toys and other objects which he shows an aversion to, and activities which he does not like. If he fails to produce the "no" sign in response to the question "Do you want (this/a) (undesired object/undesired activity)?" you can reintroduce previous prompts for this sign and then gradually fade them.

5. *Reintroduce desired objects.* After the child spontaneously signs "no" to reject a variety of foods, toys, and activities, you should then alternate between desired objects and activities for him to request with the multisign request "(Child) want x" and undesired ones for "no" trials. As you present an object or activity, you ask, "Do you want (this/a) x?" The mixed trials will teach the child when it is appropriate for him to sign

"(Child) want x" when he wants an object or activity and when it is appropriate for him to sign "no" when he does not want an object or activity.

B. **Example: Tommy learns to sign "no."** Tommy used "Tommy want x" to express his desires, but he did not use a standard symbol to communicate his refusal of an undesired object or activity. (He did demonstrate his rejection spontaneously in motoric fashion.) Therefore, we decided to teach him "no."

Prior to instruction, Tommy's teacher Arlene prepared a group of objects and activities that Tommy usually refused when each was offered to him. Included in the group were an onion, a raw noodle, a wind-up musical toy, a hit, a pinch, and a flick.

Sitting opposite Tommy, Arlene held a slice of onion before his face and asked, "Do you want this onion?" Tommy quickly averted his head and pushed away the onion with his right hand. Arlene immediately converted this action into the sign "no" by forming his right hand into a fist and moving it from side to side several times, simultaneously saying "no." After molding Tommy through the sign, she immediately withdrew the onion from his sight and then praised him with the signed and spoken statement "Good signing, Tommy."

During the early stages of teaching Tommy "no," Arlene was unable to provide an adequate manual prompt for Tommy's "no" sign while she was facing him because his rejection of both the onion and her hand were strong and emphatic. During these early trials, Benson, a colleague, stood behind Tommy. After Arlene asked, "Do you want this onion?" Benson quickly prompted Tommy through the "no" sign while Arlene simultaneously said, "no." Then immediately after Tommy (with Benson's help) signed "no," Arlene removed the onion from his sight and praised him.

Over the course of repeated trials, Benson faded his assistance. He touched Tommy's fist more and more lightly, fading his tactile prompts. Tommy began initiating the back and forth "no" movement of his fist on his own. Eventually, Benson was able to fade his manual assistance completely, and Tommy was able to produce the "no" sign spontaneously when Arlene offered the undesired onion.

When Tommy could sign "no" on his own to indicate his

refusal of the onion, Arlene taught him to sign "no" to reject other undesired objects. Using the same format, she offered him a variety of undesired objects and activities while asking "Do you want (this noodle/this music box/a hit/a pinch/a flick)?" If he did not spontaneously sign "no" but instead displayed some nonsymbolic expression of refusal, she reintroduced manual prompts for the "no" sign. She gradually faded her prompts as Tommy learned to refuse each of the undesired objects and activities by spontaneously signing "no" in response to her offers.

After Tommy learned to sign "no" to reject a variety of foods, objects, and activities, Arlene occasionally presented, interspersed with "no" trials, desired objects and activities for Tommy to request, asking the same "Do you want (this/a) x?" as she did on "no" trials. She thus taught him to discriminate those situations in which signing "no" to communicate refusal was appropriate from those in which signing "Tommy want x" was appropriate. (This would make it easier for Tommy to learn, later on, to discriminate situations in which a signed "no" to indicate refusal is suitable from those in which a signed "yes" to indicate acceptance is appropriate.)

III. **THE REQUESTS "HELP" AND "POTTY."** You teach "help" and "potty" using the same procedures as you used for "no."

A. **Teaching "help."**
    1. *Select objects with which the child needs help.* You might, for example, choose the child's jacket if he wants to and is unable to engage the zipper on his own.
    2. *Mold the child through the sign "help."* You may give the child the opportunity to perform an interesting but too difficult action—in this case, to engage the zipper of his jacket. When he struggles and then waits for your assistance or pulls your hand toward the zipper to indicate his desire for help, you can then mold his pulling hands into the sign for "help." You place his right fist on top of his left palm-up hand, position both hands about six to twelve inches in front of his waist, and move both hands upward from waist level to neck level. As you mold the child through the sign, you should simultaneously say the word "help," and immediately after molding him through the sign, give him the desired

assistance and praise him with the Signed Speech statement "Good signing."

3. *Fade prompts.* When the child begins to anticipate molding, you can gradually fade your prompts for the "help" sign. For example, to fade movement assistance after the child begins producing the upward movement of both "help" hands on his own, wait for the child to spontaneously position his hands in front of his chest. You may find the brief placement of your right fist in front of the child's chest a good prompt.

4. *Offer a variety of objects.* This might include the tight lids of jars or other containers filled with desired foods; puzzles, if the child has difficulty fitting in the pieces; articles of clothing, if the child needs assistance putting them on, removing them, or carrying out actions on them such as snapping, zipping, buckling, buttoning, and tying; wrapped, desired foods, if the child cannot remove the wrapper; doors, if the child has difficulty opening them; or a favorite food, toy, or other object placed on a high shelf the child cannot reach. If the child fails to produce the "help" sign spontaneously when faced with one of these situations, you should help him by reintroducing previous "help" prompts and then gradually fading them out.

B. **Example: Jimmy learns to sign "help."** Prior to instruction, Jimmy's teacher George searched for an activity that was difficult and interesting and one which he could repeat for a large number of trials without boring Jimmy. The interesting difficulty George found was the removal of the lid from a tightly sealed jar that contained a desired cookie. George first held the cookie (one of Jimmy's preferred foods) before Jimmy and waited for him to sign the request "Jimmy want cookie." After Jimmy made the request, George placed the cookie in the glass jar, screwed the lid on very tightly, and gave the jar to Jimmy. Jimmy attempted to open the jar. When he failed, he did one of the following: looked at George and again signed "Jimmy want cookie," pulled George's hand toward the lid of the jar, or looked to George after discontinuing his efforts at opening the jar by himself.

George responded to each of Jimmy's varied demonstrations of the need for assistance by molding Jimmy through the "help" sign and then granting Jimmy's request for assistance. When Jimmy signed, "Jimmy want cookie," George said and signed, "You have a cookie. What do you want?" Then, before Jimmy signed the request again, he molded Jimmy through the sign "help" by placing Jimmy's right fist on top of Jimmy's left palm-up hand and moving them together in an upward direction in front of Jimmy's chest. As he molded the "help" sign, George simultaneously said "help" and afterward praised Jimmy for requesting help from him.

When Jimmy pulled George's hands toward the lid of the unopened jar, George immediately molded Jimmy through the "help" sign, simultaneously saying "help," and then rewarded Jimmy with assistance and praise. He thus converted Jimmy's motor request for assistance into the explicit sign "help." Lastly, when Jimmy looked to George after ceasing his struggle to remove the lid, George asked, "What do you want?" and, before Jimmy signed, "Jimmy want cookie," George immediately molded Jimmy through the "help" sign, simultaneously saying "Help." He then granted Jimmy's request for assistance.

Over the course of a large number of trials, George faded his manual prompts for the "help" sign by touching Jimmy's hands more and more lightly as Jimmy began producing more and more of the upward sign movement on his own. Eventually George faded all tactile and other prompts completely and Jimmy spontaneously signed "help" when he needed assistance unscrewing the lid of a jar containing a cookie. After Jimmy was able to spontaneously sign "help" in this situation, George occasionally gave him a cookie he had requested in a jar with an easy-to-open lid. He did this in order to teach Jimmy to learn to discriminate those situations in which signing "help" was appropriate from those in which it was not.

Further, George taught Jimmy to generalize the "help" sign to other problematic situations, such as buttoning his coat and opening a door, by using the same instructional format. If Jimmy did not spontaneously sign "help" when faced with one of these situations but instead displayed some nonsymbolic expression of his need for assistance, George reintroduced manual prompts for the "help" sign and then gradually faded them. Eventually, Jimmy learned to sign "help" spontaneously to request assistance in a variety of problematic situations.

C. **Teaching "potty."**

   1. *Schedule regular toileting breaks.* Breaks should be at regular intervals throughout the day, for example, after language lessons, play sessions, and meals. Prior to taking the child to the bathroom, you say and sign, "It's time to go to the potty."

   2. *Mold the "potty" sign.* To mold, you lead the child to the bathroom and, while standing with him at the door, again say and sign, "It's time to go to the potty (toilet)." Then you immediately mold the child through the "potty" sign. You shape his dominant hand into a "T" (a palm-front fist with the thumb inserted between index and middle finger), and then place his "T" fist near his head at about shoulder level and shake it from right to left two times to correspond to the two syllables in "potty." As you mold the child through the sign, you should simultaneously verbalize the word "potty," and after you mold him through, praise him with the Signed Speech statement "Good signing."

   3. *Have the child sign "potty" in the bathroom.* Lead the child to the potty chair (or toilet). After removing his pants (or after the child removes them himself), you then mold him through the "potty" sign again, simultaneously saying "potty," and immediately put him on the potty chair (or toilet).

   4. *Repeat the preceding steps.* As you repeat, you can gradually fade your prompts for the "potty" ("toilet") sign. After the child has begun positioning his T-fist next to his shoulder and producing the shaking movement on his own afterward, you should assist him only in forming the T-fist. You may find that lightly touching the child's thumb and index finger as he shakes his fist next to his shoulder is a good tactile prompt to use to help him increase the clarity of his "potty" sign. As you fade prompts, the child will learn to sign "potty" spontaneously when he is standing in the entranceway to the bathroom or next to the potty chair (or toilet).

   5. *Reward and prompt spontaneous signing in new situations.* Whenever the child spontaneously signs "potty" in situations away from the bathroom, such as during a language lesson or play session, you should say "potty" as the child signs, praise him for signing, and then, without delay, take or send him to the bathroom. When

the child fails to sign "potty" in appropriate situations, you may reintroduce previous prompts and then gradually fade them. (Some children use the "potty" sign manipulatively to get out of difficult lessons or away from unpleasant situations. Only reward such manipulative signing early in training, not later on, when rewards can make this manipulative signing a problem.)

D. **Example: Tommy learns to sign "potty."** Prior to instruction, Arlene scheduled Tommy for a bathroom break once every hour, that is, after each of his 45-minute language lessons. At the termination of a sign lesson, she said and signed to him, "Signing time is finished. It's time to go to the potty." She led Tommy to the bathroom door and again said and signed, "It's time to go to the potty." Then while she said "potty," she immediately molded Tommy through the "potty" sign, praised him, and then brought him to the toilet. After helping him unsnap and lower his pants, she again prompted him through the sign "potty," simultaneously saying "potty" and praising him for the sign.

During the weeks which followed and over the course of many repeated trials, Arlene faded her assistance for Tommy's "potty" sign by systematically reducing her tactile prompts as Tommy learned to produce first the movement, then the position, and finally the hand shape on his own. Whenever Tommy signed "potty" spontaneously, either in the vicinity of or away from the bathroom, Arlene said "potty" as he signed, praised him for signing, and immediately took him to the bathroom.

IV. **TEACHING STRATEGIES.** In this section, we discuss two important strategies not previously mentioned which will help you teach the signs "no," "help," and "potty."

A. **Concentrated instruction.** You should teach the child the signs "no," "help," and "potty" through many consecutive repeated trials to help him remember the signs.

B. **Questions.** Questions are helpful in promoting generalization. When you ask, for example, "Do you want the x?" as you teach the sign "no," you help the child produce the symbolic response indicative of refusal. By occasionally asking the child "Do you want help?" when he desires your assistance, and "Do you want to go to the potty?" when he seems to need to eliminate, you also help the child attend to his desire for assistance or his need to eliminate. Again, this helps him produce the symbolic responses expressive of the states "help" and "potty," respectively. Further, by occasionally asking these questions, you provide the child with indirect information about the sign by incorporating the sign into the question.

V. **MASTERY CRITERION.** The criterion for the mastery of "no," "help," and "potty" has two levels: the child's consistent production of "articulate" versions of the appropriate sign, and the child's spontaneous use of the signs in new situations, for new purposes, or in combination with other signs. Some examples will help illustrate the spontaneous use of the signs "no," "help," and "potty." Tommy used "no" in a new situation as he signed "no" to Arlene's command "Tommy come here." He used "potty" in an egocentric fashion, a new purpose, as he signed "potty" to himself while moving in the direction of the bathroom. He used "help" in combination with other concepts to create new multisign utterances, such as "help pants" when he needed assistance raising his pants, and "help jacket" when he needed assistance putting on his coat.

It is possible for a child to achieve mastery at one level and not at the other. Consider, for example, the child who produces a precise "help" sign to ask for assistance snapping his pants during a "help" lesson but pulls your hands toward his shoes when he wants you to tie them outside of the lesson. There is also the child who consistently waves his hand back and forth several times when he needs to urinate, in whatever situation he happens to be, but does not articulate the "potty" sign precisely. Mastery of a sign is achieved when the child displays proficiency in both production and clarity of the sign and the spontaneous use of the sign in new situations. You can only be certain that he has mastered the signs "no," "help," and "potty" when he produces precisely articulated, easily understandable versions of them and when he produces them spontaneously in new situations, for new purposes, or in combination with other signs to create novel multisign utterances.

VI. **THE AFFIRMATION "YES."** You should not teach the child to sign "yes" to affirm a desire until she has mastered "no" and the multisign request "(Child) want x" and uses both spontaneously. If you teach her to affirm positive desires by signing "yes" before she knows "no" and the multisign request, you will be allowing her to make requests without learning the expressive language related to them. Therefore, teach her "yes" afterwards. The steps in teaching the "yes" sign are molding, fading, variety, and discriminating.

A. **Molding.** Present a desired object or opportunity for a desired activity to the child and ask "Do you want (this/a) x?" After the child indicates her desire for the object or activity, but before she signs it, mold her hand into and through the "yes" sign while simultaneously verbalizing the word "yes." To mold the "yes" sign, you form the hand with which the child typically signs "no" into a palm-down fist, position the fist about ten inches in front of her chest, then move the fist up and down twice. Immediately after molding the child's hand through the "yes" sign, give her the desired object or activity and praise her by signing and saying "Good signing."

B. **Fading.** You may fade your molding prompts by using structured waiting, first from the final "yes" movements, then from the "yes" position, and, lastly, from the "yes" hand shape. You shape the child's hand into a fist, position it in front of her chest, and wait for her to produce the final two up-and-down "yes" movements on her own. Then you shape the child's hand into a fist and wait for her to position it and produce the final movements by herself. Lastly, you wait for the child to form the "yes" hand shape (a fist), position it, and move it up and down twice, all on her own.

C. **Offering variety.** You should teach the child to sign "yes" to offers of a wide variety of desired objects and activities to help her generalize her use of the "yes" sign.

D. **Teaching discrimination between "yes" and "no."** Randomly offer the child desired and undesired objects and teach her to respond according to her desires. If she signs "yes" when she does not want the object or activity or "no" when she does, you can use natural consequences to provide corrective feedback: you can give her the object or activity when she signs "yes," even when she clearly does not want it, and you can remove the object or activity when she signs "no," even when she clearly wants it.

Speech Production

The goal of the speech production component of the Signed Speech Program is the development of strong, flexible, and creative speech skills. Through verbal imitation training, the nonverbal child is taught to imitatively produce a wide variety of speech sounds and to recombine these sounds in novel ways to create new sounds. (The child then becomes capable of integrating speech production and spontaneous signing to form Signed Speech.) In Chapter 6, we detail methods for teaching the child his initial sounds through verbal imitation training, and in Chapter 7, methods for teaching him syllables and words.

6

Initial Speech Sounds:
Verbal Imitation Training

I. Components of a sound: Vowels and consonants, voicing, articulation

II. The first sound

III. The second and later sounds

IV. Example: Lance's initial sounds

V. Prompts

VI. Errors

VII. Reinforcement

VIII. Mastery criterion

The goal of training in speech production is the development of strong speech skills, which is done through training in verbal imitation. The child will use these skills to learn words and to integrate those words with his spontaneous signing. In this chapter we describe a sequence of procedures for teaching the initial speech sounds; in the next, a sequence for teaching syllables and words. You need not start at the beginning of the sequence for initial sounds with each child, but rather at the point appropriate to the child's level of skill. If the child does not imitate some speech when you commence training, however, do start at the beginning.

Since the initial sounds the child learns will affect the speed and completeness with which he acquires strong speech skills, you should choose these sounds carefully. Begin training with sounds similar or identical to those the child already produces; new sounds are best built out of old ones. Ask the child's parents what sounds he utters at home and listen carefully to his vocalizations at school. Make sure that the child's initial sounds are easily distinguishable from each other, as this makes the task of learning new sounds easier. You should also, when possible, teach initial sounds that are continuants. Continuants such as "ah," "m," and "s" are good examples ("ah" is phonetically transcribed /a/, as in "lot"; "m" is transcribed /m/, as in "man"; and "s" is transcribed /s/, as in "sit"). First, continuants permit you to teach the child a new sound by merely extending an old one, as when, for example, you extend "ah" to "a-a-a-ah." Second, they make the early introduction of syllables easier because they can more easily be blended to form syllables than can noncontinuants such as "d" and "p." Finally, in teaching initial sounds, choose a wide variety of sounds and try to sample the entire spectrum of the language. The broader the range of initial sounds, the more quickly the child will develop usable sound skills.

I. **COMPONENTS OF A SOUND: VOWELS AND CONSONANTS, VOICING, ARTICULATION.** Words are composed of phonemes, that is, sounds which can signal differences in meaning. For example, "b" and "p" signal a difference in meaning between the words "bin" and "pin." Phonemes can be analyzed into distinctive features. For instance, the phonemes "b" and "p" have two common features: they are noncontinuants and labials. On the other hand, they differ in that "b" is voiced while "p" is unvoiced. You need not know the details of distinctive feature analysis to teach sounds. However, if you pay close attention to the similarities and differences between the sounds you teach, you will make better choices and develop more effective prompting strategies.

A. **Vowels versus consonants.** This distinction is basic to the structure of language. If possible, you should teach the child a vowel and a consonant as the first two sounds.

B. **Place of articulation.** The consonants "b" and "d" are articulated in different areas: "b" is produced by lip contact; "d," by the tongue tip in contact with the gum ridge behind the upper front teeth. You want to begin teaching differences in place of articulation early in training. Therefore, the third sound you teach should be a consonant different in place from the first.

C. **Voicing.** Some consonants, such as "b," "d," and "g," are voiced, and some, such as "p," "t," and "k," are unvoiced. The vocal cords are tightened and vibrate during the production of voiced consonants, but are relaxed and do not vibrate during the production of unvoiced consonants. You should teach the child an unvoiced consonant as soon as you can.

D. **Manner of articulation.** The consonants "l" and "n" are produced in approximately the same place in the mouth. They differ in that "n" has nasal resonance whereas "l" does not. Include in your instruction consonants that differ in manner of articulation (for example, ones that differ in nasality).

II. THE FIRST SOUND.

A. **Preparing the child for verbal imitation.** The two steps in preparation are instruction in noise making to raise the child's rate of vocalization, and instruction in noise making on command to teach the child to produce sounds after you produce them.

   1. *Noise making.* You should reward the child for uttering any kind of sound. Immediately after she utters a sound, give her a bite of food or a desired object, praise, and affection. If she knows the sign for the food or object, you can have her sign to request the reward. You can prompt vocalizations by pressing the child's "tummy," tickling her, or playfully jostling her.

   2. *Noise making on command.* When the child is vocalizing regularly, you should choose one of her most frequently produced sounds and begin saying it once about every 30 seconds. Choose the sound you plan to teach her to imitate first. You then reward the child with food or a desired object (possibly requested in sign), praise, and affection whenever she vocalizes during the 5-second interval immediately after you say the sound. You should reward vocalizations she produces at other times with praise and affection but not with food. In this way, you teach her to vocalize after you utter the sound, but without reducing her frequency of vocalization.

B. **Teaching the first imitated sound.** When the child is vocalizing after you, you then teach her to imitate the sound you have chosen as a vocalization prompt. This is the first step in verbal imitation training. Begin by differentially reinforcing her for uttering the sound you make. Reward her with food or a desired object when she produces either the sound you produce or one similar to or containing it, but reward only with praise and affection for other sounds. You should also provide prompts to help the child make the sound you utter. As you differentially reinforce her and provide prompts, the child will learn to imitate your sound. You may find, when you start differentially reinforcing and prompting the sound, that the child seems to fixate on a different sound. Do not hesitate to change your utterance to hers; the change will not confuse her.

It is best to remember that the child's ability to produce the sound you make is probably not true imitation. You probably could have taught her to produce the particular sound she utters in response to any sound you might have chosen. Only when she can produce each of a wide variety of sounds immediately after you utter those sounds can you say that she knows how to imitate.

III. **THE SECOND AND LATER SOUNDS.** You should teach the child to imitate her second sound after she consistently imitates her first, her third after she consistently imitates her first and second, and so forth. Over the course of training, she will learn to imitate (or at least approximate) any sound you utter. Teach each new sound first in isolation, then in alternate blocks of trials on the new sound and blocks of trials on old sounds, and finally, in randomly ordered trials on the new and on old sounds.

A. **The second sound.** You can teach the second sound as you taught the first one, uttering the sound once every 30 seconds for her to imitate. The child will very likely continue to produce her first sound after you switch to the second. You will therefore have to find an effective manual prompt to help her switch. When you find this prompt, you should use it as necessary to establish the sound firmly; then fade it.

B. **The first and second sound in blocked trials.** When the child consistently utters the second sound after you, you can switch back to a block of trials on the first sound and reteach it. Then, when she regularly says the first sound after you, switch to a block on the second sound and reteach it, and so on. As you do this, the child will relearn the alternate sound with fewer prompts and in fewer trials.

C. **The first and second sounds in random order.** After the child switches back to her first or second sound in three to five trials, you can begin uttering the two sounds in random order to teach her to imitate them discriminatively. At first the child will need prompts.

D. **The third and later sounds.** Follow the procedures outlined for the first and second sounds. As you teach successive sounds, the child will become more skillful at listening to and learning to imitate new sounds, and the character of new learning will change from a sound conversion process to more of a guessing game.

IV. **EXAMPLE: LANCE'S INITIAL SOUNDS.** To illustrate what takes place during verbal imitation training and to prepare you for a detailed discussion of the prompts you will use as you teach children to imitate sounds, we present the following example.

A. **Preparing Lance for verbal imitation training.**
   1. *Noise making.* At first, Lance babbled a limited number of sounds in an uncontrolled and unintelligible fashion. His teacher, Benson, initiated instruction in noise making by rewarding him with a piece of candy and a Signed Speech "Good talking" immediately after Lance uttered any sound (unless that sound was vegetative, that is, a sneeze, burp, or cough). During this stage, Benson did not try to teach Lance to look at him, because his primary goal was to raise Lance's rate of vocalization, not to stress eye contact. It is not necessary to teach eye contact before you begin rewarding a child for vocalizing; you can teach it along the way (see Chapter 17).

   Lance began vocalizing more and more frequently when he was rewarded with candy and was soon uttering one of his personal sounds ("ee-ah," "nah-nah-nah-nah," or "dahtn-dahtn-dahtn-dahtn") at the rate of one or two times per minute.
   2. *Noise making on command.* Benson uttered the sound "ah" once every 30 seconds and rewarded Lance when he produced any sound within 5 seconds after Benson

said "ah." The rewards were a piece of candy, affection, and the Signed Speech praise "Good talking." The sounds Lance produced at other times Benson rewarded only with affection and praise. His aim was to differentially reinforce vocalizations that immediately followed his own without decreasing the frequency of Lance's other vocalizations. Soon Lance began regularly vocalizing immediately after Benson said "ah." The majority of his vocalizations consisted of his personal sounds ("ee-ah," "nah-nah-nah-nah," "dahtn-dahtn-dahtn-dahtn," and variations thereof). Benson began teaching "ah" only after Lance consistently vocalized immediately after his instructor and produced a wider variety of sounds than he had originally.

B. **Lance's first imitative sound, "ah."** Benson choose this sound as Lance's first imitative sound for a number of reasons. First, "ah" was a component of the sounds Lance babbled on his own—"ee-ah," "nah-nah-nah-nah," and "dahtn-dahtn-dahtn-dahtn." Second, "ah" is a vowel whose production does not require articulatory movements or changes in the shape of the oral cavity. Third, it can be easily prompted by manually opening the child's mouth. Finally, "ah" is a continuant that can be extended to form a new, longer sound or blended into a syllable.

Benson prompted Lance to imitate "ah" by simply holding Lance's mouth open with thumb and forefinger as Lance vocalized after Benson. At first Lance resisted the prompt. Little by little, however, he learned to say "ah" while Benson's fingers held his mouth open, and he even started to open his mouth in anticipation of Benson's fingers. At this point, Benson began to fade the prompt. He moved successively from a forefinger-and-thumb prompt which actually pried open Lance's mouth, to gentle pressure on Lance's upper and lower lip with the forefinger and thumb, to opening the forefinger and thumb in front of Lance's face at mouth level, to simply raising the closed forefinger and thumb from his lap, to no prompt at all. The shift from manual to visual to no prompt is a sequence the teacher will repeat with each new sound.

Although Lance learned to say "ah" without a prompt after Benson said "ah," Lance occasionally said "ah" as soon as Benson merely opened his own mouth (thereby providing a visual prompt). This showed that he was watching for as well as listening to Benson's "ah." Therefore, to teach Lance to respond only to the sound of "ah," Benson occasionally covered his mouth as he vocalized, waited for Lance to say "ah" (which usually came a little late), and then gave the reward. He also occasionally opened his mouth in "ah" fashion without saying "ah," waited to see whether Lance would say "ah," and if Lance did, withheld the reward. In this way Lance soon learned to vocalize only after he heard Benson vocalize: he learned that sound, not sight, is the cue for vocalization. Many children need to be explicitly taught not to rely on visual prompts. You can teach them that mouth shape is an insufficient prompt as Benson taught Lance: by occasionally hiding your mouth with your hand as you vocalize and by occasionally providing a soundless mouth shape.

C. **Lance's second and later sounds.** Lance next learned the following sounds in order: "m," "m-m-m-m," "a-a-a-ah," "mah," "mah-mah-mah-mah," "nah-nah-nah-nah," "oh," "hah," and "h" (unvoiced).

   1. *Lance's second sound, "m."* Benson chose "m" as Lance's second sound for several reasons. He wanted the consonant "m" to follow the vowel "ah" so he could begin establishing the consonant-vowel distinction. He also chose "m" because he thought he could manually prompt it by closing Lance's "ah" mouth. Finally, he chose "m" because it is a continuant sound that can be maintained over a long period of time and, hence, can be easily extended or blended with other sounds.

     a. *"M" in isolation*—Benson began uttering "m" in place of "ah" approximately once every 30 seconds. Lance's first response was surprise: he was so used to hearing "ah" that "m" startled him. His second response was "ah." Like Lance, most children utter old sounds in response to their teachers' new vocalization prompts. Benson tried to prevent Lance from repeating the erroneous "ah" by introducing the prompt he hoped would help Lance say "m." With his forefinger and thumb, he pressed Lance's lips together as Lance said "ah." In the face of this prompt, Lance stopped vocalizing.

After Benson realized that closing Lance's mouth

would not work, he tried a different manual prompt. He pushed his horizontal forefinger between Lance's parted lips as Lance tried to say "ah." Lance pressed his lips together on Benson's horizontal forefinger to keep it from moving further into his mouth, but did not stop vocalizing. The result of simultaneously vocalizing and clamping his lips on Benson's finger was an "m." Benson's horizontal forefinger pressed against Lance's lips was thus an effective prompt, whereas the forefinger-and-thumb lip closure was not. As this example shows, finding an effective prompt is often not easy because the obvious ones do not always work. There are, however, almost always other possibilities.

When Lance was regularly clasping Benson's horizontal forefinger between his lips and saying "m," Benson began fading the prompt. He faded it first to a horizontal forefinger in front of Lance's face, then to a hand raised from his own lap with forefinger extended, then to the "m" alone.

b. *"M" and "ah" in alternating trial blocks*—Once Lance was regularly saying "m" after Benson, Benson switched back to "ah" and retaught it. He used the same manual prompt as he had originally, the forefinger and thumb that opened Lance's mouth. When Benson first switched back to "ah," Lance was a bit surprised and continued trying to say "m." Very soon, however, he responded to the prompt and converted his "m" to an "ah." When the child knows only two sounds, manual prompts at switchpoints between trial blocks serve to convert one sound to the other. As Lance began saying "ah" rather than "m," Benson began fading his forefinger-thumb prompt. He faded the manual finger prompt first to a visual finger prompt, then dropped it completely. When Lance was consistently saying "ah" after he did, Benson switched back to and retaught "m." Over successive blocks, Lance required fewer manual prompts and switched in fewer trials.

c. *"M" and "ah" in random order*—Benson introduced this stage when Lance was switching to the alternate sound in three to five trials. Lance soon learned to say "m" after Benson said "m" and "ah" after Benson said "ah." In other words, he learned to imitate "m" and "ah."

2. *Lance's next new sound, "m-m-m-m."* Benson thought he could teach this sound by merely extending Lance's "m." He uttered an "m-m-m-m" once every 30 seconds and waited for Lance to imitate him. At first Lance uttered a short "m" in response. Benson then held his horizontal forefinger against Lance's lips (the original "m" prompt) after Lance produced the short "m" for a short period and while Lance was not voicing any sound. In response to the pressure of Benson's finger, Lance extended his "m" and Benson faded his finger prompt. When Lance was regularly imitating long "m-m-m-m"'s, Benson then reintroduced short "m"'s randomly among the long ones. Lance soon learned to utter short "m"'s to Benson's short "m"'s and long "m-m-m-m"'s to Benson's long "m-m-m-m"'s.

3. *"A-a-a-ah."* Benson extended "ah" after he extended "m" because he was planning to teach Lance "mah." He held Lance's mouth open with his forefinger and thumb to show Lance how to extend the short "ah"'s to long "a-a-a-ah"'s. After Lance learned to imitate long "a-a-a-ah"'s with this manual prompt, Benson faded his prompt and began alternating between blocks of long "a-a-a-ah"'s and blocks of short "ah"'s. Then after Lance learned to switch between blocks, Benson began uttering long "a-a-a-ah"'s and short "ah"'s in random order, and when Lance mastered this step, Benson reintroduced long "m-m-m-m"'s and short "m"'s. Lance soon learned to imitate long and short "ah"'s and "m"'s in random order.

4. *"Mah": blending "m" and "ah."* Benson chose to teach Lance to imitate "mah" because he thought Lance could easily learn to blend the long "m-m-m-m" and long "a-a-a-ah" to form "mah" and because he wanted to introduce a syllable early in training. He first taught Lance to imitate "m-m-m-m" and "a-a-a-ah" in sequence, then to shorten the sounds and move them closer together in time.

   a. *"M-m-m-m" and "a-a-a-ah" in sequence*—Benson said "m-m-m-m," waited for Lance to imitate, said "a-a-a-ah," again waited for Lance to imitate, and then rewarded Lance for the two-sound sequence.

   b. *Shortened sounds closer together in time*—Benson
   shortened his "m-m-m-m" and moved his "a-a-a-ah"
   closer to it in time; then he shortened his "a-a-a-ah"
   and moved the two sounds even closer. Lance also
   shortened his sounds and moved them closer
   together in time. When Benson made his sounds very
   short and moved them very close together, Lance
   began blending the two sounds. With practice he
   soon learned to say "mah" after Benson said "mah."

5. *"Mah-mah-mah-mah."* Benson chose to teach Lance
   "mah-mah-mah-mah" after "mah" because Lance
   repeated syllables while he babbled, as in "nah-nah-nah-
   nah" and "dahtn-dahtn-dahtn-dahtn," and because Benson was planning to teach "nah-nah-nah-nah." He
   taught "mah-mah-mah-mah" by first uttering four successive "mah"s for Lance to imitate in sequence and
   then shortening the time interval between the "mah"s.
   Lance quickly learned to repeat and blend successive
   "mah"s to form "mah-mah-mah-mah." The child who
   knows how to repeat identical syllables will later find it
   easy to learn other syllables.

6. *The next new sound, "nah-nah-nah-nah."* Benson chose
   to teach Lance "nah-nah-nah-nah" after "mah-mah-
   mah-mah" for four reasons. "Nah-nah-nah-nah" was one
   of the syllables Lance occasionally uttered as he babbled. A sound the child babbles can be easy for him to
   learn to imitate. The repetitive syllable structure and
   the "ah" sound shared with "mah-mah-mah-mah" could
   also help make "nah-nah-nah-nah" easy for Lance to
   learn. Benson felt that he could highlight the difference
   in place of consonant articulation between "nah-nah-
   nah-nah" and "mah-mah-mah-mah" for Lance by using
   "mah-mah-mah-mah" as a contrast. Finally, Benson
   thought that after Lance learned about the difference in
   place of consonant articulation between "nah-nah-nah-
   nah" and "mah-mah-mah-mah," he would find other dis-
   tinctions of place of articulation easier to master.

   Benson introduced "nah-nah-nah-nah" in isolation
   after Lance had imitated a sequence of seven "mah-mah-
   mah-mah"s. Lance's repeated imitations of the old
   syllable established an auditory set that highlighted by
   contrast the difference in place of consonant articulation
   between the new and the old syllable. This made the

discrimination easier for Lance. In this way, you can use highlighting by contrast to facilitate the learning of most new sounds. When Benson first said "nah-nah-nah-nah" after seven "mah-mah-mah-mah"'s, Lance was startled and started to say "mah-mah-. . .," but before he could complete his old syllable, Benson stopped him with a combined manual and visual prompt. He placed his right index finger in Lance's open mouth underneath Lance's tongue to push the tongue up for the "n" sound and to hold Lance's mouth open. At the same time, Benson opened his own mouth, keeping his face directly in front of Lance's at eye level, placed his left index finger under his own tongue, and said "nah-nah-nah-nah." He provided this visual as well as manual prompt to draw Lance's attention to the role played by the tongue in the formation of the sound "n." Such combined manual-visual prompts tend to be more effective than either manual or visual prompts alone.

In response to his training, Lance learned first to wiggle his tongue and vocalize at the same time, then to place his tongue in the correct position, and, finally, to say "nah-nah-nah-nah." When he was consistently uttering the syllable with the full prompt, Benson faded the prompt. Lance soon learned to say "nah-nah-nah-nah" without help. At this point, Benson gradually reintroduced blocks of trials on the old syllables ("ah," "a-a-a-ah," "m," "m-m-m-m," "mah," and "mah-mah-mah-mah") and alternated them with blocks of trials on the new one. When Lance was switching from the new one to the other syllables in three to five trials, Benson switched to randomly ordered presentations. Lance quickly mastered the discriminations demanded by the switch to random ordering and was soon consistently imitating "nah-nah-nah-nah," "mah-mah-mah-mah," "mah," "m-m-m-m," "m," "a-a-a-ah," and "ah" in any order that Benson uttered them.

7. *Another new sound, "oh."* Benson chose "oh" as Lance's next new sound for two reasons. First, because it is a vowel, Benson thought that "oh" together with "ah" would possibly help establish a vowel dimension and make later vowels easier for Lance to learn. Second, Benson thought he could easily prompt "oh" by merely opening Lance's "ah" mouth wider.

Benson used his forefinger and thumb prompt to teach "oh." With it he elongated Lance's "ah" mouth vertically as Lance tried to say "ah" in response to Benson's "oh." After not too many prompted "oh" trials, Lance changed his "ah" to "oh" and Benson was able to fade his prompt. Then when Lance consistently imitated "oh" without a prompt, Benson began randomly mixing "ah"s with "oh"s. Lance soon learned to distinguish between the two sounds and to imitate each appropriately: the beginning of the vowel dimension was thus established by these trials.

8. *"Hah."* Benson chose to teach Lance "hah" because he wanted to introduce the unvoiced consonant "h" to begin establishing the voiced-unvoiced distinction. He thought Lance would easily learn "h" as a component of the syllable "hah," whose other component, "ah," he already knew. Benson introduced "hah" in the context of "ah." He uttered "hah"s and "ah"s in alternating two- and three-trial blocks for Lance to imitate. In other words, he highlighted the unvoiced "h" in "hah" by contrasting "hah" with "ah." At the same time, to help Lance find the unvoiced "h," he provided Lance with a combined prompt. He placed his finger into Lance's mouth to make Lance cough slightly in unvoiced fashion as he vocalized, and also heavily aspirated the unvoiced "h" in his own "hah" close to Lance's face.

Lance first said "ah" in response to Benson's "hah," but he soon learned to say "hah." Benson gradually faded his prompts and taught Lance to imitate "hah" and "ah" in random order.

9. *The last new sound, unvoiced "h."* Benson chose the isolated unvoiced "h" as Lance's next sound because it was contained in Lance's immediately preceding syllable, "hah," and because its mastery would help establish more firmly the voiced-unvoiced distinction. Benson thought that if Lance could imitate the unvoiced consonant "h," he could more easily learn some of the other unvoiced consonants such as "p," "t," "k," "f," and "sh."

Benson introduced "h" in highlighted contrast to "hah." He uttered "h" and "hah" in alternating two- and three-trial blocks. He also prompted "h"s by placing his finger in Lance's mouth. After two weeks of prompted trials, Lance imitated his first unvoiced "h." Benson continued contrasting "h" and "hah," always rewarding "h"'s lavishly, and after two days Lance was consistently imitating "h," but only when he was prompted. As Benson very gradually faded his prompts, however, Lance learned to imitate the unvoiced "h" without a prompt. The moral of the "h" is that some sounds take a long time to teach. If you find a prompt that looks as if it might work, stick with it—it probably will work in time.

10. *Spontaneously learned sounds.* Benson taught Lance to imitate "ah," "m," "a-a-a-ah," "m-m-m-m," "mah," "mah-mah-mah-mah," "nah-nah-nah-nah," "oh," "hah," and "h." When he tested Lance on other sounds to assess generalization, he found that Lance could imitate the long "o-o-o-oh" even though he had not been taught it. After children have learned enough sounds, they are often capable of imitating sounds other than the ones they were explicitly taught.

V. **PROMPTS.** As Lance's example shows, imitative vocalizations can be prompted in many ways: using tactile and visual prompts, highlighting by contrast, extending sounds, repeating sounds, commanding the child to vocalize, and imitating the child's own sounds.

A. **Prompting.** Prompting refers to the provision of tactile and visual cues to the child in order to help him imitate the sound the teacher utters.

1. *Tactile prompts.* Tactile prompts for a sound consist of manipulation of a part of the child's body, usually an articulator such as lips, tongue, or teeth, that plays a role in the production of the sound. A tactile prompt is usually the most effective prompt with which to begin instruction on initial sounds. (For children who know many sounds and have had experience with visual as well as tactile prompts, however, a visual prompt may be all that is required.)

Your task, as teacher, is to find a tactile prompt suited to the child with whom you are working. If the first one you try does not seem to be effective, try another: there is almost always a workable possibility. As you may recall from the example, the first prompt with which Benson tried to convert Lance's "ah" to an "m"—pressing Lance's lips together as he vocalized—failed. Lance stopped talking in response to the prompt. Therefore, Benson switched to another prompt, a horizontal index finger pressed against Lance's mouth in between his parted "ah" lips. Lance pressed his lips together on Benson's finger to reject it, but did not stop vocalizing, and thus he changed his "ah" to an "m."

Once you find an effective tactile prompt, use it as often as necessary for the child to learn to imitate the sound. The child will not consistently utter the correct sound early in training even when you help him. With practice, however, he will learn. In addition, you should let him use the prompt for some time even after he has learned to imitate the sound. By providing him with help even when he may not need it, you allow him to learn the sound thoroughly.

After the child learns to imitate the sound, you can begin fading your tactile prompt. Withdraw your hand gradually from the articulator or other part of his body.

2. *Visual prompts.* Visual prompts are either previously tactile prompts or mouth-shape prompts.

   a. *Previously tactile prompts*—As you withdraw your tactile prompt, it will change to a visual prompt. You can let it at first take the same form it had when it was tactile, then slowly foreshorten it, and then let it disappear. As you may recall from the example, Benson began fading his horizontal forefinger (the prompt for "m") by just barely removing it from between Lance's lips. He thus made it visual but still allowed it to maintain its original form, a horizontally extended digit close to Lance's lips. Next, he moved it away from Lance's lips and began crooking it in preparation for its return to his fist. In other words, he changed its form. The final form Benson had it take before making it disappear into his own lap was that of a fist slightly bent away from the lap at the wrist, with only the first two joints of the index finger crookedly extended.

   b. *Mouth-shape prompts*—After you have taught a child ten to twelve sounds, you can use the shape of your mouth and the position of the visible articulators as visual prompts. The child who has been taught many sounds will have learned—perhaps on his own, perhaps with his teacher's help—that he can use his teacher's mouth as a prompt. He will also have learned, or have been taught, that mouth shape as a vocalization prompt is secondary to the sound his teacher utters.

Another example will help explain. Benson used the shape of his mouth and tongue as a visual prompt as he taught Lance the sound "lah." He placed the tip of his tongue just above his upper lip below his nose as a visual prompt before saying "lah" for Lance to imitate. Early in training, he also prompted Lance tactilely, manually urging Lance's tongue toward the space just above Lance's upper lip. Later in training Benson showed Lance his upper-lip "lah" tongue without simultaneously providing a tactile prompt. Early in training, mouth and articulator shape are most effective when accompanied by a tactile prompt. Later they can be used either alone or with a partially faded tactile prompt.

It is best to not use mouth shape as a visual prompt until you have taught the child that it is not a sufficient prompt for vocalization. You can teach him this fact after he knows only one sound, but you may have to reteach it again after he masters his second. You teach the child that mouth shape is not a sufficient prompt by occasionally presenting a soundless mouth shape and not rewarding him for vocalizing to it. You may also occasionally hide your mouth with your hand as you vocalize.

B. **Highlighting by contrast.** You can make a new sound easier for the child to learn by contrasting it with similar known sounds. To illustrate, Benson highlighted the new place of consonant articulation in "nah-nah-nah-nah" by contrasting it with that in "mah-mah-mah-mah." "Nah-nah-nah-nah" is similar to "mah-mah-mah-mah" in syllable structure and shares with it the vowel "ah," but it differs from "mah-mah-mah-mah" in place of consonant articulation. Benson felt that the similarity between the two syllables would create a context within which Lance could easily learn about the new "n" sound and the new place of articulation. He therefore had Lance imitate a sequence of consecutive "mah-mah-

mah-mah"'s immediately prior to introducing "nah-nah-nah-nah." Lance was startled when he first heard "nah-nah-nah-nah" and thus showed that he noticed the difference in sound. After he recovered from his surprise, he started to say "mah-mah-mah-mah" to Benson's "nah-nah-nah-nah." A child will often utter the known contrast sound when a new sound is first introduced. This may be good, for the auditory differences between the known contrast sound the child utters and the new sound his teacher utters can provide the child with important negative information. He hears that his own sound is not an imitation of the new sound spoken by his teacher.

To highlight by contrast, ask the child to imitate a known contrast sound similar to the new sound several times prior to uttering the new sound. The contrast sound should, optimally, share all but one feature with the old one: vowel-consonant, place of articulation, voiced-unvoiced, or manner of articulation. The single-feature difference between the contrast and the new sound among the other feature similarities highlights what is new about the new sound. For instance, the known contrast sound might be a voiced consonant produced at the front of the mouth; the new one, a voiced consonant produced in the middle of the mouth ("d" and "g"). The known sound might be a nasal consonant produced by the lips; the new sound, a voiced nonnasal consonant produced by the lips ("m" and "b"). The old sound might be an unvoiced consonant produced at the front of the mouth, the new one an unvoiced consonant produced at the middle of the mouth ("p" and "k"). If you pay attention to and learn about similarities and differences between sounds, you will find effective contrast sounds easier to choose.

C. **Extending sounds.** You can teach a child to extend sounds by holding a tactile prompt in place after the child has stopped making the sound. The continued tactile prompt serves as a prompt to continue vocalizing. Then, after the child learns to extend a sound, he will find it easier to blend it with others. Lance, for example, easily learned to blend the sounds "m" and "ah" to form "mah" partly because Benson had previously taught him to extend "m" to "m-m-m-m" and "ah" to "a-a-a-ah."

D. **Repeating sounds.** You can teach a child to repeat sounds by teaching him to imitate the same sound a number of times in succession for a single reward and then shortening the time interval between sounds. For example, Benson taught Lance to say "mah-mah-mah-mah" by having Lance imitate a sequence of four "mah"s for his reward and then shortening the interval between "mah"s.

E. **Commanding the child to vocalize.** You can use the Signed Speech commands "Say" and "Again" as vocalization and repetition prompts, respectively, if you have previously taught the child to obey them. When the child understands these commands, it will be easier for you to practice a particular sound with him, either to strengthen it or to correct the child's pronunciation. In addition, the commands will make it easy for you to introduce partial reinforcement in a natural way. (It does not matter whether you teach him to respond to "Again" before you teach him to respond to "Say" or vice versa.)

  1. *"Again."* Teach the child to repeat vocalizations in response to the signed and spoken command "Again" in much the same way that you taught him to repeat signs. If you have already taught him to repeat signs in response to the command "Again," you will probably find it very easy to teach him to repeat sounds to it.

  a. *Imitations followed by "Again" and soundless prompts*—Ask the child to imitate a sound he knows several times in succession. Provide tactile and visual prompts for each imitation even though he can imitate without them, and reward him for each imitation but the last. Then, after he imitates the last sound and you do not reward him, immediately say and sign "Again" and provide him with tactile and visual prompts for the sound, but do not vocalize. For example, you may be teaching the sound "ah." After the child imitates your last "ah," you say and sign "Again" and prompt him manually to open his mouth for another "ah" as you show him your "ah" mouth shape, but do not vocalize an "ah." The child's previous imitations will have established a set to produce the sound. Therefore, even though you do not vocalize, he will still utter the sound when you sign and say "Again" and prompt him. You should reward him for doing so.

    b. *Removing imitations*—When, after a sequence of several prompted and rewarded imitations, the child vocalizes consistently to "Again" and the soundless prompts, you may begin removing imitations one by one from the sequence.

    c. *Fading prompts*—After the child vocalizes to "Again" and the soundless prompts after only a single previous imitation, you can begin fading the soundless prompts. He will soon learn to repeat the sound he imitated each time you say and sign "Again."

    d. *Repeated training*—It is best to repeat the training sequence with a number of different sounds to teach the child to obey the command "Again" with any sound you present.

  2. *"Say."* Teach the child to utter a sound in response to the command "Say" much as you taught him to repeat vocalizations to the command "Again."

    a. *Imitations followed by "Say"*—Without signing and saying the command "Say" prior to uttering the sound, you may ask the child to imitate a sound several times in succession, then immediately sign and say "Say" and utter the sound once more for him to imitate. His previous repetitions will have established the set to utter the sound, so he will utter it without attempting to imitate your signed and spoken "Say."

    b. *More "Say"s*—It is important to introduce the signed and spoken command "Say" more and more often prior to uttering the sound. The child will soon learn to utter the sound after you sign and say "Say" and to vocalize the sound without imitating your instruction, "Say."

    c. *Repeated training*—You should repeat the training sequence with a number of different sounds.

F. Imitating the child's sounds. The child with whom you work will probably babble sounds even when he is not imitating you because you will have rewarded him for doing so. You should occasionally imitate these babblings. He may then repeat a sound of his after you imitate it, that is, inadvertantly imitate your imitation, and you may be able to begin explicitly teaching him to imitate that sound.

VI. ERRORS. Correct the child's verbal imitation errors much as you corrected her signing errors: by providing prompts and by allowing the child to correct herself. As with signs, there are two types of errors: within-sound and between-sound errors. Within-sound errors occur when the child imitates her teacher's sound but fails to pronounce it well; between-sound errors occur when she responds with an altogether different sound. Correct the child's within-sound errors by providing prompts followed by a reward for good production. Correct her between-sound errors either with prompts or by allowing self-correction, that is, by not rewarding the child until she utters the correct sound twice. Otherwise she may merely learn to go unthinkingly through her sound repertoire.

VII. REINFORCEMENT. You reward the child for imitating sounds much as you did for signing. You may say and sign "Good talking," hug her, kiss her, or pat her on the back, and give her or ask her to sign for a desired object or activity. This signing for the reward will not confuse the child, but instead will give her the idea that signs and sounds are related. After she receives her desired object or activity, you may repeat the sound she imitated to emphasize its correctness. You should not repeat it before you give the reward, however; this could suggest to her that the correct imitation was in fact wrong and could lead to inappropriate attempts at self-correction. It could also provoke stutter-like repetitions you will later have to curb.

The child may occasionally sign during verbal imitation lessons as she imitates your sounds. This signing will not interfere with the lessons, so either ignore it or, when it takes the form of a request, occasionally grant the request. The child will eliminate this random signing on her own.

VIII. MASTERY CRITERION. You will know that the child can imitate a given sound or syllable when he consistently, that is, on 85 to 90 percent of the trials, utters it immediately after you do. After he has learned to imitate a number of sounds, he will probably begin to expand his imitative sound skills on his own. If you test him, you may find him capable of one or more of the following skills:

A. Imitating the duration of sounds other than the ones you taught him to extend.

B. Imitating the repetition of sounds other than the ones you taught him to repeat.

C. Blending sounds other than the ones you taught him to blend.

D. Imitating the volume of your sounds.

E. Imitating the pitch of your sounds.

7

Combinations of Sounds: Syllables and Words

I. Teaching strategies

II. Example: Joe learns the syllable "pem"

III. Building a vocabulary

IV. Two sample vocabularies

V. Imitation after the teacher

VI. Continued development and refinement

VII. Continued instructional support

After the child learns five to ten sounds, his verbal imitation skills will be strong enough for him to begin combining his sounds to form syllables and words. The child who can imitate syllables and words with ease is then ready to integrate his sound skills with spontaneous signing and to begin using Signed Speech. In this chapter, we detail techniques for teaching the child both syllables and words, for training him to imitate sounds after his teacher, and for refining his speech.

Syllables are linked sounds. You begin syllable instruction by systematically teaching the child to connect single sounds into syllables as soon as he can imitate two or more consonants and two or more vowels. He will probably know enough sounds to form syllables before he knows enough sounds to form meaningful words; therefore, you will probably teach actual words somewhat later. As you choose which syllables to teach, you should keep several important facts in mind. First, remember that syllables built with known sounds are easier for the child to learn than those which contain one or more unfamiliar sounds. Second, remember that syllables composed of only two sounds tend to be easier for the child to master than longer syllables, and those beginning with a consonant seem to be easier than those ending in one. Finally, note that continuants such as "m," "ah," and "s" are easier for the child to blend into syllables than are noncontinuants such as "b," "k," and "l." When possible, then, you should choose initial syllables that are composed of continuants.

I. **TEACHING STRATEGIES.** In the following sections, we outline the basic techniques for teaching syllables and words.

A. **Sequencing and blending sounds.** The primary technique for teaching syllables is to teach the child to link the individual sounds in the syllable together in sequence and then to blend the sounds together. (This strategy has already been discussed in Chapter 6.) As mentioned, it is best to choose initial syllables which begin with a familiar continuant consonant and end with a familiar vowel. For example, "sah" would be a good initial syllable for a child who knows the sounds "s" and "ah."

Let us assume that the child you are teaching can imitate the consonant "s" and the vowel "ah," that he knows how to repeat and extend sounds, and that you have chosen to teach him the syllable "sah." To begin teaching the child to sequence, sign and say "Say" and then immediately say "s"; wait for the child to verbalize "s"; then sign and say "Say" again and follow immediately with "ah"; wait for the child to verbalize "ah"; and then give him the reward. (In the descriptions which follow, the temporal relations between the teacher's vocal prompts and the child's imitative vocalized responses are schematized through spacing and punctuation.)

Teacher: "Say 's.' " . . . "Say 'ah.' " (reward)
                        | | | |
Child: "s." . . . . "ah."

You then gradually fade the signed and spoken "Say" in between the "s" and the "ah," first signing it without speaking and then removing it completely.

Teacher: "Say 's.' " . . . Say "ah.". (reward)
                        | | | |
Child: "Say 's.' " . . . Say "ah." (reward)

Teacher: "Say 's.' " . . . . . "ah.". (reward)

Child   "s." . . . . . "ah."

As you fade the "Say" before the "ah," the child learns to vocalize an "ah" in the absence of your command.

Next, shorten the interval between sounds to force blending. You have just faded the command which preceded the final sound, "ah." Now, gradually shorten the interval between the "s" and the "ah," and at the same time, since both sounds are continuants, enhance their blendability by extending them.

Teacher: "Say 's-s . a-ah.' " (reward)

Child: "s-s . a-ah."

When the interval between your "s-s" and your "a-ah" becomes very short, the child's "s-s" will begin to overlap your "a-ah" temporally. This will prompt him to switch quickly to "a-ah" and begin blending the two sounds. Now reduce the interval between your sounds to zero, that is, utter an integrated syllable rather than two separate sounds, and cease extending your sounds.

Teacher: "Say 's-ah.' " (reward)

Child: "s-ah."

Teacher: "Say 'sah.' " (reward)

Child: "sah."

As you reduce the interval between and shorten your sounds, the child will learn to blend his "s" and "ah" into the syllable "sah."

You can teach any two-sound syllable by sequencing, just as for "sah." If the initial consonant is not a continuant, however, you will not be able to rely on extension to increase its blendability. You can also teach syllables composed of three or more sounds by sequencing: you merely treat them as a series of two-sound syllables, for example, "a-b," "ab-a," "aba-da," "abada-ba." In other words, teach the child to blend the first two sounds, then the first two with the third, and so on until he has finally integrated all the sounds into a single string.

After the child masters five or six syllables, you will probably be able to teach him new ones, starting with the blending of individual sounds into a single syllable. Although blending is a very effective technique for teaching syllables such as "vee" and "sah," which are composed of continuants, you can also use it to teach syllables not composed solely of continuants, for example, "kee" and "gah." Though the consonants "k," "g," "t," "d," "p," and "b" cannot be extended, they can be quickly repeated and fitted into a modified blending format. Thus, where you would teach the child to blend the sounds in the syllable "vee" by prompting him with an elongated "v-v-v-e-e-ee," you would teach him to blend the sounds in "kee" by prompting him with a repeated "k": "k--k--k-e-e-ee." The blending sequence for "vee," a syllable beginning with a continuant, might appear as in the following description:

Teacher: "Say 'v-v-v-e-e-ee.' " (reward)
Child: "v-v. e-ee."

Teacher: "Say 'v-ve-ee.' " (reward)
Child: "v-ee."

Teacher: "Say 'vee.' " (reward)
Child: "vee."

A blending sequence for "kee," a syllable beginning with a repeatable noncontinuant, might appear thus:

Teacher: "Say 'k--k--k-e-e-ee.' " (reward)
Child: "k. e-ee."

Teacher: "Say 'k--ke-ee.' " (reward)
Child: "k-ee."

Teacher: "Say 'kee.' " (reward)
Child: "kee."

B. **Contextual prompting.** This term refers to the use of known sounds to create a context in which the child will find a new sound, a relation between sounds, or a syllable easier to learn. There are three types of contextual prompting which may be used: highlighting by contrast, assimilative prompting, and fluency enhancement.

1. *Highlighting by contrast.* This technique has already been discussed in Chapter 6 (pages 69-70). We will therefore not repeat it here.

2. *Assimilative prompting.* This refers to practice on known sounds similar to the new one immediately prior to the introduction of the new sound. Such practice makes learning the new sound easier for the child by allowing him to assimilate it to what he already knows. Two sounds can be similar in that both are vowels or consonants, articulated at the same place, voiced or unvoiced, or produced in the same manner.

   Let us assume that you would like to teach the syllable "pem." You would then have the child practice the unvoiced consonants "s" and "k" in initial position to facilitate his imitation of the unvoiced "p" in "pem." Similarly, you would have him practice the voiced consonants "d" and "n" in final positions to facilitate his imitation of the "m" in "pem." Sometimes you can have the child practice similar sounds as detached sounds and sometimes as a part of a syllable. Assimilative prompting moves the child psychologically closer to the new sound or syllable and allows him to attempt it in a supportive context.

3. *Fluency enhancement.* This refers to having the child practice a variety of old sounds in a given position in the new syllable immediately prior to introducing the new sound. Fluency enhancement frees the sounds adjacent to the given position in the syllable from prior associations. This makes it easier for the child to insert a different sound in the given position and to link adjacent sounds to it. For example, to enhance vowel fluency prior to working on "pem," you would have the child practice syllables such as "pim" and "pom." To enhance the initial consonant fluency, you would have him practice "sem" and "kem." Fluency enhancement teaches the child to treat syllable components as freely variable elements. It also serves as assimilative prompting if sounds similar to the deleted sound are inserted as variants (but not otherwise).

II. **EXAMPLE: JOE LEARNS THE SYLLABLE "PEM."** We present in detail a hypothetical example of learning a syllable to illustrate the methods just discussed.

    A. **Sequencing and blending.** First, Benson broke "pem" into its component sounds and taught Joe to say them in sequence: "p" + "eh" + "m," "p" + "em," and "peh" + "m." The strategy of using various sequences helped Joe approach syllable production in more than one way. Benson next practiced extended versions of the syllable with Joe by starting with a repeated "p": "p--p--peh-eh-m-m."

    B. **Contextual prompting.**

        1. *Assimilative prompting.* As Benson taught Joe the components of his new syllable, he had Joe practice several series of related sounds immediately prior to introducing the sound "p." Thus, to help Joe attend to and say "p," he drilled Joe on two previously learned unvoiced consonants in the following series: "s," "k," "p," "peh," "pem." Benson used the same technique with the final voice consonant "m" by having Joe practice the series "d," "n," "m," "em," "pem."

        2. *Fluency enhancement.* To help Joe produce a smooth transition between the initial unvoiced consonant "p" and the following vowel-consonant syllable "em," Benson paired "em" with two unvoiced initial consonants and had Joe utter "sem," "kem," "pem" in sequence. To ease the transition between the initial consonant-vowel syllable "peh" and the final voiced "m," Benson paired "peh" with two voiced final consonants and had Joe say "ped," "pen," "pem." Similarly, for the transition between the initial consonant "p" and the following vowel "eh," Benson had Joe practice two consonant-vowel pairs containing "p" in the series "pah," "poh," "peh," "pem." To facilitate the transition between the vowel "eh" and the final consonant "m," Benson had Joe practice two related vowel-consonant pairs, thus: "ahm," "eem," "em," "pem." Finally, for the transitions to and from the vowel, that is, from the initial consonant "p" to the vowel "eh" and from the vowel "eh" to the final consonant "m," Benson had Joe practice a variety of vowels in between "p" and "m" immediately

prior to introducing "pem." Thus Joe practiced the following series: "pim," "pom," "pem."

3. *Highlighting by contrast.* To highlight the lack of voicing in "p," Benson had Joe practice the contrasting voiced consonant produced at the same place with the lips, "b," by having Joe say the sequence "bem," "bem," "bem," "pem." Then, to help Joe attend to the place of articulation of "m," Benson had Joe practice a contrasting nasal consonant, "n," in the sequence "pen," "pen," "pen," "pem." Finally, to help Joe hear the difference between "eh" and other vowels, Benson had Joe practice the contrasting vowel "i" in the series "pim," "pim," "pim," "pem."

III. **BUILDING A VOCABULARY.** You should choose simple syllables early in training, more complex ones later on. The following guidelines will be of help as you continue to teach syllables.

A. **Increase the level of difficulty.** Teach vowel-consonant and vowel-vowel syllables (diphthongs) after you teach initial consonant-vowel syllables. Following this you may increase the number of component sounds: introduce consonant-vowel-consonant syllables.

B. **Continue teaching new sound elements.** Spend part of every lesson experimenting with new sounds. As the child progresses, she will develop speech skills that she will not show you if you do not ask her to. By eliciting these additional skills, you will both broaden the range and increase the productivity of her speech.

C. **Introduce words as soon as possible.** Words are syllables or syllable combinations with specific meanings. Begin teaching the child the sound elements of the words corresponding to her signs during verbal imitation lessons as early as possible, and teach her the words themselves as soon as she knows the component sounds. The child will probably begin adding verbal approximations to some of her signs during sign language lessons when she knows the component sounds of the words corresponding to the signs and can produce consonant-vowel-consonant syllables.

Words are taught in the same way as syllables. In addition, however, you can capitalize on their meaningfulness. You can prompt words with partially modeled signs and with their referents just as you would signs, as well as with verbal cues. On occasion the child will probably produce the signs corresponding to the words you are teaching her during verbal imitation lessons. Allow her to do so but do not require it. Until she begins spontaneously adding words or word approximations to her signs during sign language lessons on her own, she will not be ready for you to begin explicitly teaching her Signed Speech. When the signs the child produces during verbal imitation lessons prior to initiating Signed Speech appear to be requests, you should occasionally grant them; when they do not, you may ignore them or briefly comment on them in passing.

D. **Analyze each new syllable and word carefully.** The strategy of breaking a syllable into its elements and teaching these elements separately is particularly important for syllables which are more complex than they at first appear. Many apparently unitary vowels, for example, are actually two-vowel blends (diphthongs): "ai" is "ah-ee," "ow" is "ah-oo," and "ay" is "eh-ee." And some consonants are best taught as consonant combinations. "Ch," for instance, is best taught as the combination "t-sh," and "j" as the combination "d-zh" (where "zh" is the voiced version of "sh"). Teach these complex vowels and consonants as two- rather than single-element sounds. The general rule is: analyze any sound or syllable you plan to teach carefully so that you can teach it part by part if you have to.

E. **Remember that guidelines are not rules.** Sound and syllable order for a particular child will not conform to the guidelines just discussed exactly but will be determined by the following: the sounds the child babbles; the successive sounds the child is taught; the sounds the teacher tries to teach but drops because, for one reason or another, the child does not learn them; the child's occasional forgetting of previously learned sounds; the context of instruction for new sounds created by the old sounds the child knows; the child's fluctuating motivation to produce and learn sounds; and the child's tendency to imitate. The path along which a child moves as she develops productive speech skills is not completely determined by what her teacher chooses to teach. If you keep this fact in mind, you will find it easier to deal with fluctuations and regressions in speech skill acquisition.

IV. TWO SAMPLE VOCABULARIES. To show you how syllable vocabularies grow, we present below some of Benson's notes to himself on the choice of new syllables for Lance and George's orderly summary of the early sounds and syllables he taught Jimmy. Benson's notes focus on problems and experimentation, George's, on mastery and progress.

A. **Benson's notes on Lance.**

Oct. 13—Lance occasionally says "oh" to "ah," so I am trying to build the "oh-ah" discrimination. His unvoiced "h" is still not perfect, so I still occasionally use the finger-in-the-back-of-the-mouth prompt. I am looking for an easy new sound for Lance and have tried "bopm"; it seems to work a bit. It is a good sound because it is a syllable Lance babbles to himself. It also contains a voiceless consonant, "p"; and Lance may view it, I think, as an approximation of the word "popcorn."

Oct. 15—Lance is starting to aspirate "h" at the beginning of all his sounds, so I only reward him with food when he doesn't introduce one. I'm still working on "bopm" (but Lance hasn't got it yet), and am thinking of teaching "ball" (a sign Lance almost knows).

Oct. 18—I introduced "mo," "ho," "no," and "wah-wah-wah" today and Lance seems to be getting all of them, the "wah-wah-wah" by contrast with his well-practiced "oh-oh-oh." I'm also reteaching the "mah-mah-mah-mah," which Lance seems to have partially forgotten. Lance still hasn't mastered "bopm."

Oct. 20—I'm still working on "ball" and "bopm." Since Lance is having difficulties, I'm accepting as an approximation to "bopm" any sound that contains a "b" or a "p," and as an approximation to "ball" any sound that contains a "b" or an "l."

Oct. 30—I introduced "woah" today and Lance had no trouble with it.

Nov. 3—"Nah-nah-nah-nah" is sometimes a good sound to try before "bopm." This is probably because Lance occasionally repeats "bopm"'s to himself with the same rhythm pattern with which he imitates "nah-nah-nah-nah."

Nov. 4—I have reintroduced Lance's self-stimulatory "dotn," which I earlier tried to teach him control over but failed. Perhaps his partial knowledge of "bopm" will make it easier for me to teach him "dotn": "dotn" is just "bopm" transferred from the front to the middle of the mouth.

Nov. 7—I began teaching Lance to say "baby," "daddy," "nee," "mee," and "wee" today and he didn't have any problems with the syllables.

Nov. 10—It seemed like time for a new sound, so I started teaching Lance the unvoiced "p." Perhaps his knowing how to say "bopm" will make "p" easier for him to learn. In searching for the best way to present "p" I hit on repetition: I found Lance more willing to say "p" after I said "p-p."

Nov. 11—I tried to teach Lance to imitate "hi," but he only said "ai" ("ah-ee"). Since "ai" is a new sound for him, however, I changed my "hi" to an "ai" and taught him "ai." Lance still hasn't learned "p."

Nov. 13—I introduced "dee," "deetun," "beepem," "doe," "done," "bai," "day," and "doo," and Lance seemed to do well with all of them. "Dee" and "deetun" probably grew out of the "dotn" he just mastered, and "beepem" out of his knowledge of "bopm."

Nov. 15—Lance has "p" under control, so I started to teach "pee" and "pop," both of which didn't prove difficult. I also introduced, and only had a little trouble with, "why" ("oo-ah-ee") and "tee."

Benson's notes to himself show that teaching syllables is not a straight-line process, but one with detours, regressions, and repetitions.

During the last two weeks of instruction described above, Lance began adding verbal approximations to his signs during sign language lessons. He started by humming along with his signs, moved on to vowel-only word approximations, then to vowel approximations with a final consonant or syllable, and lastly, after about three more months of instruction, to complete words.

Benson's notes convey the flavor of instruction but do not describe with precision the syllables Lance mastered or when he mastered them. To show more clearly the progression of sound and syllable mastery prior to the initiation of Signed Speech, we next present George's summary of Jimmy's progress during verbal imitation lessons prior to his addition of word approximations to his signs. The summary tells what month Jimmy mastered a sound (but not when the sound was introduced, how often Jimmy forgot a sound and had to relearn it, and what sounds were tried out and then dropped).

B. George's summary of Jimmy's progress.
September—"ah," "m"
October—"k," "mah," "oh"
November—"mama," "wha" ("oo-ah"), "ow" ("ah-oo"), "ahm," "ohm," "oak," "kah," "koh," "loo," "keh"
December—"uh," "h" (unvoiced), "doo," "tsipah" (almost "chip," a food whose sign Jimmy knew), "key," "dah," "dee," "bah," "t" (unvoiced)
Jimmy began adding word approximations to his signs in December. Like Lance, he began adding them at about the time that he began learning consonant-vowel-consonant syllables and after he could imitate most of the component sounds of the words whose approximations he began to add to his signs.

V. **IMITATION AFTER THE TEACHER.** As you teach syllables, it is important to have the child imitate your sounds after you complete them rather than imitate them echoically by "shadowing" you as you say them. If the child can imitate sounds he remembers hearing, he has greater control over his voice than if he shadows sounds. Some nonverbal children who are taught to speak through verbal imitation tend to imitate the teacher echoically. For example, the child says the "Da" in Daddy while his teacher is saying the "dy."

If the child with whom you work shadows, you should teach him to imitate sounds after you complete them by combining signed and spoken prompts in a repetition-based format. You would initiate this training only after he could imitate a wide variety of syllables.

A. Repetitions. Have the child repeat a sound he knows well, for example, "ah," several times in succession, commanding him to imitate with a signed and spoken "Say" each time.

Teacher: "Say 'ah.' " . "Say 'ah.' " . "Say 'ah.' " (reward)
Child:　　　　"ah." . . . . ."ah." . . . . . . "ah."

B. Unvoiced mouth-shape prompts for the last sound. Have the child repeat the series again but do not voice the last sound: sign and say "Say" and merely provide a mouth-shape cue for the sound.

Teacher: "Say 'ah.' " . "Say 'ah.' " . "Say" ah . . (reward)
Child: "ah." . . . . . "ah." . . . . "ah."

You will find that after the child overcomes his initial surprise, his set to repeat the sound will lead him to utter it when he sees your unvoiced mouth-shape prompt. This repetition in the absence of a vocal prompt is his first step toward production of the sound after you on the basis of remembered information.

C. **Shortened sequences of repetitions.** After the child is consistently uttering the sound to your mouth-shape prompt, you can gradually remove repetitions from the sequence until only one voiced sound remains.

Teacher: "Say 'ah.' " . "Say" ah . . (reward)
Child: "ah." . . . . . . "ah."

D. **No mouth-shape prompts.** After the child learns to utter the sound to your mouth-shape prompt after only one prior imitation, you can cease providing the prompt. Merely sign and say "Say."

Teacher: "Say 'ah.' " . "Say ." . . . (reward)
Child: "ah." . . . . . . "ah."

The child's set to imitate and his prior practice at imitating in the absence of a vocal prompt will lead him to imitate even in the absence of a mouth-shape prompt.

E. **Sounds in short bursts.** After the child is consistently uttering the sound to the command "Say" without a mouth-shape prompt and after only one prior vocal imitation, you can begin saying the sound in a short, quick burst.

Teacher: "Say 'ah.' " . . . (reward)
Child: "ah."

Your burst will be too short for him to shadow, so he will have to imitate the sound after you complete it. If he has difficulty imitating bursts, you can mix in some "Say" plus mouth-shape trials. When the child consistently imitates you after you complete the sound, you can gradually lengthen your bursts and begin uttering normal-length sounds. You may find it helpful to reintroduce burst trials occasionally to remind the child not to shadow.

You should teach the child to imitate a wide variety of sounds after you. Once he can do so on the basis of remembered information, he will, on his own, generalize his ability to new sounds, syllables, and words. It is important not to force him to imitate every sound after you, however, especially if the sound is a difficult one: too much pressure will only impede generalization. Once again, your goal is to promote spontaneity in the learning of new sounds, syllables and words.

VI. **CONTINUED DEVELOPMENT AND REFINEMENT.** You should continue intensive speech instruction using verbal imitation even after the child has mastered a wide variety of sounds, syllables, and words. The goal is the development of productive speech skills which the child will then be able to link to signs in Signed Speech and finally use alone as verbal language. "Productive" means that the child can easily produce a wide variety of familiar and novel sounds and recombine old sounds in new ways. The child will only develop this capacity if you continue intensive speech instruction beyond the time when she can produce the words corresponding to her signs, through her development of Signed Speech, and well into, or beyond, the time when she begins to use verbal language. In the present section, we discuss speech refinement, the continued instruction with which you will be concerned after the child learns to pronounce words. Speech refinement includes instruction in new sounds, two-word phrases, and loudness.

A. **New sounds.** As the child's sign and word vocabulary grows, she will come in contact with sounds she does not know. Previously nonverbal children tend to have difficulty with the following: consonant clusters, such as "st," "tr," "pl," "str," "spl," and "spr"; final consonants; fricatives, such as "sh," "th" (in thin), "th" (in then), "v," and "z"; two-sound vowels (diphthongs), such as "ai" ("ah-ee"), "ow" ("ah-oo"), and "ay" ("ah-ee"); and back-of-the-mouth, or velar, consonants such as "k," "g," and the back "r."

1. *Consonant clusters.* Consonant clusters such as "spl" and "thr" are typically the last sounds mastered by both normal and speech-delayed children. For the child who was once nonverbal, these sounds are especially difficult, so it is best to teach them through sequencing, that is, part by part. Begin instruction by having the child repeat the cluster components in sequence, as in "s" + "p" + "l"; then teach her to blend them in a single unit, in this case, "spl." It is important to be especially patient when you teach difficult consonant-to-consonant transitions.

2. *Final consonants.* Children tend to find word-final consonants difficult to learn. This is especially true of unvoiced final consonants, such as the "p" in "map"; final consonant clusters, such as the "zle" in "puzzle"; and, most notably, unvoiced final consonant clusters, such as the "st" in "rest." A good prompt to use with final consonants is exaggeration, which can take the form of repetition, extension, increased loudness, or vowel addition.

   a. *Repetition*—Repetition as a technique to exaggerate initial consonants was mentioned in the discussion of blending. Repetition can also be used for the purpose of exaggeration with a difficult final consonant such as the "p" in "cup."

   Teacher: "Say 'cup--p--p.' " (reward)
   Child: "cu". ."p."

   b. *Extension*—This is used not only to facilitate sequencing and blending as discussed earlier, but also for exaggeration. With a difficult final unvoiced consonant, such as the "s" in "pass," extension for the purpose of exaggeration might appear thus:

   Teacher: "Say 'pass-s-ss.' " (reward)
   Child: " pa ".."ss."

   This is a useful technique for exaggerating and facilitating the blending of complex vowels such as "ai" ("ah-ee"), as well as for exaggerating final extendable consonants.

c. *Increased loudness*—An increase in loudness is a good way to exaggerate any sound except an unvoiced one. For instance, the voiced "n" in "man" might be increased in loudness for emphasis as it is extended, thus: "maN--N--N." Increases in loudness are often accompanied by extension or repetition because it is easier to increase the loudness of a sound when it is extended or repeated than when it is not.

d. *Vowel addition*—This is a type of exaggeration especially useful with unvoiced and noncontinuous final consonants, such as the "t" in "cat." Vowel addition with "cat" might appear thus:

> Teacher: "Say 'catuh.' " (reward)
>
> Child: "catuh."

The added vowel ("uh") exaggerates the difficult sound ("t") by creating a vocal context within which the child can more easily attend to and learn the difficult sound. After the child masters the new sound, the added vowel can be faded.

3. *Fricatives.* Unvoiced sounds, such as "th" (in "thin"), "f," "s," and "sh," and voiced sounds, such as "th" (in "then"), "v," "z," and "zh" (the voiced version of "sh") are fricatives. They share the same manner of production, air rushing through a narrow passage. Fricatives, as a group, are difficult for previously nonverbal children to learn. You can use exaggeration by extension and manual prompts (formation of the child's mouth into the proper mouth shape) to make them easier for the child to learn.

4. *Two-sound vowels (diphthongs).* "Ai" ("ah-ee"), "ow" ("ah-oo"), and "ay" ("eh-ee") are two-sound vowels (diphthongs). Previously nonverbal children typically only learn two-sound vowels after they learn the component single vowels. Two-sound vowels should therefore be taught as blends.

5. *Back-of-the-mouth consonants.* Back consonants, such as "g" and "k," are not easy to shape, which makes it difficult to use successive approximations to teach them. You should therefore try to find manual, visual, and contextual prompts you think will help the child learn back consonants, and repeat these prompts even in the face of 8 to 10 days of apparent failure. With back consonants, the

transition from inability to produce the sound to mastery is often abrupt and may follow a period of little or no apparent progress. Manual prompts which involve the insertion of the teacher's fingers into the child's mouth are particularly useful with back consonants.

B. **Two-word phrases.** It is a good idea to provide the child with explicit instruction in uttering two-word phrases, even though she will come to do so naturally as she integrates signs and speech. You teach two-word phrases as syllable strings with a pause in the middle. To show the child that any two words can be combined in this way, have her practice a wide variety of such phrases. It is important to not practice much beyond the point at which she begins consistently imitating two-word phrases during verbal imitation lessons, however: too much practice may begin to encourage echolalia.

C. **Loudness.** Loudness is a basic dimension of speech, and the child who has control over it will have more productive speech skills than the child who does not. Teach loudness explicitly, even though the child will probably already have gained some control over the dimension on her own as a function of her practice with sounds. Because loudness is most easily taught through the presentation of contrasting pairs of sounds, it is a good idea not to begin instruction until the child can produce a variety of words and some two-word phrases. We schematize contrastive pairing by using upper-case letters to represent loud sounds and lower-case letters to represent soft sounds.

Teacher: "Say 'AH.' " . . "Say 'ah.' " (reward)
Child: "AH." . . . . "ah."

Teacher: "Say 'ah.' " . . "Say 'AH.' " (reward)
Child: "ah." . . . . "AH."

As you present the child with pairs of sounds which differ only in loudness, you should utter loud-soft and soft-loud pairs in random order and use a variety of the sounds the child knows well. After the child can control loudness, you may be able to help her express her emotions by teaching her to yell or whisper when she is angry.

VII. CONTINUED INSTRUCTIONAL SUPPORT. It is best to continue speech instruction for as long as you work with a child. The child who was nonverbal rarely outgrows the need for the support speech instruction provides and the demands it makes.

Signed Speech

Signed Speech is what is new about the Signed Speech Program. Many children who are taught sign language and speech production as independent skills begin adding words to their signs on their own; some subsequently move from simultaneous signs and words, that is, Signed Speech, to words alone. In Chapter 8 we describe techniques for teaching the nonverbal child who begins speaking as he signs to use Signed Speech for all of his communications, that is, to simultaneously say and sign every utterance he produces. In Chapter 9 we describe techniques for teaching the child who begins fading the signs from his Signed Speech on his own to speak without signing.

8

Signed Speech:
Integration of Signs and Words

I. Critical speech skills: Imitation and pronunciation

II. Facilitating the initiation of Signed Speech

III. Teaching strategies

IV. Stuttering errors

V. Building a vocabulary

VI. Duration of Signed Speech instruction

After a child begins using multisign utterances spontaneously and after he can imitate syllables and words, he is likely to begin spontaneously adding words or word approximations to his signs, that is, to begin using Signed Speech. The day the child begins integrating signs and sounds is a day composed only of dramatic moments, and hearing the child begin to speak as he signs is a compelling and rewarding experience. The speech children first add to their signs varies from child to child. Low-functioning children typically initiate Signed Speech by adding undifferentiated singsong vowel accompaniments to their signs, higher level children typically add one or more words or word approximations to their signs; and both typically begin by adding vocal accompaniments to the final sign in an utterance. Once a child begins talking as he signs, he tends to continue. Signed Speech is a robust phenomenon that is not easily suppressed. The more it is used, the more the spontaneity of the signs transfers to and becomes an integral part of the words; after several months of spontaneous communication in simultaneous signs and words, the child will be ready to begin fading his signs and moving on to verbal language.

In the present chapter, we specify techniques for teaching the child to simultaneously say and sign his utterances. We discuss the speech skills critical to the development of Signed Speech and the prompts the teacher should use to stimulate it. Then we detail the techniques for teaching Signed Speech explicitly and for dealing with errors the child is likely to make. Last, we consider the introduction of new concepts and the duration of Signed Speech instruction.

I. **CRITICAL SPEECH SKILLS: IMITATION AND PRONUNCIATION.** The strength of the nonverbal child's speech skills determines how easily and well he will learn Signed Speech. It is, therefore, very important for you to help him develop these skills before initiating Signed Speech instruction, to continue intensive speech training during instruction in Signed Speech, and, in particular, to make certain the child masters the speech skills critical to the development of Signed Speech. Intensive speech skill training must include refinement of old speech skills as well as the introduction of new ones, as specified in Chapter 7. The child should be able to imitate a wide variety of learned and unlearned sounds, syllables, and words. Children who lack strong speech skills tend to have discrimination and vocalization problems that interfere with the development of Signed Speech. Maintenance of speech skills requires constant teacher attention, even after the child is using Signed Speech for all of his communications.

Two sound skills in particular are critical to the development of Signed Speech: imitating sounds after the teacher and pronouncing sign words.

A. **Imitating sounds after the teacher.** The child's ability to imitate your sounds after you complete them, in other words, to imitate after you on the basis of remembered information, will give him the voice control and vocal spontaneity necessary for the integration of speech with spontaneous signing. This ability will facilitate the initiation of Signed Speech.

B. **Pronouncing sign words.** The child who can pronounce the words corresponding to the signs he knows is likely to begin uttering those words, or their approximations, as he signs. Some children can learn to pronounce sign words before they begin adding these words to their signs on their own; others learn to pronounce sign words after they initiate Signed Speech. Nevertheless both of these groups of children learn to use Signed Speech spontaneously.

II. **FACILITATING THE INITIATION OF SIGNED SPEECH.** The following two techniques are helpful in stimulating Signed Speech in a child.

A. **Speak as the child signs.** Prior to his initiation of Signed Speech, and during the period when the child is signing without speaking, you should speak the corresponding word as the child produces the sign. Your concomitant speech will stimulate the child to produce sounds along with his signs, because he has already learned to imitate sounds. Your speech will also help him learn the associations between signs and words.

B. **Maintain syllable-sign-movement correspondences.** You can do this best by teaching the child to produce the same number of final sign movements as there are syllables in the corresponding word. Thus, if the final movement of the child's "cookie" sign consists of a tap of the right fist on the upturned left palm, you should teach the child to tap twice, once for each of the two syllables in the word "cookie." As he produces his first tap, you pronounce the first syllable, "coo," and as he produces his second tap, you pronounce the second syllable, "kie." (Also, you should tap twice and articulate one syllable per tap whenever you sign and say "cookie.") To correct the child when he taps only once, you prompt him to tap again and withhold your concomitant vocalization of the second syllable, "kie," until he produces the second tap. To correct him when he tries to tap more than twice, you grasp his hands and hold them still, all the while remaining silent.

III. **TEACHING STRATEGIES.** The techniques which we describe for teaching Signed Speech are based on two guidelines and follow a natural progression of instructional procedures. We first present the two guidelines and then discuss each of the procedures in detail.

A. **Wait for the child to initiate Signed Speech before explicitly teaching it.** The child's spontaneous initiation of words or word approximations to his signs is a more accurate gauge than your judgment of whether or not his speech skills are strong enough to bear the weight of Signed Speech. In addition, he is more likely to feel free to use Signed Speech if he imposes it on you than if you impose it on him.

B. **Place less emphasis on the sounds than on the signs of Signed Speech and follow the child's lead.** The most serious interference in the development of Signed Speech is excessive instructional emphasis on the sounds in Signed Speech. This emphasis makes the child's task of learning to speak spontaneously as he signs very difficult. When the child first initiates Signed Speech, sounds are weaker communicative tools than signs, and they remain weaker until the time he begins using Signed Speech for all of his communications. For this reason, when the child begins adding words to his signs, it is best to refine the sounds he produces only during verbal imitation lessons. During signing and Signed Speech lessons you want to encourage but not force him to speak as he signs. In this way, you help him take an active role in learning the consistent and spontaneous use of Signed Speech. After the child's Signed Speech has become strong and spontaneous you can begin placing instructional pressure on the sounds.

You can best maintain a level of instructional emphasis on sounds that will help the child develop Signed Speech by following his lead. This means not working with the child on a particular sound or word addition to Signed Speech until he makes the addition on his own.

C. **Instructional procedures.** Instruction in Signed Speech follows a natural progression: differential reinforcement of Signed Speech during sign language lessons, accompanied by sound refinement during verbal imitation lessons; prompting of speech during sign language lessons; structured waiting to stimulate Signed Speech; "Say-and-sign" lessons; and word refinement during Signed Speech lessons. By using these techniques, you can help the child move from incomplete and infrequent to consistent use of Signed Speech. The child will probably initiate it himself by adding a word or word approximation to the last sign in an overlearned or single-sign utterance. With your instruction, he will then gradually begin increasing the number of signs in an utterance to which he adds speech, as well as the proportion and variety of utterances to which he adds speech. At the same time, he will also gradually increase the precision and clarity of his Signed Speech words. Eventually he will learn to use complete and clearly articulated Signed Speech for all of his communications.

1. *Differential reinforcement and sound refinement.*
    a. *Differential reinforcement of Signed Speech*—You may begin instruction by responding more positively and quickly to signed utterances with speech added than to those without it. Introduce differential reinforcement when the child begins regularly adding a particular word or sound to the utterance on 50 percent or more of the occasions that he produces the utterance. For example, when he adds the word to his signed request, you should grant the request immediately and praise him with a signed and spoken "Good talking and signing," a smile, and physical affection. When he signs the request without the word, you should respond less quickly and less positively. However, to keep the child's spontaneous utterance rate high, you should continue rewarding him for spontaneously signed utterances. Your differential positive reinforcement will lead the child to add speech more frequently to both the utterances you reinforce differentially and those you do not.

    As the child begins adding speech to a larger proportion of his signed utterances, he will simultaneously begin adding speech to a larger number of the signs in each utterance. For example, from speaking only as he produces the last sign in one utterance, he will progress to speaking as he produces the last two signs in several utterances, then the last three signs, and so forth. You should adjust your differential positive reinforcement to his speech additions. When he begins adding speech to the last two signs rather than only to the last one, differentially reinforce him for this improvement. As mentioned, you may take 50 percent as the cutoff point for readjusting your reinforcement criterion. When the child begins adding speech to the last two signs of an utterance on 50 percent of the occasions that he produces the utterance, you shift from differentially reinforcing him for speaking with the last sign to differentially reinforcing him for speaking with the last two signs. The shift will help him increase both the number of signs per utterance to which he adds speech and the proportion and variety of utterances to which he adds speech.

It is critically important that in the early stages of training you differentially reinforce Signed Speech without regard to its form, that is, without regard to how clearly the child speaks as he signs. All that matters at the beginning of Signed Speech instruction is that the child learn to speak as he signs, not that he learn to speak precisely. Therefore, do not attempt to refine his speech as you differentially reinforce him for Signed Speech or you will interfere with, rather than facilitate, its development. The child will begin refining the words in his Signed Speech on his own as you continue teaching him new sound skills and refining old ones during his verbal imitation lessons.

b. *Sound refinement during verbal imitation lessons—*You should continue intensive verbal imitation lessons independent of Signed Speech lessons, both as you teach Signed Speech and beyond. Teach the child first to clearly pronounce the words he attempts to speak as he signs and pay special attention to difficult sounds. Your instruction in the pronunciation of sign words during verbal imitation lessons will make it easier for the child to refine his Signed Speech on his own. You should also continue teaching new sounds, syllables, and words, since the more speech the child knows, the easier it will be for him to integrate his speech with spontaneous signing. Last, you should make certain the child can imitate sounds after you complete them so he has the voice control necessary for the integration of signs and speech. This may mean reteaching the skill.

During verbal imitation lessons, reinforce the child for producing the corresponding signs as he imitates words: sound-instigated Signed Speech is as welcome as sign-instigated Signed Speech.

2. *Prompting speech during sign lessons.* After the child is adding words or word approximations to 60 percent or

more of his signed utterances, you can begin explicitly prompting speech when he begins to sign without speaking. Say and sign "Say" to the child before you speak the words corresponding to the signs without words in an utterance. The child has been responding to this command as a speech prompt for some time during verbal imitation lessons. For this reason, it will stimulate him to speak. When he adds speech to a sign in response to your "Say," you should not speak for him, but continue speaking for him if he does not add speech. You should reward the child more quickly when he adds speech after you prompt him than when he does not, but you should also remember to continue rewarding him even when he does not add speech. In short, do not require the child to add speech in response to your prompting.

3. *Structured waiting to stimulate Signed Speech.* When the child is adding words or word approximations to one or more of the signs in 70 percent or more of his utterances, you can begin using structured waiting. Wait for the child to add words to one or more of his signs before rewarding him, and thus frustrate him into Signed Speech. The two forms of structured waiting to use are merely waiting and disallowing signing.

a. *Merely waiting*—This term refers to ignoring signed utterances not accompanied by words. When you do not respond to one of the child's signed utterances, he will tend to repeat it with some change. By waiting until his change includes the addition of words, you can frustrate him into Signed Speech.

For example, if Tommy were to sign "Tommy want cookie" without speaking at the same time, you would withhold your response to his request until he repeated it and added one or more words or until he repeated a variant such as "Tommy want candy" and added one or more words.

The typical child tends to produce variants as he adds words early in Signed Speech instruction because he does not understand that you want him merely to add words, not to change his utterance in some other way. Respond to his variants when the child speaks as he signs, and not otherwise. You may find that he occasionally changes his utterance completely, with or without adding words, to obtain your response. He may, for example, change "Tommy want cookie" to "This book." You should respond to completely changed utterances only when the child speaks as he signs, just as you would to other variants with words.

It is important to introduce merely waiting gradually: abrupt introduction may hinder spontaneous communication. If the child's spontaneous utterances decrease in frequency when you introduce merely waiting, you should reinstate responses to signed utterances and then reintroduce merely waiting after the frequency of spontaneous signing rises. Merely waiting channels the energy of frustration into the child's efforts at communicating and thereby helps him incorporate more speech into his spontaneous signing.

b. *Disallowing signing*—Disallowing signing means preventing the child from signing until he begins to speak at the same time. You can disallow signing by firmly taking hold of and immobilizing the child's hands when he begins just signing (without speaking) an utterance to which he normally adds words. You then release his hands as soon as he starts to speak. Disallowing signing frustrates the child more than merely waiting, so you should introduce it only after the child is responding well to merely waiting.

A caveat concerning structured waiting: previously nonverbal children find Reference, or naming, harder to learn than the Expression of Desires, and use reference statements much less frequently than requests. It is, therefore, best not to use structured waiting to frustrate the child into adding words to reference statements (descriptions).

4. *"Say-and-sign" lessons.* After the child begins saying a word or word approximation with every sign in an utterance and when he simultaneously speaks and signs 80 percent or more of his utterances, you may introduce "Say-and-sign" lessons. The purpose of these lessons is twofold: to improve the child's Signed Speech, and to teach him to use Signed Speech on command. You should set aside one lesson period per day for teaching the child to "Say and sign" on command.

"Say-and-sign" lessons are a variant of verbal imitation lessons. Instead of commanding the child merely to imitate a word, however, you also command him to imitate the sign corresponding to the word. The compound command "Say and sign" will be new to the child, so you will have to teach him to respond to it.

a. *The command with a desired object*—Present a desired object, x, to the child, and before he requests it, say and sign "Say and sign 'x.' " The sight of the desired object and your spoken and signed command-and-imitative-prompt ("Say and sign 'x' ") will lead the child to imitate your signed and spoken "x." Reward him for saying and signing "x" by giving him the x. As you repeat the training sequence, the child will learn to obey the command "Say and sign 'x' " consistently when you accompany the command with the sight of the desired object.

b. *The command alone*—Next, gradually fade the object. You want the child to be able to imitate the sign-and-word in the absence of the object. Teach the child to "Say and sign" on command each of the Signed Speech concepts he knows. You should not, however, teach him to imitate multiconcept Signed Speech utterances, because you do not want imitation to interfere with spontaneous production. For this reason also, you should teach no more than one "Say-and-sign" lesson per day and only continue the lessons for about a month. You may feel free to reintroduce the lessons if the child starts omitting some of the words that normally accompany his signs.

5. *Refining the words in Signed Speech.* When the child is regularly signing and saying each concept in almost all the utterances he produces, his Signed Speech will be strong enough for you to refine the words as he speaks them. You will now be able to interrupt his Signed Speech to help him refine his pronunciation during Signed Speech lessons, rather than waiting for verbal imitation lessons. Prior to this point, attempts to correct and improve the pronunciation of the words in Signed Speech as the child speaks and mispronounces them will probably only interfere with the development of Signed Speech.

To correct a mispronounced or unclearly pronounced word, you repeat the word correctly for the child immediately after he completes his utterance, give him the signed and spoken command "Again," and prompt the first sign-word in the utterance both vocally and manually. Then, after he repeats the utterance correctly, you can reward him.

To further improve pronunciation, teach the child to utter his syllables in time with his sign movements. To do this, you gently prompt him with your hands to slow down when he talks or signs too quickly and to speed up when he talks or signs too slowly. The closer the correspondence between the child's words and signs, the more quickly he will develop Signed Speech.

Some children move through the Signed Speech instructional progression utterance by utterance. They learn to use Signed Speech for one utterance or for a small cluster of utterances, then to use Signed Speech for another slightly larger cluster of utterances, and so forth. Other children move through the progression sign by sign. They learn to sign and say one sign per utterance, then two signs per utterance, and so forth. And many children move through in both ways. You will find it easy to adapt the instructional progression to the way in which the child with whom you are working learns Signed Speech. If you teach carefully and if you do not rush through the progression, the child will learn to use complete and clearly articulated Signed Speech for all of his communications and will increase his frequency of spontaneous utterances in the process.

IV. **STUTTERING ERRORS.** We mentioned before in Chapter 4 that most children "stutter" in sign at one time or another, and we described methods for eliminating such stuttering. Most children also stutter in Signed Speech at one time or another. Signed Speech stutters can be more troublesome than sign-only stutters, for a child may maintain different stuttering patterns in each mode. For example, as a child signs "Tommy want . . . want . . . want . . . ," he might simultaneously say "Tommy . . . Tommy . . . Tommy . . . Tommy . . . Tommy . . . ." The techniques described in Chapter 4 for overcoming sign stutters can be adapted for use with Signed Speech stutters. However, others may also be needed. One particularly useful for word stutters is stopping speech, and a technique particularly helpful for sign-and-word stutters is stopping both signing and speech.

A. **Stopping speech.** Cover the child's mouth with your hand to force him to produce only one word per sign. For example, if Tommy were saying "Tommy . . . Tommy . . . Tommy" as he signed, "Tommy want cookie," you would cover his mouth with your hand when he began to repeat "Tommy" as he signed "want," but you would allow him to sign "want cookie." You would then uncover his mouth and wait for him to repeat his request in complete Signed Speech. After you stop his speech, you should provide the child with the vocal and manual prompts he needs to repeat his request. You may find that when you stop a child's speech he ceases signing. In this case, you should uncover his mouth when he ceases signing and wait for him to repeat his utterance in complete Signed Speech.

B. **Stopping both signing and speech.** To do this, you cover the child's mouth and grasp and immobilize his hands when he begins stuttering. After 10 to 15 seconds, you uncover his mouth and release his hands and wait for him to repeat his utterance in complete Signed Speech. Then reward him. After you stop his signs and words, you should provide the child with the vocal and manual prompts he needs to repeat his utterance.

In sign-and-word stutters, the onset of word stuttering typically, but not always, precedes that of sign stuttering. If the child begins stuttering in words but completes the signed portion of his utterance without stuttering, treat his utterance as a word-only stutter. If he begins stuttering in sign after you cover his mouth, however, immobilize his hands for 10 to 15 seconds and wait for him to repeat his utterance in complete Signed Speech. If the child begins stuttering in sign first (the atypical event), immediately immobilize his hands. With almost all sign-first stutters, immobilizing the hands will lead the child to cease talking. Allow 10 to 15 seconds to pass after the child ceases talking, then allow him to repeat his utterance. If he continues talking after you immobilize his hands, allow him to talk until he begins to stutter in words (the usual occurrence), then cover his mouth, wait 10 to 15 seconds, and allow him to repeat his utterance in complete Signed Speech. If he completes his utterance in words alone without stuttering, you should reward him immediately.

V. **BUILDING A VOCABULARY.** You should continue introducing new concepts and complex versions of old concepts as you teach Signed Speech. Most children learn new concepts in sign and only later add words even after they have begun using Signed Speech for most of their communications. Therefore, you should allow the child with whom you are working to learn new concepts in sign alone at first, if that is his tendency, and to add speech to the concepts on his own when he is ready. After he begins adding the word to the new sign on his own, you may treat the resulting Signed Speech concept a bit more gently for a while than you would other instances of Signed Speech by not placing much instructional pressure on it. The new concept to which the child adds a word is doubly fragile: both the sign and the word are new.

Many children do not begin learning new concepts in Signed Speech, that is, do not simultaneously sign and speak their first attempts to produce a new concept, until after they have used Signed Speech for a considerable time. When a child begins learning new concepts in Signed Speech, change your sign language lessons to Signed Speech lessons. In other words, begin teaching new concepts (and complex versions of old concepts) as sign-word pairs rather than as signs alone.

VI. **DURATION OF INSTRUCTION.** Continue teaching new concepts in Signed Speech until the child begins speaking without signing. He will probably not begin speaking without signing until after he has been consistently communicating in complete, well-formed Signed Speech for 5 or more months.

9

Verbal Language: Fading Signs
from Signed Speech

I. Facilitating the fading of signs

II. Teaching strategies

III. Complicated utterances and new concepts

After the child has been using Signed Speech for many months, he will begin occasionally speaking without signing, that is, he will begin fading the signs from his Signed Speech on his own. You can help him move from spontaneous Signed Speech to spontaneous verbal language by appropriately structuring the fading he initiates. You should not allow him to fade signs too soon, however. Many months of Signed Speech are required for the transfer of spontaneity from the signs to the words of Signed Speech. For this reason, you should begin helping the child fade his signs only after he speaks without signing 10 percent of the time or more and after some of his purely verbal utterances are as complex, creative, and appropriate as his "best" Signed Speech utterances.

I. FACILITATING THE FADING OF SIGNS. The techniques we describe follow three guidelines: strengthen the sound skills necessary for unsigned speech; wait for the child to initiate unsigned speech on his own before explicitly teaching it; place gradually increasing instructional emphasis on unsigned speech and follow the child's lead.

A. Strengthen the speech skills necessary for unsigned speech. As you help the child fade signs from his Signed Speech, you should also improve his speech skills. The spontaneity of the speech in Signed Speech is initially dependent on the greater spontaneity of the signs. Therefore, removal of sign supports weakens speech and makes the explicit strengthening of speech skills a necessity.

B. **Wait for the child to initiate unsigned speech before explicitly teaching it.** The child's initiation of unsigned speech is the best measure of his readiness for instruction in unsigned speech. By waiting for him to indicate when he is ready, you avoid interfering with the natural growth of the spontaneity of unsigned speech and help the child understand that unsigned speech is his own personal communication tool.

C. **Place gradually increasing emphasis on unsigned speech and follow the child's lead.** Consolidation of unsigned spontaneous speech can be disrupted by too early attempts to refine words and by premature removal of sign supports. Allowing the child to use sign supports for a longer time than he needs them is better than forcing him to give up his sign supports too soon.

II. **TEACHING STRATEGIES.** The three guidelines—speech strengthening, child-initiated fading, and gradual increases in instructional emphasis—suggest a natural progression of instructional techniques for moving from spontaneous Signed Speech to spontaneous verbal language. These steps are, in order: removing the signing requirement during Signed Speech lessons and strengthening speech during verbal imitation lessons; teaching the child to speak without signing those utterances from which she begins fading signs on her own; and strengthening and refining the child's purely verbal utterances.

A. **Removing the signing requirement and strengthening speech.** You may do this when the child begins regularly speaking without signing on her own. As we mentioned earlier, however, it is better to begin teaching unsigned speech later rather than sooner, so do not rush to remove the signing requirement.

1. *Removing the signing requirement during Signed Speech lessons.* To do this, merely allow the child to speak without signing, that is, cease asking her to sign when she speaks without signing. It is time to remove

the signing requirement when the child regularly (10 to 20 percent of the time) speaks an utterance without signing; when some of her purely verbal utterances are as complex as her complex Signed Speech utterances; and when some of her purely verbal utterances are as novel as her novel Signed Speech utterances, that is, when they represent a new linguistic construction the child invents or contain incidentally learned new words. Removing the signing requirement allows the child to learn the acceptability of unsigned speech on her own and helps her feel that the unsigned speech she develops is her own personal communication tool.

You should continue using Signed Speech to communicate with the child even after you remove the signing requirement. If you begin speaking to her without signing, she may be imitatively tempted to try producing more speech without signs than she is able to. Lastly, it is best to keep the period during which you allow the child to spontaneously speak without signing short (about 2 weeks). The point of removing the signing requirement is to allow the child to learn the acceptability of unsigned speech on her own, not to allow her to learn to stop working at communicating.

2. *Strengthening speech during verbal imitation lessons.* When you remove the signing requirement, the child's speech will, without its sign supports, probably deteriorate slightly. The child will probably speak more softly, less distinctly, more slowly, and in a less coordinated and rhythmic fashion than she did when she also signed. At the same time, she will probably also begin occasionally losing her train of thought, discontinuing utterances before she completes them, and stuttering more often.

To strengthen speech during this period, you can teach the child to speak more loudly and quickly. By so doing, you help her hear and remember what she says more easily and also help her put more effort into speaking. Initially, you can instruct the child in loud speech and quick speech during verbal imitation lessons rather than as she speaks without signing. This will allow her to generalize her strengthened speech from verbal imitation lessons to purely verbal utterances on her own, and thus allow her to learn that she herself can overcome the difficulties these utterances present. (Later you can begin strengthening and refining the words in the child's purely verbal utterances as she speaks.)

a. *Instruction in loud speech during verbal imitation lessons*—When you remove the signing requirement during Signed Speech lessons, you should reintroduce instruction in loudness during verbal imitation lessons to reacquaint the child with loudness discriminations and to teach her to speak loudly. After she is speaking most of her utterances without signing, you can prompt loud speech during her unsigned speech.

b. *Instruction in quick speech during verbal imitation lessons*—After the child can imitate loud and soft speech on command, you can teach her to imitate speech uttered either quickly or at a normal rate. Teach her first to repeat two words you utter at a normal speech rate; then, two words you utter quickly; then, two words you utter either quickly or at a normal rate; and finally to repeat the same word twice, either quickly or at a normal rate.

For example, you might utter two words, such as "house up," for the child to imitate. You should pair words that do not normally occur together in everyday conversation, such as "house" and "up," rather than ones that do, such as "want cake" or "this dog." You do not want the child's imitations to interfere with her spontaneous speech. (If the child shadows your speech, reintroduce training in imitating after you; if she imitates only the second word in the pair, do not reinforce her, but wait until she imitates both words.) After the child imitates the two words you utter (you earlier taught her to imitate two-word phrases), teach her to imitate ten to twelve more word pairs.

After the child can imitate normal rate (normal interval) pairs, gradually reduce the interval between the two words until you are finally asking the child to imitate pairs with a near-zero interword interval. Do not allow the child to shadow. She may initially produce pairs at normal rate in response to your quickly spoken short interval pairs, but you should not reinforce her for these errors. Although she will not find short interval pairs as easy to master as she did normal interval pairs, she will eventually learn to imitate them as well.

When the child can easily imitate quickly spoken pairs, you can reintroduce normal rate pairs. Switch back and forth between blocks of normal rate and quickly spoken pairs. When she can switch to the alternate pair in three to five trials, you should begin uttering quickly spoken and normal rate pairs in random order.

Finally, when the child can easily imitate quickly spoken and normal rate pairs in random order, you can begin occasionally uttering pairs composed of one word repeated twice, either quickly or at a normal rate. You might, for example, utter the pair "house, house" quickly and then at a normal rate. As the child learns to respond to differences in rate unaccompanied by a difference in words, gradually increase the proportion of consecutive pairs that differ in rate but are composed of the same words. You will know that the child has mastered quick speech when she can accurately imitate word pairs composed of one word that you utter either quickly or at a normal rate in random order.

B. **Teaching the child to speak without signing those utterances from which he begins fading signs on his own.** The child imitates loudly and quickly on command during verbal imitation lessons, and you have allowed him to speak without signing when he wishes for about 2 weeks. Now, you can teach him to speak without signing those utterances from which he began fading signs on his own. You may begin explicitly teaching the child to speak an utterance without signing after he speaks it without signing 50 percent of the time. Because children fade signs in different ways, you will have to adjust this criterion to the child's style of fading. Some children fade signs by proceeding sign by sign, some fade signs by proceeding utterance by utterance. In general, most children fade signs from more practiced and frequently used utterances before they fade them from less practiced and less frequently used ones.

As you fade signs, you should always follow the child's lead: do not teach him to speak without signing an utterance from which he has not begun fading signs on his own. You can begin explicit instruction in speaking without signing by prompting the child not to sign and by preventing him from signing. You can then gradually fade your prompts not to sign and also your sign prevention.

1. *Prompt the child not to sign and prevent signing.* To do this, ask the child "What do you want?" speaking but not signing your question. You want the child to know that speaking without signing is acceptable, and you also want to show him how to do it. Your unsigned speech will serve as a prompt. If he begins to answer your spoken question in Signed Speech, you then prompt him not to sign by saying, but not signing, "Talk. Don't sign. Put your hands down." If he does not start speaking without signing, you should repeat the spoken question "What do you want?" If he begins to sign, prevent him from signing. Grasp his hands, place them in his lap, hold them there, and wait for him to speak. You will find that the child will begin speaking without signing more signs per utterance and more utterances as you continue telling him not to sign and continue preventing him from signing.

2. *Fade prompts for not signing and fade sign prevention.* Start with sign prevention, the hand restraint, then move backwards to prompts, and your commands not to sign. As you fade your prompts for not signing and your manual efforts at sign prevention, the child will learn to speak without signing.

C. **Strengthening and refining the child's purely verbal utterances.** You may begin explicitly strengthening and refining the child's purely verbal utterances when 80 percent of them contain no more than one signed and spoken concept.

1. *Strengthening.* This refers to prompting the child to speak more loudly or more quickly. When he forgets what he is saying and garbles an utterance and/or speaks too softly and slowly, you can prompt him to repeat the utterance more loudly or quickly. As you have previously taught him to speak loudly and quickly during verbal imitation lessons, you will be able to introduce loud speech and quick speech prompts without disrupting the flow of purely verbal utterances.

a. *Loud speech*—To prompt loud speech for garbled verbal utterances, you first shadow the child's utterance in a loud voice. After he increases the loudness of his utterance in response to your loud shadowing, you ask him in a loud voice to say the utterance again louder. You may ask him, for example, to "AGAIN, LOUDER, SAY 'GO' " after he softly speaks the garbled phrase, "Go toy play play. . . ." After the child can repeat utterances loudly on command when you provide a first-word imitative prompt, you then teach him to respond to the loud command "AGAIN, LOUDER" without a first word imitative prompt. We suggest that you continue prompting loud speech throughout the period of sign fading and for 2 to 3 weeks thereafter.

    b. *Quick speech*—Introduce quick speech prompts after the child can respond easily to loud speech prompts by using a format similar to that for loud speech. Repeat quickly the ungarbled portion of the child's garbled utterance; ask the child for a quick repetition with "Again, quicker, say '(first word)' "; and teach him to obey the command "Again, quicker."

  2. *Refining.* Refining refers to correcting the child's mispronunciations as he speaks. Use the techniques outlined in Chapters 6 and 7 on instruction in speech skills.

III. COMPLICATED UTTERANCES AND NEW CONCEPTS.

Even after the child is speaking most of his utterances without signing, he may tend to fall back on signs as a source of support for verbal language when he produces complicated utterances or uses new concepts. When he does, he is likely to use an abbreviated form of Signed Speech: words accompanied by foreshortened, or miniaturized, signs. For example, when he speaks a complicated utterance such as "Tommy want Arlene's cookie on box" or when he uses a new concept such as "under" to verbalize the answer "Candy under table" in response to the question "Where is the candy?" he may produce foreshortened signs as he speaks. These signs appear to be partially internalized signs. Like fully formed versions, they are good memory supports for speech, so allow the child to use both them and fully formed signs when he produces complicated utterances or uses new concepts. This will make it easier for him to produce such utterances and will not interfere with his fading of signs from simpler utterances.

You should also allow the child to learn new concepts in

Signed Speech. For example, when teaching the concept "under," you should sign "under" as you say the word and allow the child to both sign and say "under," as well as to sign and say the old concepts which may accompany it, such as "candy" and "table" in the phrase "Candy under table." (Do not, however, sign the old concepts yourself.) Teach new concepts in Signed Speech throughout sign fading and for a little while after, even if the child tends to speak new concepts without signing. Your signs will, as redundant prompts, make learning new concepts easier. After he has mastered a new concept, however, cease signing it as you say it.

You will know that the child is relying fully on speech to communicate when he ceases signing in foreshortened fashion with complicated utterances and new concepts and begins learning on his own, in incidental fashion, the verbal functors which you do not explicitly teach him, for example, "the," "a," and "of," and verbal inflections, such as "ing," the plural "s," and past tense endings.

Linguistic Functions

The goal of the linguistic functions component of the Signed Speech Program is to develop the social uses of language beyond the Expression of Desires. In it we describe methods for teaching and encouraging spontaneous use of four crucial, and increasingly complex, linguistic functions: Reference (description); Person Concepts (people's names, possessive terms, and labels for emotions and actions); Inquiry (the use of language to gain information); and Abstraction (the use of language to reflect on itself). In Chapter 10, we detail methods for teaching Reference; in Chapters 11 and 12, methods for teaching Person Concepts; in Chapters 13 and 14, methods for teaching Inquiry; and in Chapters 15 and 16, methods for teaching Abstraction.

10

Reference: A New Linguistic Function

   I. The Reference function
  II. Single-sign reference: Answering "What is this?"
 III. Example: Jimmy learns single-sign reference
  IV. The reference statement: "This x"
   V. Example: John learns the reference statement
  VI. Encouraging initiated reference
 VII. Example: Jimmy initiates reference
VIII. Teaching strategies
  IX. Mastery criteria

You teach Reference, a new linguistic function, to enable the child to describe his world and to understand others' descriptions, and to provide the child with the tool he will need to learn other linguistic functions (Person Concepts, Inquiry, and Abstraction). The child should be introduced to Reference after he has learned to express his desires in discriminative signed requests. With Reference, he will now learn to describe objects and activities rather than to request them.

Two considerations are important for you to remember as you teach this function. First, you should be aware that the discrimination between requests and descriptions is the basic goal of your instruction in Reference. Second, because nonverbal children rarely initiate Reference (describe objects) on their own, you may find that Reference remains a secondary linguistic function for the child as compared to the Expression of Desires. Only by teaching him to describe objects and activities, however, will you be able in the future to teach him other important concepts and linguistic functions (Person Concepts, Inquiry, and Abstraction) that are unrelated to his strong desires.

I. **THE REFERENCE FUNCTION.** There are three stages in teaching Reference to a child: reference in isolation, discrimination between reference and requests, and encouragement of initiated reference.

   A. **Reference in isolation.** Teach the child single-sign reference in isolation initially and, later, the two-sign reference statement "This x"; do not allow the child to make requests.

   B. **Discrimination between reference and requests.** Introduce alternating blocks of reference and request trials and gradually decrease the number of trials per block as the child begins switching to the alternate function in fewer trials. When the child can move freely between the two functions, that is, when he switches to the alternate function in three to five trials, you may then introduce randomly ordered trials on the two linguistic functions.

   C. **Encouragement of initiated reference.** After the child learns to discriminate between reference and requests, encourage him to initiate reference on his own by teaching him to describe objects in the absence of a question from you.

II. **SINGLE-SIGN REFERENCE: ANSWERING "WHAT IS THIS?"** After the child has learned to use "(Child) want x" to request ten to twelve different objects, you may introduce single-sign reference, first in isolation, then as discriminated from requests.

   A. **Single-sign reference in isolation.** You should teach the child to describe with a single sign the objects she can appropriately request. At the same time, prevent her from making the requests: each time she correctly describes an object, immediately reward her with a different object from the one she has described, without allowing her to request her reward.

1. *The first single-sign reference.* Present an object, then sign and say the reference question "What is this?" Point to and touch the object with your "this" sign to focus the child's attention on it. Then immediately mold the child through the appropriate sign while simultaneously saying the corresponding word. Immediately after you have molded her through the sign, you should reward her with a strongly desired object different from the object she just described. Do not allow her to request her reward. Praise the child affectionately with a signed and spoken "Good signing" as you give the reward. You should repeat the procedure until the child begins signing the description before you mold her through it, then gradually fade your molding. Introduce new single-sign references after the child is regularly describing the first object in response to the question "What is this?"

2. *The second and later single-sign references.* You teach the second and later single-sign references in isolation first, then in alternating blocks of trials on the new reference and trials on old references, and finally, in randomly ordered trials on both the new and all the old references. As you teach the child to discriminate between single-sign references, always remember to prevent her from requesting her rewards: you want her to focus her attention exclusively on Reference, the new linguistic function.

B. **Discrimination between single-sign references and requests.** Begin teaching this discrimination after the child regularly produces correct single-sign references to eight to ten objects when asked "What is this?" Alternate between blocks of reference trials in which you ask "What is this?" and request trials in which you ask "What do you want?" (Within each block of reference or request trials, present objects in random order.) As the child begins switching to the alternate function in fewer trials, gradually decrease the number of training trials per block. Introduce randomly ordered reference and request trials when she can switch to the alternate function in three to five trials. Ask the questions "What is this?" (reference) and "What do you want?" (request) in random order as you present randomly chosen objects from among those single-sign references the child knows. (Reward the child with what she requests on request trials.) The child will gradually learn to discriminate between single-sign reference (describing objects) and requests (asking for objects).

III. **EXAMPLE: JIMMY LEARNS SINGLE-SIGN REFERENCE.** We present Jimmy's initial learning of single-sign reference to illustrate methods for working through problems that may confront you as you teach single-sign reference.

A. **Single-sign reference in isolation.** Jimmy's teacher, George, began teaching Jimmy his first single-sign reference by showing him a book and asking "What is this?" Jimmy's first response was to sign the request "Jimmy want book." To help him overcome his tendency to request rather than describe, George introduced the following procedures.

1. *Immediate molding.* George employed immediate molding to discourage Jimmy's tendency to request. He presented an object, such as a book, and asked, "What is this?" As he signed "this," he pointed to and touched the book with his extended "this" finger. He then immediately molded Jimmy's hands through the sign "book." His molding prevented Jimmy from signing the request "Jimmy want book" and, at the same time, provided Jimmy with tactile prompts for the correct response. The "book" sign is made by opening two palm-together hands outward without separating them as if to suggest an opening book. To mold Jimmy through this sign, George grasped the backs of Jimmy's hands, positioned them at chest level, pressed the palms together (with the fingers pointing toward George), then opened the palms outward (still keeping their inner edges touching). He then faded from completely molding Jimmy through the sign, to lightly touching the backs of Jimmy's hands, to holding his own extended hands out at chest level (without touching Jimmy), to holding only one of his hands at chest level, to barely lifting that one hand from his lap, to simply asking the question "What is this?" As George faded from tactile prompts to visual prompts to the reference question alone, Jimmy learned to describe the object *book* with the sign "book."

2. *Teaching less preferred objects first.* George taught ini-

tial single-sign references for objects relatively low on Jimmy's list of preferred objects. He first taught Jimmy to describe books, blocks, dolls, and drums—objects Jimmy rarely requested—and only later taught candy, cookie, drink, and chips—objects Jimmy requested frequently. By focusing first on less preferred objects, George increased Jimmy's receptivity to single-sign reference, since he was less likely to sign "Jimmy want x" when he did not strongly prefer the x.

3. *Discriminative reinforcement.* Throughout lessons on single-sign reference, George rewarded Jimmy with an object different from the one Jimmy had just described and prevented him from requesting his reward. Thus, George might reward Jimmy with a piece of candy for correctly describing a book. The discrepancy between the object Jimmy described and the reward he received weakened Jimmy's initial tendency to request the objects he was asked to describe. His not being allowed to request that object helped him learn that the name he had signed was functioning to describe rather than request the object.

As George taught Jimmy his second and later single-sign references, he continued to employ immediate molding when necessary to prevent Jimmy from requesting the object. He continued to reward Jimmy with objects different from the one he had described and continued to prevent requests. And he continued to teach reference to less preferred objects. The second object Jimmy learned to refer to (describe) was a doll. It was chosen because of the dissimilarity between the sign components, perceptual properties, and sound elements of the concept "doll" and those of Jimmy's first single-sign description, "book." George taught Jimmy to describe "doll" first in isolation, and then taught the discrimination between "doll" and "book." George then alternated between blocks of trials on "doll" and trials on "book," gradually decreasing the number of trials per block. When Jimmy was switching to the alternate reference in three to five trials, George began randomly ordering "book" and "doll" trials. Because Jimmy had previously learned to discriminate between requesting books and requesting dolls, he learned to discriminate between referring to books and referring to dolls relatively quickly and easily. George then introduced new single-sign references and Jimmy soon learned to describe each of the objects he had previously learned to request.

B. **Discrimination between single-sign references and requests.** George began instruction in discrimination by alternating between a block of trials on the reference and on the request question. When he introduced blocked trials, Jimmy at first confused the two functions. He frequently answered the question "What do you want?" with a single-sign reference, "x," and the question "What is this?" with the request "Jimmy want x." To teach Jimmy to refer and request appropriately, George used an exaggerated verbal prompt. He asked the reference question "What is THIS?" with the word "THIS" greatly increased in loudness and duration, but he asked the request question "What do you want?" using a normal questioning intonation. Jimmy attended to George's exaggerated vocal "THIS" and learned to answer blocked reference questions with single-sign references. He then began switching easily between single-sign references and requests. When Jimmy was switching to the alternate response in three to five trials, George began uttering the two questions in random order, still exaggerating the word "THIS" in his signed and spoken reference questions. He presented various objects and randomly asked either, "What do you want?" or, "What is THIS?" When Jimmy was answering the randomly ordered questions correctly with the aid of George's exaggerated "THIS," George faded the exaggerated prompt. He began asking "What is this?" in a normal questioning intonation. He also began exaggerating words other than "this" on occasion in both reference and request questions to teach Jimmy that exaggeration was irrelevant to correct answers. Jimmy soon learned to answer George's questions correctly regardless of the manner in which they were intoned. In other words, he learned to discriminate between using language to refer to objects and using language to obtain objects.

IV. **THE REFERENCE STATEMENT: "THIS X."** You should teach the reference statement "This x" only after the child can respond consistently with the appropriate single-sign reference or request when you randomly ask, "What is this?" or, "What do you want?'' You teach "This x" in isolation first, preventing requests, and then teach the discrimination between reference statements and requests.

A. The reference statement in isolation.

1. *The first reference statement.* Teach the first reference statement in isolation, preventing the child from making requests and using one of the objects whose single-sign reference he knows well. Present the object, sign and say "What is this?" and then immediately mold the child through the reference statement "This x." Teach him to sign "This" by pointing to and touching the object with his extended index finger. His pointing and touching will help him to focus attention on the object and will give the "This" sign a concrete meaning. Immediately after you mold the child through "This," you should mold him through the sign for the object, simultaneously saying the word he is signing. Then immediately after you mold him through the reference statement, you should reward him with a desired object other than the one he described, without allowing him to request either the object described or his reward. Praise him with a signed and spoken "Good signing" as you reward him.

   Begin to fade your molding when the child begins to sign "This" in anticipation of your molding. First fade molding of the object name while continuing to mold "This," then gradually fade your molding of "This." Fade from complete molding to a partial tactile prompt, to a visual prompt, to the reference question alone. As you do so, the child will learn first to sign "This" with your help and the single-sign description on his own, then to sign the entire reference statement "This x" on his own. Your signed and spoken "this" in "What is this?" will serve as an imitative prompt for the child's signed "This."

2. *The second and later reference statements.* You can teach the child his second reference statement after he masters his first one, using another of the objects whose single-sign reference he knows well. Teach the statement in isolation initially, with immediate molding that you gradually fade. After the child learns to respond to the reference question with the second reference state-

ment without any prompt, teach him to discriminate between his first and second reference statements. Alternate between blocks of trials on the first and second reference statements, then move to randomly ordered trials on the two statements. Introduce and teach later reference statements as you taught the second one: in isolation initially, then in alternating blocks on the new and on old reference statements, and finally, in a series of randomly ordered trials on the new and all old statements.

B. Discrimination between reference statements and requests. Teach the child to discriminate between the reference statement "This x" and the request "(Child) want x" after he uses the reference statement with the eight to ten objects he formerly described with a single sign. Alternate between blocks of trials on the reference statement and on the request and shorten the blocks as the child begins switching to the alternate form in fewer trials. When the child is switching to the alternate form in three to five trials, you may begin asking the questions "What is this?" and "What do you want?" in random order. As the child learns to discriminate between reference statements and requests, his understanding of Reference will increase.

V. **EXAMPLE: JOHN LEARNS THE REFERENCE STATE-MENT.** To illustrate methods for working through difficulties you may encounter as you teach the reference statement "This x," we present an example: how Arlene taught John the reference statement.

A. **The reference statement in isolation.** During early lessons, John tended to omit "This" and simply sign "x" when answering the question "What is this?" Arlene employed two strategies in addition to immediate molding to help John overcome this difficulty.

1. *Exaggeration.* Arlene exaggerated the word "THIS" in her signed and spoken reference question by increasing the loudness and duration of her spoken "this" and by enlarging the final movement of her signed "this." John used her exaggerated loudness and sign as a prompt for his signed "This." As Arlene gradually faded the exaggerated "this," John learned to sign "This x" rather than "x."

2. *Self-correction.* After John began omitting "This" from his "This x" less frequently, Arlene began allowing self-correction: when John answered the question "What is this?" with only the single-sign description, Arlene signed and said, "Sign again" or simply, "Again." Arlene's command served as feedback to John. It told him to change his statement in some way but did not provide him with a model.

B. **Discrimination between reference statements and requests.** After Arlene taught John to use the reference statement with the eight to ten objects he formerly described in a single-sign reference, she taught him to discriminate between the reference statement "This x" and the request "(Child) want x." Because he had previously learned to discriminate between single-sign references and requests, John mastered the new discrimination easily.

VI. **ENCOURAGING INITIATED REFERENCE.** The typical nonverbal child rarely initiates reference statements on his own, even after considerable instruction in Reference. Therefore, it may be necessary for you to encourage initiated reference explicitly. By "initiated" we mean "spontaneous and un-prompted." Of course, you should reward the child for any self-initiated reference statements he makes. However, you should also introduce explicit instruction in initiated reference after the child can answer the reference question with the reference statement "This x" (with less than 10 percent error for eight to ten objects). To explicitly encourage initiated reference, first fade the reference question, then fade the pointing prompt, and then encourage the extended use of initiated reference.

A. **Fade the reference question.** To initiate reference on his own, the child will need to be able to produce a reference statement in the absence of your reference question. To help him learn, gradually fade your reference questions by using structured waiting. Wait for the child to respond with the reference statement when you present an object and draw his attention to it only by pointing.

Prior to introducing structured waiting, you should establish the child's set to produce reference statements by running through a block of five or more consecutive reference trials in which you ask the reference question

"What is this?" You should then introduce structured waiting by following this block with a shorter block of one or two trials in which you simply point to the object and wait for the child to respond. During these structured waiting trials, your pointing to the object will prompt him to describe it. To facilitate responses during structured waiting trials, you can introduce response-provoking prompts. For example, you might tap the object emphatically or form a partial sign for the object.

After the child is regularly producing reference statements during the short structured waiting block, gradually increase the number of trials in the block. As you do so, the child will learn to initiate reference to an object on his own when you present the object and point to it. Accept single-sign reference when first prompting initiated reference so as not to extinguish the response, but require the full reference statement later on.

B. **Fade the pointing prompt.** To initiate reference on his own, the child will also have to produce reference statements when no one is pointing to the object. Fade the pointing prompt after you fade the reference question. Employ structured waiting: present an object without pointing to it and without asking the reference question, and wait for the child to respond. Alternate between blocks of five or more trials with the pointing prompt to establish a reference statement set, and blocks of one or two trials without the pointing prompt. Gradually increase the number of trials in the no-pointing block as the child learns to describe without the prompt. As you fade, the child will learn to initiate reference to objects you present completely on his own, without the pointing prompt or the reference question.

C. **Encourage the extended use of initiated reference.** Introduce procedures to help the child extend his spontaneous use of initiated reference. Occasionally present an object in a novel situation, such as inside a closed box; and occasionally present two or more objects at once for him to describe. In addition, you can have him describe pictures (photographs, picture cards, posters, pictures in books) as well as objects.

VII. **EXAMPLE: JIMMY INITIATES REFERENCE.** When George began to teach Jimmy initiated reference, structured waiting was ineffective as a technique for fading the reference question "What is this?" even when George provided referent and imitative prompts as he waited. Jimmy simply did not respond with the reference statement until George asked the reference question. Therefore, George introduced an intermediate signed and spoken prompt less explicit than the reference question but more explicit than either a referent or an imitative prompt. Instead of asking "What is this?" George merely signed and said "Sign" as he pointed to the object. Jimmy soon learned to initiate reference when George presented an object, pointed to it, and signed and said, "Sign." George then gradually faded the command, and Jimmy learned to initiate reference on his own.

After Jimmy began to initiate reference regularly during language lessons, George introduced procedures to encourage Jimmy to initiate reference outside language lessons. He encouraged Jimmy to describe a variety of objects in a variety of settings for a variety of people. Of course, he also praised Jimmy for all spontaneous reference statements, even when reference was not the task on which he and Jimmy were working.

VIII. **TEACHING STRATEGIES.** As you teach Reference, you may follow the strategies described below.

A. **Choice of objects.** Use less preferred objects first. This will weaken the child's tendency to make requests. Introduce the new objects the child learns to request so that he will learn to refer to them as well. Teach the child to describe anything which captures his interest but which he has not yet learned to request, such as toys, school materials, or activities. Finally, extend instruction in reference to objects that, in your judgment, play a significant role in the child's life, such as eating utensils, clothing, furniture, and body parts.

B. **Emphasis on variety.** As you teach a child Reference, you should present a variety of objects in a variety of settings, exposing him to numerous exemplars of each object. As George taught Jimmy to describe toy building blocks, he presented wooden and plastic blocks of different sizes, shapes, and colors. By exposing the child to a variety of exemplars as you teach Reference, you help insure appropriate generalization. You also help insure generalization by asking the child to refer to objects in a variety of settings and for people other than yourself. George asked Jimmy to describe objects during walks outdoors, during play periods, during lunch, during transitions between activities, and so forth. Further, whenever possible he had other people ask Jimmy to describe.

C. **Use of combined prompt.** The combined prompt can be used during any phase of sign language instruction, but it is particularly helpful during instruction in Reference. The combined prompt is a combination of a referent prompt, the sight of the object, and a partial imitative prompt, the modeling of a part of the sign. Let's look at how Benson used a combined prompt to teach Lance to describe a shoe. To sign "shoe," one forms the hands into fists, holds the fists in a palm-down position at chest level, and taps the thumb sides of the fists together. Benson presented a shoe to Lance, signed "What is" as he normally did, but changed his "this?" sign into a partial-sign combined prompt. He tapped the shoe with the thumb side of his palm-down fist instead of pointing to it with his index finger. Lance recognized the palm-down tapping fist as part of the sign for "shoe" and soon learned to sign "shoe" when Benson signed and said "What is this?" with the combined prompt. Benson then gradually transformed his fist back into an extended index finger to recapture his normal "this" sign. As Benson faded the combined prompt, Lance learned the single-sign reference, "shoe." The combined prompt focuses the child's attention on two sources of information, the sight of the object and the partial sign, and is particularly effective for teaching single-sign reference.

D. **Use of exaggeration.** As the examples demonstrate, you can help the child who has difficulty discriminating between the reference and the request question by vocally (and manually) exaggerating the word (and sign) "THIS" in the reference question "What is THIS?" It will likely be easy for the child to discriminate between exaggerated reference questions and normal request questions. After he learns to answer exaggerated reference questions and normal request questions in random order, fade your exaggeration. You should then occasionally exaggerate other words (and signs) in both questions to teach him that exaggeration is irrelevant to the correct response.

IX. **MASTERY CRITERIA.** As mentioned previously, one of the primary goals of instruction in Reference is to teach the child the difference between the use of language to describe, and the use of language to express a desire. The criteria for the mastery of single-sign reference, reference statements, and initiated reference reflect this goal.

A. **Single-sign references.** You will know that the child has mastered single-sign references when he discriminates between the reference question "What is this?" and the request question "What do you want?" The nonverbal child rarely describes objects on his own. Therefore, we do not include the spontaneous generalization of single-sign references in the mastery criteria, but we do consider it an important indication of the child's interest in Reference.

B. **The reference statement.** You will know that the child has mastered the reference statement "This x" when he employs it consistently to answer the reference question "What is this?" and when he discriminates it from the request in response to the request question "What do you want?" Again, we do not include the spontaneous generalization of reference statements in the criteria for mastery, but consider it an important measure of the child's interest in Reference.

C. **Indications of initiated reference.** It is not likely that the typical nonverbal child will master initiated reference even with extensive instruction and encouragement. The typical nonverbal child will initiate reference on his own during the structured language lessons in which you teach initiated reference, and some children will occasionally initiate reference on their own outside of the structured lessons. But only the exceptional nonverbal child will learn to employ Reference with the spontaneity and freedom that he employs requests. Rather than working for mastery, therefore, you should work towards increasing the child's frequency of use and interest in initiated reference.

11

Person Concepts I:
Names of People and Possession

I. Names of people: "Who is this?"

II. Possession: "Whose x is this?"

III. Discrimination between names as labels and as possessive terms

IV. Person concepts in order of difficulty

V. Errors

VI. Teaching strategies

VII. Mastery criteria

After the child learns to respond to the reference question "What is this?" with the reference statement "This x," you may begin teaching her Person Concepts. As you teach these concepts, you will also be teaching the child to pay very close attention to people: to the physical characteristics which differentiate one person from another (when teaching names); to the relationships between people and objects (when teaching possession); to the movements people engage in and the way people feel (when teaching actions and emotional states); to the way a statement or request can be directed to a specific person (when teaching direct address); and to the way a person's attention can be obtained (when teaching the vocative, that is, calling). Teaching the child to understand and use Person Concepts will help her develop an interest in and capacity for linguistic social interactions with people and, consequently, will help her learn language from them on her own. Further, for the child who is socially unresponsive and pays only minimal attention to people (like the autistic child), teaching language whose use requires close attention to people is likely to increase attentiveness to others and social responsiveness. The importance of thorough and extensive instruction in Person Concepts cannot be overemphasized.

We have divided Person Concepts into two groups. This chapter will discuss name signs and the use of people's names to express possession; the following chapter will deal with actions, emotions, direct address, and calling. We present more detailed instructional procedures for name signs and possession to emphasize the special necessity for thorough and varied instruction in the first concepts in this new language area.

I. NAMES OF PEOPLE: "WHO IS THIS?" The steps to follow in teaching name signs are, in order: expressive use of name signs (the child's name, then her teacher's name, then the discrimination between the two name signs, then other name signs); receptive understanding of name signs; and discrimination between the expressive use and receptive understanding of name signs.

A. Expressive use of name signs.
1. *The child's name sign.* Previously you taught the child to use her name sign expressively as part of the request "(Child) want x." Now you will teach her to use it to refer to herself with the reference statement "This (Child)." As you may recall from Chapter 4, the child's name sign is formed by placing her dominant hand, shaped into the first letter of her name, on or near a part of her body which emphasizes an outstanding feature (such as striking eyes) and then moving the hand in rhythm with the syllables of her spoken name (which you say as she signs).
a. *Molding*—As you sit across from the child, ask her "Who is this?" Touch her chin with the tip of your "this" index finger as you say "this." Because she has already mastered the reference statement "This x," she will probably begin to respond to your question with the sign "This." If she does not, you should mold her through the sign, making sure, by prompting, that as she signs "This," she touches her chin with her "This" index finger. Then you immediately mold her through her name sign. As you do so, you should say her name. Afterward, you should praise

her with the Signed Speech statement "Good signing" and reward her with affection and the opportunity to make a request.

b. *Fading name sign prompts*—You may gradually fade
your prompts for the child's name sign after she
begins spontaneously signing "This." Begin with
movement, then position, then hand shape prompts,
and tactile, then visual, then verbal prompts. As you
fade these prompts, the child will learn to sign "This
(Child)" when you ask the signed and spoken question "Who is this?" and touch her chin with your
"this" index finger.

c. *The whole-child concept*—Many nonverbal children
have only a limited concept of what constitutes a person. When the child first learns her name sign she
believes it refers only to the part of her body which
the "this" index finger of her teacher's "Who is
this?" touches. Therefore, after she can respond to
your chin-touching "Who is this?" without prompts,
you should teach her that her name sign refers to all
parts of her body and to her body as a whole by
touching a different part of her body, such as her
forehead, legs, or neck, with your "this" index finger
each time you ask the question "Who is this?" Teach
the child to sign "This (Child)" in response to your
question when you touch any part of her body, and
teach her to touch the body part with her "This" index finger as she signs "This (Child)." As you repeat
the procedure, the child will learn that her name sign
refers to all parts of her body and to her body as a
whole and will sign "This (Child)" when you touch a
previously untouched part of her body and ask your
question, "Who is this?"

2. *The second name sign: Teacher's name.* After the child
masters her own name sign to refer to herself, you can
introduce her to your (Teacher's) name sign. Your name
is a good second name sign because the teacher is an important person to the child and because teacher and
child frequently interact.

Begin with your name sign in isolation, employing the
same procedures you used to teach the first (Child's)
name sign. You should be especially sure to teach the
child that your name sign refers to all parts of your

body. Next you can teach the child to discriminate between her own name sign and yours. You first ask the
question "Who is this?" throughout a block of trials
touching only the child while saying "this," then ask the
question touching only yourself, and so forth. When the
child switches easily to the alternate sign (in three to
five trials), you randomly touch either her or yourself as
you ask, "Who is this?" When the child responds correctly, you should praise her with the Signed Speech
statement "Good signing" and affection (and, occasionally, the opportunity to make a request). If she uses
the wrong name sign as she signs, "This (Person)," you
then say and sign, "No. Put your hand on your lap."
After the child follows your directive, ask your question
again and reintroduce previous prompts for the name
sign; gradually fade your prompts as the child learns to
respond without them.

You may need to reintroduce touching different parts
of the child's and your own body when you begin randomly ordering trials on the two name signs during
discrimination training. Random trials may confuse the
child at first and lead her to fall back on her originally
limited concept of a person. If during these trials you
need to reintroduce touching a variety of body parts,
start by touching different parts of each of your bodies,
for example, the child's chest and your leg, or the child's
arm and your neck, and gradually move to the touching
of identical parts. You will probably only have to reintroduce touching of a variety of body parts briefly.

A special "tip": the combined prompt is very effective
for strengthening the association between the name
sign and the person to whom it refers. To form the combined prompt, change the "this" at the end of the question "Who is this?" to make it resemble the name sign
of the person to whom the question refers. For example,
if the name sign involves a tapping motion, you might
sign "this" with a tapping motion as you touch the person, or if the name sign employs a closed fist, you might
sign "this" with a closed fist. You would then gradually
fade your combined prompt "this" into the normal
"this" sign (an extended index finger) as the child learns
to make the discrimination between his own and his
teacher's name sign.

3. *Other (new) signs.* You can teach the next name signs using the same procedures you employed with the first and second, following the same guidelines. You should make certain that the child learns to discriminate between each new and all old name signs and that she associates each new name sign only with the person to whom it refers. Try to choose signs that meet the following criteria.

   a. *Name signs that refer to important persons in the child's life*—Such people might be her parents and siblings, and those with whom she interacts on a regular basis.

   b. *Name signs whose hand shape, position, and movements differ substantially from the child's name sign*—For example, if the child signs her name by tapping her (dominant) "M" hand on her temple once for the single syllable in her name, "Meg," a good new name sign to teach, the name of a friend or relative, might be positioned on the chest, shaped into a first letter different from "M," and might move in a circular fashion twice on the signer's chest (for the two syllables in the new name).

   c. *Name signs which correspond to spoken names that sound different from the child's spoken name*—Two features of a new spoken name which can be used to determine how different the child's spoken name is from the new name are the individual sounds (phonemes) which make up the names and the number of syllables in the names.

4. *Pictures of people.* After the child can sign "This (Person)" to refer to five to seven people, you can teach her to name pictures of the people whose name signs she knows when you ask the question "Who is this?" This will help the child generalize name signs to new situations by providing her with an alternative representation to which to link name signs and by strengthening her linguistic-conceptual memory for people.

   If the child has difficulty learning to respond to pictures, discontinue instruction and try again when you are teaching Inquiry (Chapters 13 and 14). The language the child masters in the interim will probably make learning to respond to pictures of people easier. Even so, you may still have to teach her to refer to the image of a person in a mirror before you will be able to teach her to refer to a picture of the person.

B. Receptive understanding of name signs.
    1. *"Touch (Child)."* After the child can use his own name sign expressively to refer to himself, you can teach him to touch himself when you give him the Signed Speech command "Touch (Child)." This will give him receptive understanding of his name sign. Say and sign "Touch (Child)" while sitting opposite the child, then manually prompt him through the act of touching his own extended index finger to his own chin, cheek, chest, or other body part. You may gradually fade your prompts for the child's touching response by reducing your tactile and visual prompts.
    2. *"Touch (Teacher)."* After the child can use your (Teacher's) name sign (his second name sign) expressively to refer to you, teach him to touch you when you give the Signed Speech command "Touch (Teacher)."
    3. *Receptive discrimination.* Give the child the commands "Touch (Child)" and "Touch (Teacher)" in alternating blocks; then when he switches easily between blocks, give the commands in random order. When he touches the appropriate person, praise him with the Signed Speech remark "Good touching." When he makes an error, say and sign "No" and tell him to put his hands on his lap. Then give him one of the commands again and use prompts to facilitate appropriate touching. Gradually fade your prompts as the child learns to touch without them.
    4. *New name signs.* Teach the child to touch on command each person whose name sign he has learned to use expressively, and teach him to discriminate receptively (in his touching) between each new and all of the old name signs. For example, teach him to respond to the command "Touch (Person 3)" with Person 3 sitting beside you as you give the command. Then have him "Touch (Person 3)" when you alternate between blocks of "Touch (Person 3)" trials and blocks composed of "Touch (Child)" and "Touch (Teacher)" trials. And, last, teach him to "Touch (Person 3)" when you randomly order touching trials on Person 3, Teacher, and Child.
    After the child learns to "Touch (Child)," "Touch

(Teacher)," and "Touch (Person 3)" when you give the commands, teach him to respond when Person 3 gives them. You should continue instruction until the child is able to touch appropriately any of the people whose name signs he can use expressively when any of those people commands him to.

5. *Pictures of people.* After the child can obey the command "Touch (Person)" when (Person) refers to any one of five to seven people, you can teach him to touch pictures of people on command. Place on a table next to the child photographs of the people and teach him again to obey the command "Touch (Person)." You start with one photograph, then add another, and another, and so forth, until the child is searching through photographs of all of the people whose name signs he knows in order to touch the person named in the command. Mastery of the receptive name sign task with pictures will provide the child with an alternative representation (pictorial) for name sign referents (people) and make it easier for him to generalize his receptive knowledge to new situations. As we mentioned earlier, you should not press the child to learn to respond to pictures if he seems to be having difficulties: wait until you are teaching Inquiry.

C. **Discrimination between expressive use and receptive understanding of name signs.**

1. *Discrimination between sign and command.* After the child masters the response to the question "Who is this?" and to the command "Touch (Person)," you then teach him to discriminate between the name sign question and the name sign command. Alternate between blocks of trials on the expressive question and blocks of trials on the receptive command. Then, when the child learns to switch to the alternate response in three to five trials after a block switch, begin randomly ordering trials on the question and the command.

2. *Errors.* You may find, as you teach the discrimination, that the child signs "This (Person)" in response to the command "Touch (Person)" or touches the person in response to the question "Who is this?" Both errors can be corrected.

   a. *"Touch (Person)" errors*—When the child signs "This (Person)" in response to the command "Touch (Person)," his signed statement will most likely be correct. Since he saw and heard you give the command, the person he names will likely be the person named in the command. For this reason, do not correct him by saying "No": this would indicate that his statement was incorrect. Instead, sign and say "Yes, this is (Person); put your hands in your lap." Then, after the child puts his hands in his lap, restate the command "Touch (Person)" and prompt the child through the correct response. Fade your prompts as the child learns to touch the appropriate person without them. (You may have to teach the child how to put his hands in his lap.)

b. *"Who is this?"* errors—When the child touches the person you point to in response to the question "Who is this?" simply shape his touching response into the sign "This" and then prompt him to sign the individual's name. Gradually fade your prompts as he learns to respond appropriately without them.

II. POSSESSION: "WHOSE X IS THIS?" Teach the use of name signs as possessive terms in the following order: expressive use of name signs as possessive terms; receptive understanding of name signs as possessive terms; discrimination between the expressive use and receptive understanding of name signs as possessive terms; and discrimination between names as labels and names as possessive terms. We stipulate that you teach the use of name signs as possessive terms rather than possessive pronouns because name signs have concrete physical referents (the person) which do not change when the speaker changes. We also suggest that possessive pronouns be taught (as an Abstraction) well after the child knows how to use name signs as possessive terms (see Chapter 15).

A. **Expressive use of name signs as possessive terms.** Teach name signs as possessives after the child can use five to seven name signs expressively and receptively.

1. *"This (Child) x."* First teach the child to use her own name sign as a possessive term in the statement "This (Child) x." Select several desirable foods whose signs the child knows. Place one of the foods, for example, a piece of cookie, next to the child on her chair, on her lap, or in her hand, and say and sign "This is (Child)'s cookie."

Then ask "Whose cookie is this?" and prompt the child through the signed statement "This (Child) cookie." You need not prompt her through the "'s" sign marker after you prompt her through her name sign. Do say and sign the possessive "'s" marker yourself, however, as you prompt—that is, say "(Child)'s." Praise the child with a signed and spoken "Good signing" after you prompt her through "This (Child) cookie" and allow her to request the cookie. (Let her use her name sign as a possessive term as she requests the cookie if she wishes. If she uses the wrong name sign in the request, however, do not reward her; merely tell her to repeat the request by saying and signing "Again" and prompt her through the correct name sign.) You should gradually fade your prompts for the possessive name sign as the child begins to respond correctly to the question "Whose cookie is this?" on her own.

2. *"This (Teacher) x."* After the child can use her name sign as a possessive term to refer to "(Child) x," here, "(Child) cookie," teach her to use your name sign as a possessive term to refer to "(Teacher) cookie." Place a piece of cookie on your chair, on your lap, or in your hand, say and sign "This is (Teacher)'s cookie," and then eat the cookie. This will pique the child's interest. Then take another piece of cookie, again place it on your chair, on your lap, or in your hand, and ask "Whose cookie is this?" Now, prompt the child through the signed statement, "This (Teacher) cookie," while saying "This (Teacher)'s cookie." Then praise the child with a signed and spoken "Good signing" and allow her to request your piece of cookie. Gradually fade your prompts for the child's use of your name sign as a possessive term as she learns to respond to the question "Whose cookie is this?" on her own.

3. *Discrimination between the child's and your name sign as possessives.* You should alternate between blocks of trials on (Teacher)'s cookie and blocks of trials on (Child)'s cookie. Then, when she can switch to the alternate block in three to five trials, randomly order trials. Randomly place a piece of cookie on either your chair (lap, hand) or the child's chair (lap, hand) and ask "Whose cookie is this?" When the child signs, "This (Child/Teacher) cookie" appropriately, praise her and

allow her to request the cookie. When she fails to do so, sign and say "No; put your hands on your lap." Then, after she follows your directive, ask the question again and reintroduce prompts to obtain a correct response. Gradually fade prompts as the child learns to respond correctly on her own.

4. *Expressive use of possessive name signs extended to a variety of domains.*

   a. *Possessives with a variety of objects*—After the child can describe one desirable food (or other object) possessively as either "(Child) food" or "(Teacher) food," teach her to describe possessively a variety of desirable foods, toys, and other objects, employing the procedures outlined above. The child will soon learn that possession applies not only to one desirable food but to all foods and objects.

   b. *Possessives with articles of clothing and body parts*—Next, you can teach the child to describe possessively articles of clothing and body parts, that is, to respond appropriately to the questions "Whose (article of clothing) is this?" and "Whose (body part) is this?" Employ the procedures outlined above to teach the child to sign the statement "This (Child/ Teacher) (article of clothing/body part)." Instruction on possessives with articles of clothing and body parts will teach the child that possession applies to objects which, though they are not necessarily desired, are nevertheless clearly possessed.

   c. *Possessives with a variety of people*—Teach the child to describe possessively objects belonging to any one of the individuals whose name signs he knows.

5. *Possessive requests.* After the child can describe objects using possessive name signs, teach her to express possession in a request. Hold a favorite food, for example, a piece of banana, in your hand and ask "Whose banana is this?" After the child signs "This (Teacher) banana," praise her and ask "What do you want?" (or "Whose banana do you want?"). If the child does not spontaneously sign "(Child) want (Teacher) banana," prompt her through the signs and then reward her with the piece of banana she just requested. (Prior to this point you allowed the child to make requests possessively or not, as she wished.) Gradually fade your prompts

as the child learns to sign "(Child) want (Teacher) banana" on her own.

a. *Possessive requests with a variety of objects and individuals*—Teach the child to request possessively a wide variety of foods and objects to help her generalize the use of the possessive request. Next, teach her to request foods and objects possessively from a variety of individuals so that she learns to use the possessive request with any of the people whose name signs she knows.

b. *Importance of possessive requests*—It is extremely important that you teach these thoroughly. The majority of the child's spontaneous utterances are likely to be requests, that is, expressions of desire, rather than reference statements. She is therefore much more likely to generalize her use of name signs as possessive terms (and any other new concept you teach her) to new situations and purposes if you teach her to use name signs (and any other new concept) in requests. We cannot overstress this point.

c. *The possessive sign marker "'s"*—It is important to not teach the sign marker "'s" unless the child begins learning it incidentally on her own. Earlier instruction in the use of this marker will only confuse her. To teach "'s," physically prompt the child through the marker after she signs the "(Person)" in the statement "This is (Person)'s x" and the request "(Child) want (Person)'s x"; then gradually fade your prompts as she learns to sign "'s" on her own.

B. **Receptive understanding of name signs as possessive terms.**
   1. *"Touch (Child)'s (body part/article of clothing)."* After the child can sign the statement "This (Child) (body part/article of clothing)" in response to the question "Whose x is this?" you can teach her to respond to the Signed Speech command "Touch (Child)'s (body part/article of clothing)." Fade prompts by reducing tactile and visual prompts as the child learns to touch the body part (or article of clothing) you name.

   You should teach the child to respond receptively to body parts and articles of clothing before desirable foods and toys to prevent her strong desires to request (or merely grab) foods and toys from interfering with instruction. (Later you will teach her to respond receptively to foods and toys.) While sitting across from the child, sign and say "Touch (Child)'s (body part/article of clothing)," then manually prompt her through touching the named body part or article of clothing with her extended index finger. Initially teach the child to touch only one body part or article of clothing.

2. *The second possessive command: another body part or article of clothing.* Next you insert a second body part or article of clothing into the command "Touch (Child)'s (body part/article of clothing)" and teach the child to respond appropriately. Manually prompt the child through the touch, then gradually fade your prompts.

3. *Discrimination between commands.* Give the child the commands in blocks and then randomly order them; reintroduce previous prompts if discrimination training confuses the child, then gradually fade the prompts.

4. *A variety of possessive commands with the child as possessor.* After the child masters the first two commands, you may introduce a variety of possessive commands where the child is the possessor and different body parts and articles of clothing of hers are the objects possessed. Follow a similar instructional strategy as that outlined previously, teaching the response to each new command first in isolation, then in alternating blocks on the new and on all old commands, then randomly ordered with all old commands.

5. *"Touch (Teacher)'s (body part/article of clothing)."* After the child masters "Touch (Child)'s (body part/article of clothing)" with a variety of objects, you can teach her to respond to a command where the teacher is the possessor, that is, you teach her to "Touch (Teacher)'s (body part/article of clothing)."

6. *Discrimination between teacher and child possessive commands.* Give the child the commands "Touch (Child)'s x" and "Touch (Teacher)'s x" in alternating blocks of trials, then in random order. You may need to reintroduce manual prompts at various points in discrimination training.

7. *Possessive commands with a third person as possessor.* Next teach the child to respond to the command "Touch (Possessor)'s (body part/article of clothing)" where the possessor is a third person whose name sign the child

can use expressively in possessive fashion. After she masters the third person command in isolation, practice it in trials alternating with opposite blocks composed of teacher and child commands, and then give the three commands in random order. This exercise will teach the child to discriminate between child, teacher, and person possessive commands.

8. *Possessive commands with other people.* When the child can discriminate among the three commands just discussed, you can teach her to respond to more possessor commands. Teach the child to discriminate among "Touch (Possessor)'s (article of clothing/body part)" commands by giving each new command in isolation first, then in blocks alternating with blocks on old commands, and then randomly ordered with old commands. Prompt the child, then gradually fade your prompts as she learns to respond appropriately. Teach the child to "Touch (Possessor)'s (body part/article of clothing)" with a variety of possessors and a variety of body parts or articles of clothing (as the object possessed).

9. *"Touch (Possessor)'s food."* The child can then learn to respond to possessive food commands, that is, to "Touch (Possessor)'s (food)." Have each of the people sitting in your small group (the child, you, the child's mother, another child) hold up a piece of the same food, or place a piece on her lap. Each person holds up the same food, such as a pretzel, so that the possessor in "Touch (Possessor)'s (food)" is the only varying and informative term in your command. Give commands in random order, randomly inserting the names of the different possessors. Prompt the correct response when necessary. After the child can respond correctly to the command "Touch (Possessor)'s (food)" with one food, you can complicate the task by having each person in the group hold a different or more than one type of food, and randomly insert into your commands the various different foods possessed (as well as the names of the various possessors). The child will probably find the task more interesting if you occasionally give her the command "Take (Possessor)'s (food)" rather than "Touch (Possessor)'s (food)." After the child responds appropriately to a command, allow her to request (or take) the food named from the possessor specified.

C. **Discrimination between expressive use and receptive understanding of possession.**
   1. *Discrimination.* Present expressive possessive questions and receptive possessive commands first in alternating blocks, then in random order.
   2. *Errors.* The child may produce any one of a number of errors during this part of her training. She may insert an incorrect possessor or an incorrect object possessed into her signed response; she may respond with the signed request "(Child) want (Possessor)'s x" to the reference question "Whose x is this?" or with the reference statement "This (Person)'s x" to the request question "Whose x do you want?" She may respond to the command "Touch (Possessor)'s x" by touching an incorrect possessor or an incorrect object possessed; or she may take a named possessor's object in response to the "Touch" command or touch a named possessor's object in response to the "Take" command. Finally, she may respond to one of the expressive questions by touching or taking, or to one of the receptive commands by signing a possessive request or description. If the child produces any of these errors repeatedly, she probably needs additional training on the error-relevant possessive response(s) or discrimination(s), expressive or receptive, that she supposedly learned previously.

   To determine what to reteach, first pinpoint the child's repeated error, then return to that step in the training procedures which teaches the response or discrimination, and then reteach it. For example, if the child repeatedly signs "This (Teacher) x" instead of "This (Child) x" in response to the question "Whose x is this?" when the question refers to an object the child possesses, you should reteach "This (Child) x" and the discrimination between "This (Child) x" and "This (Teacher) x." After the child once again masters the response and the discrimination, you may return to the instruction which you had temporarily suspended on the discrimination between the expressive use and receptive understanding of possessive name signs.

III. **DISCRIMINATION BETWEEN NAMES AS LABELS AND AS POSSESSIVE TERMS.** Up to this point you have taught names and possession and the child has learned to make increasingly complex discriminations within each of the two domains. Now teach him to discriminate between the use of name signs as labels and name signs as possessive terms. When he can perform the tasks described next, you can be reasonably certain that he has mastered this discrimination, for the performance demands a precise understanding of the complex differences between the two usages.

Sit across from the child, preferably among a small group of people. Have each person in the group hold one or more of the child's favorite foods, and present the following expressive questions and receptive commands in random order:

"Who is this?"
"Touch (Person)."
"Whose x is this?"
"Whose x do you want?"
"Touch (Person)'s x."
"Take (Person)'s x."

To further help the child discriminate between the use of name signs as labels and as possessives, teach him to give objects possessed by one person to another person. In a small group similar to the one just described, teach the appropriate response to each of the following commands, first in isolation, then in alternating blocks on the various commands to give, and lastly, in random order:

"(Person) wants x."
"(Person A) wants (Person B)'s x."
"Give x to (Person)."
"Give (Person A)'s x to (Person B)."
"Give (Person A) (Person B)'s x."

IV. **PERSON CONCEPTS IN ORDER OF DIFFICULTY.** As you teach names and possession and the child's understanding grows, you will be teaching him more and more difficult discriminations. The instructional formats discussed previously presented in detail the specific discriminations you would teach the child. We here present these discriminations in order of increasing complexity to give you a clearer picture of the sequencing of discriminations for instruction.

A. **Name signs as labels.**
    1. *"This (Child)."*
    2. *"This (Child)"/"This (Teacher)."*

3. *"This (Child)"/"This (Teacher)"/"This (Person 3)"/etc.*
4. *Response to "Touch (Child)."*
5. *Response to "Touch (Child)"/"Touch (Teacher)."*
6. *Response to "Touch (Child)"/"Touch (Teacher)"/"Touch (Person 3)"/etc.*
7. *"This (Person)"/response to "Touch (Person)."*

B. **Names as possessive terms.**
   1. *"This (Child) x."*
   2. *"This (Child) x"/"This (Teacher) x."*
   3. *"This (Child) x"/"This (Teacher) x"/"This (Person 3) x"/ etc.*
   4. *"(Child) want (Person) x."*
   5. *"(Child) want (Person) x"/"This (Person) x."*
   6. *Response to "Touch (Child)'s x."*
   7. *Response to "Touch (Child)'s x"/"Touch (Teacher)'s x."*
   8. *Response to "Touch (Child)'s x"/"Touch (Teacher)'s x"/ "Touch (Person 3)'s x"/etc.*
   9. *Response to "Take (Person)'s x."*
   10. *Response to "Take (Person)'s x"/"Touch (Person)'s x."*
   11. *"This (Person) x"/"(Child) want (Person) x"/response to "Touch (Person)'s x"/response to "Take (Person)'s x."*

C. **Discrimination between names as labels and as possessive terms.**
   1. *"This (Person)"/response to "Touch (Person)"/"This (Person) x."/"(Child) want (Person) x"/response to "Touch (Person)'s x"/response to "Take (Person)'s x."*
   2. *"This (Person)"/response to "Touch (Person)"/"This (Person) x"/"(Child) want (Person) x"/response to "Touch (Person)'s x"/response to "(Person A) wants (Person B)'s x"/response to "Give x to (Person)"/response to "Give (Person A)'s x to (Person B)"/response to "Give (Person A) (Person B)'s x."*

V. **ERRORS.** The child may produce any one of a multitude of possible errors as he learns names and possession. You will find it helpful to follow these guidelines in correcting them.

A. **Give feedback.** Let the child know that his response was not accurate. If it was clearly wrong, say and sign "No," and then repeat your question or command. The child will in no way be psychologically "damaged" if you indicate that he made a mistake; rather, he will learn that your "No" is a signal to alter his response. If the child did not respond correctly to your question or command but produced an action or utterance response which, in isolation, would be appropriate (for example, accurately labeled his shoe in response to your command to "Touch (Child)'s shoe," say and sign "That's right; put your hands in your lap." Then, after he places his hands in his lap, repeat your question or command and prompt the correct response.

B. **Use repetition.** After you correct an error, you should present your command or question repeatedly over the course of several consecutive trials so that the child has the opportunity to practice the correct response several times in a row. Also, after you move to new commands and questions, you should occasionally present again old commands or questions on which the child made errors to make certain that he is still able to produce the correct response.

C. **Anticipate and prevent errors.** Preventing errors is the strategy of choice when other error correction strategies are ineffective. Prevent the child from repeating an error by prompting the correct response before he has a chance to repeat his mistake. Do not try to anticipate all errors, however: on occasion you should also provide the child with direct negative feedback in the form of a "No." This tells the child which of the alternative responses he tries is not correct and fosters self-correction.

VI. TEACHING STRATEGIES.

A. **Concentrated instruction.** Whatever a child's learning rate, he will learn most easily when instruction on a specific language task is concentrated. The child who learns slowly may take hundreds of consecutive trials each day, over a 2-week period, to learn the utterance "This (Child)"; the child who learns more quickly may take less than a hundred consecutive trials, in one day, to learn the same utterance.

B. **Use of prompts.** You will find that prompting the correct response initially, then gradually fading prompts over the course of repeated trials, will make it easier for the child to learn names and possession. The following are some sug-

gested prompts.
1. *Visual sign prompts.* When teaching the child to produce a sign in response to "Who is this?" you can prompt him by forming your "this" sign into the hand shape for the name sign of the person to whom you are pointing. When teaching the child to touch a particular person in response to the command "Touch (Person)," you can have the person referred to sign his name sign (without speaking) as the child searches for the correct person to touch.
2. *Receptive and expressive response prompts.* Use receptive responses which the child executes appropriately to prompt expressive responses which the child has yet to master, and vice versa. For example, if the child has mastered the receptive "Touch (Child)'s x" response but is still learning the expressive "This (Child) x" response, you can give the command "Touch (Child)'s x" and then, after he correctly touches the x, ask, "Whose x is this?" The "(Child)'s" in your receptive command will prompt him to insert the sign "(Child)" into his expressive response to your expressive question.
3. *Tactile movement prompts.* You can manually shape the child's hands through a chain of signs to help smooth transitions between one sign and the next in his multisign responses to expressive questions. Similarly, you can gently push his hands in the correct direction to help him respond to receptive commands.

C. **Varied instruction.** The child will be more likely to generalize names and possessive terms and the multisign utterances which contain them if you teach him names and possessive terms in a variety of ways. For example, you probably would do well to teach him to sign "This Mama" by touching any part of his mother and asking "Who is this?"; to teach him that "Daddy" refers to the photograph of his father as well as to the real person; and to teach him that "This (Person) x" can be used to describe any one of a number of objects possessed by any one of a number of persons.

You can also promote response generalization to new situations and settings by asking the same questions and commands outside language lessons as those you ask during language lessons. For example, at lunch time you might sign and say to Ricky, "John wants a napkin" to encourage

Ricky to give John a napkin. When Ricky is about to depart for home and his mother is waiting at the door for him you might sign and say, "Sign 'Hi' to Mommy."

D. **Expressive and receptive language tasks.** Teach the child both to sign "This Mommy" and to touch Mommy on command; both to sign "This (Child) shoe" and to touch his shoe on command; and both to use his name to make a request ("(Child) want x") and to respond appropriately to your requests ("(Teacher) want x"). By teaching him to demonstrate his understanding both expressively and receptively, you help him attain a broader, more generalized knowledge of names and possessive terms (and of any other complex concepts you teach).

E. **Inserting possessive terms in requests.** It is extremely important to teach the child to insert possessive terms in personal requests of the form "(Child) want (Person) x." This is one of the most powerful ways to promote generalization because the expression of personal desires motivates much of the typical nonverbal child's use of language. If you teach him to use possessive terms when he makes personal requests, therefore, he is likely to begin generalizing his use of the possessive to new situations, both in descriptions and in requests. If you teach the child to insert *any* concept he learns, simple or complex, into personal requests, he is much more likely to begin generalizing the concept to new situations. We cannot overstress the importance of teaching the child to use new concepts in combination with his expressions of desire.

VII. **MASTERY CRITERIA.** The following criteria relate to the mastery of names and possession.

A. **Name signs as expressive labels.** The child can be said to have mastered a name sign as an expressive label when he does the following.
   1. *He produces the sign movement, position, and hand shape clearly, without prompts.*
   2. *He consistently and accurately associates a particular name sign with a particular person.*
   3. *He spontaneously and appropriately generalizes the use of the name sign: produces it in new situations; uses it*

for new purposes; or combines it with other signs to form novel utterances.

B. **Multisign expressive utterances, such as "This (Person),"**
   "This (Person) x," and "(Child) want (Person) x." The child
   can be said to have mastered these when he does the
   following.
   1. *He chains the signs in the multisign utterance in the cor-*
      rect order and makes smooth transitions from one sign
      to the next.
   2. *He spontaneously and appropriately uses the multisign*
      utterance.
   3. *He spontaneously and appropriately generalizes the use*
      of the utterance: produces it in new situations; uses it for
      new purposes; flexibly inserts into it the signs he knows
      (for example, he signs "This (Possessor) (object pos-
      sessed)" with an object possessed which he was not ex-
      plicitly taught to insert in the utterance).

C. **Receptive understanding of name signs and possessive**
   terms. The child can be said to have receptive understanding
   when he does the following.
   1. *He consistently and appropriately responds to com-*
      mands containing names and possessive terms.
   2. *He responds appropriately when you give him one of the*
      commands in a new situation.

12

Person Concepts II: Actions, Emotions, Social Greetings, Direct Address, and Calling

   I. Actions

  II. Emotions: Happy, sad, angry, and tired

 III. Social greetings: "Hi" and "Bye-bye"

 IV. Direct address

  V. Calling a person by name

 VI. Teaching strategies

After the child learns the possessive use of names, teach him the labels for people's actions and emotional states. Teach him to respond to the question "What is (Person) doing?" with the signed utterances "(Action)," "(Person) (action)," and "(Person) (action) (object)." Also, teach him to respond to the question "How is (Person) feeling?" with the signed utterances "(Emotion)" and "(Person) (emotion)." Finally, teach him to respond to commands containing action and emotion concepts such as "Touch the person who is eating" and "Touch the person who is sad." As you teach action and emotion concept, also begin teaching the child to sign "Hi" and "Bye-bye" and to use names to address people directly and to call them to him.

I. ACTIONS.

A. Expressive use of action signs.

1. *The first action sign: An action of personal interest.* The first action sign to teach the child is one which describes an action that interests him and involves the motion of his entire body. For these reasons, "jump" is a good sign to teach.

   a. *Modeling and prompting the action and its sign—* Begin instruction by modeling the action of jumping while the child watches. Then ask the question "What is (Teacher) doing?" and model the response to the question by signing "jump" and simultaneously saying "jumping." (At this stage you need not sign the "ing" marker.)

   Execute the action again, ask "What is (Teacher) doing?" and then prompt the child through the action sign "jump" as you simultaneously say "jumping." You should praise the child with the Signed Speech statement "Good signing." Gradually fade your prompts for the child's "jump" sign as the child learns to sign "jump" on his own in response to the question "What is (Teacher) doing?"

   b. *Other actors—*You should also teach the child to use the action sign to describe the action when actors other than yourself execute it. While another person, child or adult, engages in jumping, you can ask, "What is (Person) doing?" and teach the child to describe the individual's action with the sign "jump." (Remember to say "jumping" as you prompt or partially prompt the "jump" sign and as the child produces it on his own.)

2. *The second action sign.* In deciding which action sign to teach next, you should choose a sign for a familiar action which the child appears interested in watching, and whose referent action is as different as possible from the referent action of the first action sign you taught. For example, if the referent action of the first action sign involved the entire body, such as jumping, you might choose "drink" as the second sign, since its referent action involves only the hands. You should also choose a sign whose hand shape, position, and movement differ markedly from those of the first action sign, and whose corresponding word differs significantly from the corresponding word of the first action sign.

   First teach the second action sign by itself, employing

the same procedures you used to teach the first action sign. Then, after the child masters the second action sign, teach him to discriminate between the first and second action signs. You engage in either of the two actions while asking "What is (Teacher) doing?" first in alternating blocks of trials on the two actions, then in randomly ordered trials. When the child produces the correct action sign in response to your question, you then praise him with the Signed Speech statement "Good signing." When he makes an error, you should say and sign "No, put your hands on your lap." After the child follows this directive, ask the question again and reintroduce prompts for the correct action sign. As the child learns to discriminate between the two action signs, you can gradually fade prompts.

3. *Other action signs.* You may use the same procedures you used to teach the first and second action signs, making certain that the child correctly discriminates each new action sign from those previously learned. You should teach the child to produce from five to seven action signs appropriately in response to the question "What is (Person) doing?"

4. *Pictures of actions.* You might vary instruction on action signs by presenting pictures of a person engaged in each of the five to seven actions for the child to describe. After the child learns to produce the sign for the action represented in the picture, he will probably find it easier to generalize his use of action signs to new situations.

5. *"(Person) (action)."* Next, teach the child to sign "(Person) (action)" instead of merely "(action)" in response to the question "What is (Person) doing?" You do this by prompting him to produce the name sign before he signs the action label. Remember to say the corresponding words as he produces each sign (with prompts or on his own). Start with one person engaging in one particular action, then have one person engage in each of a variety of actions, and, last, have each of several people engage in each of a variety of actions. The child will gradually learn to sign "(Person) (action)" to describe a variety of actions by a variety of people.

6. *"(Person) (action) (object)."* Teach the child to add the sign for the object-acted-on to his utterance so that he signs "(Person) (action) (object)" instead of "(Person) (ac-

tion)." As you prompt him to add the sign for the object-acted-on and then gradually fade your prompts, the child will learn to sign "(Person) (action) (object)" (as in "Tommy eat cookie" and "Patrick hug doll"). It is important to verbalize the corresponding words as the child produces the sign. You should begin instruction with one object-acted-on and add new objects only after the child learns to use old ones in his action descriptions.

A good method for prompting the entire three-sign action-response when the child leaves out the sign for the object is to ask the question "What is (Person) (action)-ing" after the child responds with just "(Person) (action)." For example, if John were eating a cookie, you would ask, "What is John doing?" and if he signed "John eat," you would then ask, "What is John eating?" to obtain, "John eat cookie."

B. Receptive understanding of action signs.

    1. *Responding to action commands.* As you teach the child to describe your and other people's actions, you can also begin building his receptive understanding of action signs. Start by teaching the child to engage in a specified physical action on command. For example, you might teach the child to jump in response to the command "(Child), jump" or to take a drink in response to "(Child), drink." To obtain the correct response to your command, you initially prompt the child through the appropriate action and then, over the course of repeated trials, fade your prompts. For example, you might prompt the child to jump by beginning to lift him and modeling a jump yourself. You can use prompting to teach the child to respond to a variety of action commands.

    After you teach the child to engage in specified actions on command, you can use his receptive knowledge to help him generalize the expressive use of action signs to new situations. Have him describe his own spontaneous actions outside as well as inside the classroom. Prompt him initially if he needs help.

    2. *Responding to action pictures.* Place two or more action pictures on the table in front of the child and teach him to "Touch the picture of the (Person) (action)-ing." Use prompts to teach him to search for and touch the correct picture in response to your directive. Over the course of

repeated trials, you may then gradually fade your prompts. Eventually the child will search for and touch the correct action picture in response to your command with a variety of actions.

C. **Signing action commands.** Next you may teach the child to sign action commands. The typical nonverbal child enjoys controlling his teacher's and other people's behaviors whenever he can. You can use his pleasure in control to motivate him to use and generalize action signs to new situations by teaching him to give you and other people action commands. For example, you might tell him, "Sign 'jump,' " prompting him if necessary, and jump as he commands you to when he signs. Have the child give you one action command first, then give you any one of the action commands whose signs he knows, then give other people action commands as well.

After you teach the child to produce commands containing the action signs you taught him, you may also teach him to produce commands containing "Give." His experience with the other action signs will allow him to understand that "Give" refers to an action. Teach the child first to give the command "Give x," then "Give x to (Child)." These commands provide the child with an action-centered alternative to requests and allow him to enjoy controlling the giving of the giver as well.

II. **EMOTIONS: HAPPY, SAD, ANGRY, AND TIRED.**

A. **Expressive use of emotion signs.**
1. *The first emotion sign.* The first emotion sign to teach the child should refer to an emotion which intrigues him. Some children, for example, are quite intrigued with the crying of another child and tend to learn to label the affective state "sad" very quickly. If the child does not demonstrate an interest in one of the four emotions previously listed—happy, sad, angry, or tired—choose one arbitrarily.
a. *Modeling and prompting the emotion and its sign*—Let's assume you have chosen to teach the sign "happy" first. You would begin instruction by making a very happy smiling face, asking as you smile "How is (Teacher)?" and then modeling the correct emotion sign, "happy," and simultaneously say-

ing "happy." Next, you make a very happy face again and ask, "How is (Teacher)?" Prompt the child through the "happy" sign as you simultaneously say "happy" and praise him with the Signed Speech statement "Good signing." Gradually fade your prompts for the child's "happy" sign as the child learns to sign "happy" on his own in response to the question "How is (Teacher)?" and the sight of your happy face.

   b. *Other people*—To give the child a generalized understanding of the concept "happy," teach him to describe the happiness of other people. While another person, child or adult, produces a happy face, ask "How is (Person)?" inserting the person's name, and have the child describe the person's affective state with the sign "happy." It is important to say "happy" as you prompt or partially prompt the "happy" sign and as the child produces it on his own.

2. *The second emotion sign.* Follow the same procedures you used to teach the first emotion sign as you teach a second emotion sign, such as "sad." After the child masters the second emotion sign, you can teach him to discriminate between his two emotion signs. Make either a happy or a sad face and ask "How is (Teacher)?" When the child produces the correct response, praise him with the Signed Speech statement "Good signing." When he makes an error, sign and say "No, put your hands in your lap." After he follows your directive, you can ask the question again and reintroduce previous prompts for the correct emotion sign, then gradually fade them once again.

3. *Other emotion signs.* You can teach the emotion signs "angry" and "tired" using the same procedures you used to teach the first and second emotion signs. You should make certain that the child discriminates each new emotion sign from previously learned emotion signs. Your goal is to teach him to produce each of the signs—"happy," "sad," "angry," and "tired"—on his own in appropriate situations when asked "How is (Person)?"

4. *Pictures of emotions.* To vary the child's task, you can present pictures of people with each of the four facial expressions and ask "How is (Person)?" Mastery of this task will help the child generalize the use of emotion

signs to new situations.

5. *"(Person) (emotion)."* Now the child can learn to sign "(Person) (emotion)," that is, to specify the person as well as describe the emotion. To teach this longer response, prompt the child through the person's name sign before he begins signing the emotion label in answer to your question. Say the corresponding name and emotion as he signs the name sign and the emotion sign. You can gradually fade your name sign prompts as he learns to sign "(Person) (emotion)" on his own. After he can sign "(Person) (emotion)" appropriately when one person produces any of the four facial expressions, you then teach him to respond when any one of several persons produces any of the four facial expressions.

B. **Receptive understanding of emotion signs.**
  1. *Making faces.* Make a face which depicts the emotion sign (and simultaneous word) you produce. Give the command "(Child), make a (emotion) face," prompt the child to respond, then gradually, over the course of repeated trials, fade your prompts. For example, when you tell Joe to make a happy face, you might prompt him to smile by pushing up gently on the corners of his mouth as you tickle him and model a smile (and perhaps push up on the corners of your mouth occasionally). You can fade your prompts as Joe learns to smile on his own after you sign and say, "Joe, make a happy face." You may also occasionally want to hold a mirror in front of Joe as he makes a happy face so he can observe the similarities between the happy faces of others (which he can describe) and the happy face he makes himself. You should teach the child to make the appropriate face in response to each of the four emotion commands: "(Child), make a (happy/sad/angry/tired) face."

  When the child can make emotion faces, you can use this receptive knowledge to help him generalize expressive emotion signs to new situations. Ask him to label his own spontaneous emotions outside as well as inside the classroom; provide prompts when necessary.
  2. *Responding to emotion pictures.* After you teach the child to describe actual emotions, you can teach him to touch pictures representing emotions, a receptive variation on the emotion task. To do this, you place two or

more emotion pictures in front of the child and sign and say "Touch the picture of the person who is (emotion)." You may use prompts to teach the child to search out and touch the correct picture in response to your directive. Gradually fade your prompts as the child learns to search out and touch the correct emotion picture on his own in response to the directive with each of the four emotions whose signs he knows.

C. **Signing emotion commands.** You may be able to use the child's pleasure in controlling people's behaviors to motivate him to use and generalize emotion signs to new situations. Teach him to give "make a face" commands. For example, you might tell him to "Sign '(Teacher) happy,' " prompting him if necessary, and smile and laugh as he commands you to. If the child seems to learn, teach him to give you one emotion command first, then to give you each of the emotion commands whose signs he knows, then to give other people emotion commands as well. (You may wish to teach him to sign "Be (emotion)" as an alternative command to "(Teacher) (emotion).")

III. SOCIAL GREETINGS: "HI" AND "BYE-BYE."

A. **"Hi."** When the child arrives at school in the morning, you can greet him with a signed and spoken "Hi." (You may use a simplified version of the adult "Hi" sign: place the fingertips of your palm-down signing hand on the signing hand side of your forehead, and then move your hand briskly away from your forehead.) After you sign and say "Hi," you then prompt the child to sign "Hi" in response by molding his dominant hand into the "Hi" sign and simultaneously saying "Hi." Gradually fade your prompts for the child's "Hi" sign during the weeks which follow, as the child learns to say "Hi" on his own in response to your "Hi."

To give the children in your class additional practice with the "Hi" sign, you might schedule a "Hi time" for them prior to the first language lesson in the morning. As children and staff sit in a circle, take each child, one at a time, to each person in the circle. While the child stands in front of the person (child or staff member), prompt him (from behind) through the "Hi" sign. (A staff member positioned behind a seated child who receives a "Hi" can prompt that child through the "Hi" sign in response.) Fade your prompts gradually as the child begins intiating the "Hi" sign on his own. (To foster eye contact during "Hi time," praise the child and reward him with affection for making eye contact with the person to whom he signs "Hi.")

B. **"Bye-bye."** When the child is leaving at the end of the school day, you can sign and say "Bye-bye" to him. (The "Bye-bye" sign consists of two waves of the dominant hand.) After you sign and say "Bye-bye," prompt the child to respond by molding his dominant hand through the "Bye-bye" sign and simultaneously saying "Bye-bye." During the weeks which follow, you can gradually fade your prompts for the child's "Bye-bye" sign as he learns to produce it on his own in response to your "Bye-bye." (To foster eye contact, also praise the child and reward him with affection whenever he makes eye contact as he signs "Bye-bye.")

IV. **DIRECT ADDRESS.** Now you can teach the child to use name signs for the purpose of direct address as he greets a person. After he signs "Hi" or "Bye-bye," you immediately prompt him through the name sign of the person he is addressing. For example, when he is greeting his mother, prompt him to sign "Mama" after he signs "Hi." (Remember to verbalize the corresponding words as he signs.) Fade your prompts for the name sign as the child learns to sign "Hi, (Person)" or "Bye-bye, (Person)" on his own when addressing someone.

You can promote the mastery of direct address in greetings by appropriately modeling the utterances "Hi, (Child)" and "Bye-bye, (Child)" as you address the child. For example, when John arrives at school in the morning, you can say and sign, "Hi, John," and when he leaves at the end of the day you can say and sign, "Bye-bye, John."

V. **CALLING A PERSON BY NAME.**

A. **Calling one person by name.** Teach the child to call a person by name after he learns to sign the names of several individuals; for this you will need the assistance of another adult whose name sign the child knows. You and the child are seated facing each other on one side of the room while the other adult (for example, the child's mother) sits on the other side of the room holding a tray which contains some of the child's favorite foods and toys (clearly visible to the child). Tell the child to call the person, that is, to "Call Mama," and then provide a complete imitative prompt (a large name sign and a loud verbalization of the name) and whatever manual prompts the child needs. After the child "calls out" the adult's name in sign (and perhaps simultaneously says it), the adult on the other side of the room rewards the child by immediately bringing the child the tray of desired foods and toys and asking "What do you want?" The child then makes a request and the adult gives him the desired object. Gradually fade your prompts as the child learns to "Call (Person)" when you ask him to. You should make sure that each time the child appropriately calls (on his own or while being prompted), the adult called quickly approaches the child and asks what he wants.

B. **Other people.** After the child learns to call one adult, teach him to call other adults and children whose name signs he knows, so that he learns to call a familiar adult or child when he wants something.

C. **Responding to being called.** A receptive variation on the calling task is to teach the child to come when someone calls his name. To teach this response, you call the child from a distance, perhaps from across the room, and have another person prompt him to come to you immediately. As the person assisting fades the prompts over the course of many trials, the child will learn to respond to your call by coming to you immediately on his own. You can then teach him to respond to other people's calls if you wish. Reward the child for coming by allowing him to make a request.

VI. **TEACHING STRATEGIES.** As you teach actions, emotions, social greetings, direct address, and calling, use the teaching strategies detailed earlier in Chapter 11. These strategies are now outlined briefly along with some suggestions for how you might apply them when teaching the person concepts discussed in this chapter.

A. **Facilitating mastery.** Teach in a concentrated fashion and use a variety of prompts.
   1. *Concentrated instruction.* Provide the child with repeated instructional trials to help him learn to pro-

duce the sign, utterance, or action response on his own.
2. *Variety of prompts.*
   a. *Visual prompts*—When teaching the child to "Make a (emotion) face," you can model the facial expression to prompt the child initially.
   b. *Indirect prompts*—When teaching the child to sign the person's name after a greeting, such as "Hi, Mama," you can ask, "Who is this?" and then, after he signs, "Mama," tell him to "Sign 'Hi' to Mama."
   c. *Tactile prompts*—When teaching the child direct address, you can mold the child's hand(s) through the name sign of the person he is addressing after he signs "Hi" or "Bye-bye" on his own.

B. **Promoting generalization.** You should capitalize on the variety of concept-relevant situations inside and outside the lesson to reinforce use and understanding. Ask concept-relevant questions and give concept-relevant commands in a wide variety of situations, and teach both expressive and receptive language skills. Here are some examples.
  1. *Variety of concept-relevant situations.* If during a lesson the child takes special notice of a person entering or leaving the classroom, you might have the child sign "Hi" or "Bye-bye" to that person.
  2. *Questions and commands.* If, outside the language lesson (for example, at lunch or during group games), another child or the child himself begins to cry, laugh, throw a temper tantrum, or fall asleep, you might ask the child the same question you ask him during language lessons when teaching emotions: "How is (Person)?"
  3. *Expressive and receptive language.* For example, you can teach the child to jump in response to your command as well as to sign "jump" to describe this action; to make a happy face in response to your command as well as to sign "happy" to describe this emotion; to respond to as well as initiate a greeting; and to come when someone calls him as well as to call another person.

C. **Discriminations among person concepts.** You should teach the child to discriminate among actions, emotions, names, and possession. After the child masters action and emotion signs, you might ask the following questions and give the following commands to him in random order, to make cer-

tain he can discriminate among person concepts.
1. *"Who is this?"*
2. *"Touch (Person)."*
3. *"Whose x is this?"*
4. *"Touch (Person)'s x."*
5. *"What is (Person) doing?"*
6. *"(Child), (action)."*
7. *"Touch the picture of the person who is (action)-ing."*
8. *"How is (Person)?"*
9. *"Make a (emotion) face."*
10. *"Touch the picture of the person who is (emotion)."*

D. **Correcting errors.** Use a correction procedure which the child can clearly and easily understand.
   1. *Give feedback.* Give feedback in the form of "No" (Signed Speech) when the child makes an error.
   2. *Use repetition.* Use repetition to provide the child with practice on the correct response.

13

Inquiry I: Language-guided Search for Hidden Objects

I. Searching for hidden objects on command

II. Mastery criteria

Inquiry should be taught after the child masters name signs. The purpose of teaching Inquiry is to encourage the child to use language on her own to obtain information. The child's skill in using language to obtain information will then provide her with a tool for learning new language concepts.

Normal children employ language to obtain information and to solve problems. Children who are severely language handicapped, however, do not often ask for information or search for missing objects. To help the handicapped child use language in these ways, teach her to search for hidden objects, to answer questions about the locations of hidden objects, and to ask questions. As you teach, you will be giving the child a new linguistic function and will be placing a greater emphasis than before on receptive language.

We have divided Inquiry into two chapters. In the present chapter we outline procedures for teaching the language-guided search for hidden objects. In the next chapter, we describe instruction in question-answering and question-asking.

I. SEARCHING FOR HIDDEN OBJECTS ON COMMAND.
Begin by teaching the child to obey the command "Touch the x" when x is an object hidden in one of several containers or locations. Essentially you are teaching two skills: a receptive language skill (understanding the command "Touch the x") and a search skill (active search for the hidden object). As the child

masters these skills, she will learn to use your command to activate her memory of the hidden object and to maintain that memory as the goal of her search.

As we noted, the time to begin teaching the child to search for hidden objects is after she masters name signs (for three or more people). You should teach her to search for hidden objects in three steps: first, to obey "Touch the x" when the x is visible and within reach; second, to discriminate between the command "Touch the x" and the question "What is this?"; and, finally, to obey "Touch the x" (or "Find the x") when the x is hidden (that is, to search for a hidden x).

A. **"Touch the x."** Place one object for the child to touch on a tray or small table between you and the child, say and sign "Touch the x," and then immediately mold the child through touching the object. Have her touch a strongly desired object and reward her for touching it by saying and signing "Good" or "Good touching" and allowing her to hold (or eat) the object. Gradually fade molding prompts as the child learns to touch one object on command; then one by one teach her to touch other desired objects on command.

B. **Discrimination between "Touch the x" and "What is this?"** After the child can touch any desired object whose sign she knows, you may begin alternating between blocks of trials on the command "Touch the x" and on the reference question "What is this?" Gradually decrease the number of trials per block. When the child can switch her responses in three to five trials, you can begin randomly presenting the command and the question.

C. **Search for a hidden x.** First direct the child to touch one of two visible objects, then to search for an out-of-sight but uncovered object, and, finally, to search for a hidden object. (The instructional tasks we suggest here do not exhaust the great variety of search tasks it is possible to teach; feel free to develop your own as you teach, remembering to start with simple ones and move gradually to more complex ones.)

1. *Touching one of two objects.* Place two objects on a tray or small table between you and the child. By signing and saying "Touch the x," direct her to search out and touch one of the two objects; if necessary mold the child through the correct response and then fade your

molding prompts. You should direct her to touch only one of the two objects first, then alternate between blocks of trials on each of the two objects, and then randomly direct her to touch one or the other of the two objects. Throughout training, it is good also to randomize the position of objects on the tray. The child will then learn not to respond to irrelevant position cues.

When the child can touch either of the two objects with ease, you can then replace one of them with a third object and teach her to touch this object on command when it is one of the two objects in front of her. Continue replacing objects so that she learns to touch one of any two objects in her sign repertoire. Then teach her to touch one of three, four, five, and finally six objects when you sign and say, "Touch the x." The child's ability to touch one of a number of visible objects is her first search skill.

2. *Searching for out-of-sight but uncovered objects.* Remove objects from the tray and place them in various locations near the child but out of her immediate sight: locations she has only to turn her head to see. You can teach her to search for and touch these nearby objects, assisting her with prompts when necessary, and as her search skills develop, you can place the objects in a greater variety of locations throughout the work area.

3. *Simple search for a hidden object: The cup game.* The cup game is a good first task because it is simple: the child merely searches for an object hidden under an upside-down cup. It will probably pique her interest in search and, in developmental terms, will help her bring her object concept skills and interests to bear on search-related tasks. Teach the child to search first for partially hidden objects, then for completely hidden objects, and then complicate her search tasks in a variety of ways. (As you teach the cup game, continue having the child search for a wide variety of out-of-sight but uncovered objects, such as people and pictures.)

a. *An object partially hidden under a cup*—You begin by placing an object on a tray between you and the child. As she watches, you cover half the object with a paper cup so it is partially hidden. Then you direct the child to search for and touch the object by signing and saying "Touch the x." If necessary, introduce and fade tactile prompts to help her search out the partially hidden object. You should teach the child first to search for and touch half-hidden objects she sees you hide, and then introduce half-hidden objects she does not see you hide.

b. *A completely hidden object*—Over successive trials, gradually decrease the portion of the object visible to the child until she is searching for and touching objects completely hidden under the cup. You should practice this with a variety of objects.

c. *Two or more cups*—Next, you hide an object under one of two cups as the child watches you and teach her to search for and touch the object. After she masters this task, you introduce cup movement as a distracting prompt: before you say, "Touch the x," move the cup under which the object is hidden around on the table, keeping the object hidden under it. After the child learns to search out an object hidden under a previously moved cup, stop moving that cup and introduce movement of the other cup (under which the object was not hidden) as a distracting prompt. As the child learns to find and touch an object hidden under either one of the two cups, you should gradually fade prompts. Then have the child search for an object which you have hidden under one of three, four, or five identical cups.

4. *Complicated search for hidden objects.* You can complicate the child's task by having her search for one or more objects hidden in one or more containers and locations. For example, you might hide a toy car in a shoe box, under an old towel, under an upside-down cup, or in the middle of a pile of blocks on the table. Now when you ask the child, "Find the car," she will have to search through three containers and in three locations to obey your command.

There are many other ways of gradually complicating search tasks to develop the child's search skills. You can allow the child to watch you hide the object and later prevent her from watching. You can hide objects in containers and locations on the table near the child and then begin hiding them in containers and locations in other parts of the work area. Or you can begin by asking the child to search for only one object and later ask her to hold in memory and search for two objects. (Before teaching the child to search for two objects, teach her to search for the one object you name after you hide two objects.) As you gradually increase the complexity and variety of the searches you demand of the child, her search skills will grow and the likelihood of her using them spontaneously outside search lessons will increase. An early sign of growth in search skills is that the child repeats to herself the name of an object for which she is searching.

5. *Search for people.* You may follow procedures similar to those you used to teach search for objects. Start by having the child touch one of several people near her, then teach her to search for and touch people farther away, and finally have her search for and touch people out of easy visibility (such as in another room). Teaching the child to search for people helps her to integrate her knowledge of person concepts with her inquiry skills.

6. *Search with pictures.* As with other objects, you first present two clearly visible pictures and ask the child to touch one. After the child learns to touch one of five or six clearly visible pictures, you then teach her to hunt through a pile of pictures, one on top of the other, in response to the directive "Find the x." All the pictures except the top one will be hidden objects. Next, you teach the child to look through picture books to find and touch pictures of objects. This kind of search helps her integrate an alternative mode of representation into her inquiry skills.

7. *Search generalization.* Whenever possible, you should encourage the child to use search skills outside the structured language lessons. For example, you may teach her to search for objects and people outdoors, throughout the school or treatment center, or in her own home. Introducing a variety of settings will help her generalize language-guided search.

The typical nonverbal child does not have the inquisitiveness of a normal child and is therefore not as motivated to engage in search. You can greatly help her develop and generalize her search skills, therefore, by placing her in social situations that arouse inquisitiveness. For example, if the child is accustomed to passing out cookies and juice to her classmates at snack time, puzzles at puzzle time, or paper and crayons at drawing time, you can hide the items she normally distributes in an easy-to-find place and prompt her to find them. Similarly, if she has her own favorite lesson or activity, you can have her search for the materials, toys, and rewards she needs to carry it out. The more often the child's inquisitiveness is aroused, the more likely she is to engage in search on her own and generalize this inquiry skill to new situations.

II. **MASTERY CRITERIA.** The first criterion for mastery of a search skill is consistent and accurate use of the skill on command. The second and more important criterion is spontaneity. You will know that the child has taken her first steps toward spontaneous search when you see her looking for a hidden object on her own, possibly with an accompanying egocentric sign or word for the object.

14

Inquiry II: Answering and Asking Questions of Location

I. Question-answering: "In" and "on"

II. Question-asking: "Where is x?" and "What is this?"

III. Lesson variety

IV. Mastery criteria

As we mentioned in the first chapter on Inquiry, the reason for teaching the language-handicapped child inquiry skills is to promote his spontaneous use of language to obtain information. In the present chapter, we detail steps for teaching the child question-answering and question-asking. As he learns to answer questions about the locations of hidden objects, he will begin linking his own language to search; as he learns to ask questions about objects' locations and names, he will learn to use his own language to obtain information.

   I. **QUESTION-ANSWERING: "IN" AND "ON."** After the child can search on command for a variety of hidden objects in a variety of settings, you can teach him to answer questions about the locations of the objects for which he searches, first the hidden ones located in containers and then the visible ones located on other objects. Start with objects in containers to allow the child to tie his question-answering about objects in containers to his ability to search for hidden objects on command; this will help him link language to the need for information.

    A. **The location concept "in."** Teach this concept in two steps:

first teach the child to place objects in containers on command, and then teach him to answer questions about objects hidden in the containers. The child thus gains a receptive understanding of the locative concept "in"; then, as he learns to answer questions about objects hidden "in," he gains the expressive use of both the concept "in" and question-answering.

1. *Receptive understanding of "in."* Teach the child to respond to the command "Put the x in the y."

   a. *The first object*—Place an object such as a toy car in a container such as a box on the table near both you and the child. Then simultaneously sign and say "Put the x in the y" ("Put the car in the box"). Prompt the child through placement, that is, grasp his hands and physically mold them through placing the car in the box. You should praise him for his placement by providing him with affectionate physical contact, kind signs and words, and a desired object. Then fade your prompts as the child learns to obey "Put the x in the y."

   b. *A variety of objects in a variety of containers*—After the child can consistently place one object in one container, you can help him generalize his receptive understanding of "in" by using many objects and many containers. You can gradually increase the complexity of receptive tasks as follows: introduce new objects one at a time for placement in one container; introduce new containers one at a time; present two or more objects at a time and tell the child to place a particular one in the one container in front of him; present one object and tell the child to place it in a particular one of two or more containers; present two or more objects and two or more containers and tell the child to place a particular object in a particular container; and present two or more objects for the child to place in two or more containers.

   c. *Discrimination*—You should assess whether or not the child discriminates the command "Put the x in the y" from your other questions and commands (such as "What is this?" "Touch the x," and "What do you want?"). If the child confuses the spatial location command with your other commands and questions, teach him to discriminate it from them.

2. *Expressive use of "in."* This means that the child will learn to search for an object and then to describe its location by signing "X in y." You should teach the child first to answer questions about the location of an object you hide in a container as he watches, then to search for and describe the location of an object you hide when he is not watching.

a. *An object hidden as the child watches*—Place an object such as a car in a container such as a box as the child watches. Then ask the child "Where is the x?" ("Where is the car?") and prompt him to sign "In y" ("In box") by grasping his hands and molding them through the signs. Gradually fade your prompts as the child learns to sign "In y" by himself. Teach him first to sign "In y" when you hide an x in any one of a variety of containers (or y's): a box, a shoe, an opaque jar. Then, after the child consistently signs "In y" without a prompt when you hide the x in any one of a variety of y's, teach him to sign the complete phrase "X in y" in answer to your location questions.

After he can answer the question "Where is the x?" about one object, x, in any one of a variety of containers by signing "X in y," introduce other objects, also in a variety of containers. Increase the complexity of question-answering tasks until the child can answer "in" questions about the location of one of two objects, each of which you hide in its own container as he watches. Teach him first to describe the location of one object after he watches you hide it in one of two, three, or four containers; then teach him to describe the location of one of two objects you hide as he watches in one of two, three, or four containers.

After the child can describe the location of one of two hidden objects, assess whether or not he discriminates the location question "Where is the x?" from other questions and commands, including the command "Put the x in the y." If he confuses "Where is the x?" with other questions or commands, you will then have to teach him to discriminate this question from the others.

b. *An object hidden when the child is not watching*—Hide an object in the single container in front of the child when he is not watching, ask him the question

"Where is the x?" and prompt him to search for and describe the location of the hidden object. As he learns to search and describe on his own, you can gradually fade your prompts.

When the child consistently searches for and describes the location of an object you hide when he is not watching in the single container in front of him, you may introduce a second container and teach the child to search for and describe the location of the object you hide when he is not watching in one of the two containers in front of him. Do the same with three and, later, four containers. Then you may gradually extend the domain of search and description by teaching the child to search for and describe the location of objects you hide in a variety of places and containers in the lesson room.

B. **The location concept "on."** After the child can answer questions about hidden objects located in containers, he then can learn to answer questions about visible objects located on other objects.

    1. *Receptive understanding of "on."* Teach the child "Put the x on the y" in the following stages: when only the two objects x and y are on the table in front of him; when the two objects, x and y, and one other object are present; when x, y, and two other objects are present; and, last, when x, y, and three other objects are present.

    2. *Expressive use of "on."* Teach the child to sign "X on y" appropriately in answer to the question "Where is the x?" Using a variety of y's, first teach the child to sign "On y" and then "X on y" when only x-on-y is in front of him. Then gradually increase the complexity of his task: direct him to sign "X on y" when x-on-y and a-on-b are present; when x-on-y and a-on-y are present; and when x-on-y, a-on-y, and a-on-b are present.

C. **Receptive discrimination between "in" and "on."** To teach this discrimination, you can begin to alternate between blocks of "Put the x on the y" and "Put the x in the y" commands. After the child learns to switch to the alternate response in three to five trials, you then begin presenting "on" and "in" commands in random order. The child will gradually learn to put the object "on" or "in" and you will be able to fade your prompts.

D. **Expressive discrimination between "in" and "on."** Alternate between blocks of "Where is the x?" questions with an x-on-y, and blocks of "Where is the x?" questions with an x-in-y. (Place the x "on" or "in" as the child watches and use a variety of objects and containers.) After the child learns to switch his answer within three to five trials, you can begin placing an x "on" or "in" y in random order. The child will gradually learn to describe the object as "on" or "in," and you will be able to fade your prompts.

E. **Additional spatial location concepts.** You may next introduce and teach additional spatial location concepts such as "beside" and "under" by using procedures similar to those outlined above for "in" and "on." "Beside" is good to teach after "in" and "on" as a general descriptor for nearness-without-contact; "under" tends to be hard for children to discriminate from "in," perhaps because both concepts specify contact and partial visibility. However, if the child has difficulty mastering the receptive and expressive discriminations between "in" and "on," do not introduce additional concepts. Such difficulties suggest that differences among spatial location concepts are not of personal interest and meaning to the child and that he will be unlikely to differentiate among the concepts appropriately in his spontaneous utterances.

F. **Location requests: "(Child) want object-location-object."** To foster spontaneous use of spatial location concepts, you should teach the child to use them in extended requests: to sign "(Child) want x in y," "(Child) want x on y," and so forth. This will link location concepts to the child's desires and make them personally meaningful.
   1. *"(Child) want x in y."* Place an object the child strongly desires, such as a cookie, in a container and ask the child "Where is the x?" ("Where is the cookie?"). Immediately after the child responds, "X in y" ("Cookie in box"), praise him and ask "What do you want?" Then prompt him to lengthen his "(Child) want x" request, for example, "Tommy want cookie," to include the spatial location concept. In other words, you should teach him to sign the extended request "(Child) want x in y." The

child will gradually learn to sign the extended request with the location on his own, and you will be able to fade your prompts.

2. *Other spatial location concepts in the extended request.* You teach the child to insert the other spatial location concepts you have taught him, such as "on" and "under," into the extended request "(Child) want x (location) y." If he fails to learn, you may have to again teach him to discriminate between the various extended location requests.

II. QUESTION-ASKING: "WHERE IS X" AND "WHAT IS THIS?" Now the child is ready to ask questions to obtain information, first about the locations of hidden objects, then about the names of hidden or unfamiliar objects. You can use the child's question-answering (search and describe) skill as the base on which to build his new question-asking skill.

A. "Where is x?" You teach the child to ask "Where is x?" to learn the location of a hidden, desired object from you without actively searching himself. First you hide an object when the child is not watching, then say "Find the x." Before he can begin searching for the object as you previously taught him to, however, you sign and say "You ask me 'Where is x?' " and prompt him through the signed question "Where is x?" Then you tell him where the object is located by signing and saying "X in y," prompt him through the finding of the object, and reward him for finding the object.

As the child learns to sign it on his own, you can gradually fade your prompts for the "Where is x?" question: tactile sign prompts first, then the 'Where is x?' in "You ask 'Where is x?' " then "You ask" itself. You may find that you have to keep signing "You ask" as a prompt until well after the child can do without tactile prompts; in fact, you may even find that the child does not become interested enough in asking questions to sign them without "You ask" as a prompt. In any event, however, you should train him to ask about the locations of a wide variety of objects in a wide variety of settings: in school, on the playground, and, if possible, at home.

B. "What is this?" Teach the child to ask "What is this?" to discover the name of a hidden or unfamiliar object.

1. *Names of hidden objects.* To pique the child's interest in asking about an object's name, you link asking for the object's name to requesting a hidden object. Show the child a box containing six to ten objects he desires and, without allowing him to see which object you remove, take one object, for example, a ball, from the box and conceal it behind a screen between yourself and the child. Then immediately set the box aside and ask the child "What do you want?" When he begins to display some interest in the hidden object, to reach toward the screen and sign "(Child) want . . . ," or merely to look longingly at the screen, you then prompt him to ask you for the name of the hidden object. You sign and say "You ask 'What this?' " and prompt him to sign "What this?" Then immediately provide the name of the hidden object ("ball"), praise the child with "Good asking," and again inquire "What do you want?" When the child signs the appropriate request ("(Child) want ball"), give him the desired object and then praise him again with "Good asking."

Repeat the previous step with a variety of objects from the box to teach the child to ask for the name of any hidden object. Fade your prompts as the child learns to ask for the name on his own, first tactile sign prompts, then the 'What this?' in "You ask 'What this?' " then the command "You ask."

Allow the child to name rather than request the object behind the screen after you tell him its name. Some children are as interested in naming as in requesting. You may want to ask the child interested in names "What is this?" instead of "What do you want?" at the start of a trial and "What is this?" at the trial's end.

2. *Names of unfamiliar objects.* Present an object whose name the child does not know and ask "What is this?" When he shows some interest in the object, reaches toward it, or begins to sign "This. . . ." to describe it, prompt him to ask for the unknown name: sign and say "You ask 'What this?' " and prompt him to sign "What this?" Then provide him with the object's name by signing (for instance, "tractor"), praise him with "Good asking," and ask him the question "What this?" Help him sign the answer ("This tractor" or "tractor"), then help him request the object with "(Child) want tractor" or

"Want tractor" if he seems interested in the object. Fade tactile sign prompts first, then the 'What this?' in "You ask 'What this?' " then the command "You ask." You may find that the child does not become interested enough in asking for the names of unfamiliar objects to do so without the command; help him generalize his name-asking skill by teaching him to ask for the names of a wide variety of unfamiliar objects.

III. **LESSON VARIETY.** Present question-answering and question-asking lessons in a wide variety of ways to broaden the child's understanding of inquiry. Teach spatial location concepts using as many desired objects and containers as possible; place objects in "natural" locations outside of the lesson room to promote generalization of inquiry; and use people as desired objects by asking questions such as "Where is Kurt?" After the child has a firm grasp of question-answering, you should feel free to introduce new questions and tasks related to old concepts. You might ask questions such as "What is on the y?" and "Who is in the y?" instead of "Where is the x?" and "Where is Kurt?"

A particularly good way of introducing lesson variety is to take advantage of situations which arise naturally, for example, whenever the child seems to be searching for an object. This will help him transform his nonlinguistic search into language-guided inquiry. For example, you might ask the child to ask you where the snack cookies he wants to give out to his classmates are. By encouraging him to use his question-asking skills to solve his problems, you help him tie them to his natural inquisitiveness. This promotes the spontaneous use of inquiry skills.

IV. **MASTERY CRITERIA.**

A. **Answering questions about location.** You can establish a specific mastery criterion for each question-answering skill. You can stipulate, for instance, that a certain percent of correct responses over a specified period of time or number of trials indicates mastery of the discrimination of the expressive use of "in" from that of "on." The most important indication of mastery, however, is spontaneous and appropriate use of the skill (as in the spontaneous description, "Kurt on table" or the spontaneous request, "Tommy want candy in box").

B. Question-asking. You can also establish a criterion for mastery of each question-asking skill, for instance, that a certain percent of correct question-asking responses over a specified time, or number of trials, indicates mastery of "What this?" Only when you observe the child asking questions spontaneously in everyday situations, however—when, for example, he spontaneously asks, "What this?" as a new person enters the room or, "What paper?" when he has a set of crayons and wants paper—will you know that the child has begun to internalize and generalize question-asking and to make the skill his own.

15

Abstraction I: "I," "My," "Your," "No," and "Yes"

I. The personal subject: "I"

II. Personal possessives: "My" and "your"

III. Affirmations and denials: "Yes" and "no"

After the child can use spontaneously the linguistic functions discussed in the preceding chapters, he will be ready to learn more abstract language concepts and skills. In this chapter, we describe methods for teaching the language concepts "I," "my," "your," "no" (to deny the truth about a question), and "yes" (to affirm the truth about a question). In Chapter 16 we detail procedures for teaching initial sight-reading and number skills.

Personal pronouns, both as the subject of an utterance ("I") and as possessive terms ("my" and "your") are abstract concepts. Their meaning changes with the speaker: I am "I" when I sign or speak but "you" when you sign or speak; an object I possess is "my x" when I sign or speak and "your x" when you sign or speak. "Yes" and "no," when used to affirm or deny the truth of a proposition in a question (such as "Is this a book?") are also abstract concepts: they refer to the relation between the proposition in the utterance and the state of the world, not to the state of the world directly.

The concepts and skills discussed in the present chapter will enlarge the child's capacity to understand and use complex linguistic concepts and constructions (such as those involved in pretend-play and conversation) and will provide tools for memory expansion. When the child begins using these concepts spontaneously, you will know that he has begun to think abstractly.

I. **THE PERSONAL SUBJECT: "I."** Begin teaching the child to use the sign "I" in place of "(Child)" in the multisign request "I want x" after he begins using people's names spontaneously as possessive terms.

   A. **The child as "I."** Offer a desired object to the child, ask "What do you want?" and wait for him to begin his request. Before he can produce his name sign, however, you should mold him into and through the sign "I" while simultaneously saying "I": shape his name-sign hand into the manual letter "I" and move it to the center of the child's chest. After he signs "I" with your help, prompt him to sign the remainder of the request, "want x." Then praise him in Signed Speech for his request and provide him with the desired object. You should occasionally allow him—and even encourage him—to sign "I, (Child), want x" as he makes the transition from "(Child) want x" to "I want x." This will teach him the equivalence between "I" and his name sign and will help him give "I" a physical (name-sign) meaning.

   You may fade your prompts in backward fashion, first from "want x" and then from "I." After the child begins signing "I want x" spontaneously, require him to use "I" in all of his requests.

   B. **The teacher as "I."** After the child is employing "I want x" spontaneously in a wide variety of situations, you can teach him that "I" refers to you, the teacher, when you sign and speak. This will give him a receptive understanding of "I" and teach him that "I" refers to whoever is using it, not only to the child himself. To do this, place foods, toys, and other desirable objects on the table next to the child and simultaneously say and sign "I want x," then prompt him to give you the object you request. You then gradually fade your prompts as the child learns to give you the correct object on his own. Finally, you should teach the child to respond to "I want x" requests from a variety of people (staff, parents, peers).

II. **PERSONAL POSSESSIVES: "MY" AND "YOUR."** These concepts should be taught after the child masters the expressive use and receptive understanding of "I." You begin with the receptive understanding of "my" and "your," teaching the child to "Touch my x" and "Touch your x," and then move to the expressive use of "my" and "your."

A. **"Touch your x."** You should begin instruction with "your." Teach the child to obey the signed and spoken command "Touch your (Child)'s x" where "(Child)'s" is the child's name and x is the name of a body part or article of clothing. You insert the child's name to allow him to use his knowledge of his name as a possessive term. In this way you give "your" a physical meaning and teach him the equivalence between "your" and the person addressed. Prompt the child through the correct response to the command, gradually fading your prompts as he begins to respond on his own. Then after the child is consistently obeying the command "Touch your (Child)'s x," you may gradually fade the redundant "(Child)'s" by saying and signing only "Touch your x."

B. **"Touch my x."** Next you teach the child to obey the signed and spoken command "Touch my (Teacher)'s x" where "(Teacher)'s" is your name sign. Then fade the redundant "(Teacher)'s" from the command.

C. **Discrimination between "my" and "your."** Give the child both the commands "Touch my x" and "Touch your x," first in alternating blocks and then in random order. You may have to reintroduce the redundant "(Child)'s" and "(Teacher)'s," along with other prompts, during discrimination training.

D. **Expressive use of "my" and "your."**
   1. *"This my x."* Ask, while pointing to an article of clothing of the child's or a body part, "Whose x is this?" You may prompt the child to sign "This my x" initially, and then gradually fade your prompts. You should occasionally allow him to sign "This my (Child)'s x" if he wishes to: this will help him give a physical meaning to his expressive "my."
   2. *"This your x."* Initially prompt the child to sign "This your x," then gradually fade your prompts. As with "my," you should occasionally allow the child to sign "This your (Teacher)'s x" if he wishes to.
   3. *Expressive discrimination between "my" and "your."* Ask "Whose x is this?" and touch either one of the child's body parts or articles of clothing or one of yours,

first in alternating blocks of consecutive "my" or "your" trials, then in randomly ordered "my" and "your" trials.

E. Review. Give the child some review by randomly presenting the commands "Touch my x" and "Touch your x."

F. Discrimination between expressive use and receptive understanding of "my" and "your." This is the last step in "my/your" instruction. Sensitive prompting is extremely important at this time because the child may become confused as you teach him the difference between "Touch (my/your) x" and "Whose x is this?" questions. Teach this discrimination as you would others, by blocking and then randomly ordering expressive and receptive trials, and be prepared to provide prompts to minimize errors. Teach the child to discriminate between the expressive and receptive "my" first, then between the expressive and receptive "your," and, finally, between the expressive and receptive "my" and "your" in combination, in blocked and then in randomly ordered trials.

G. Visual prompts for "my" and "your." A quick movement of your "my" or "your" signing hand toward the possessor of the x specified in the command "Touch (my/your) x" is a good visual prompt for person-touching receptive possessive responses. For expressive possessive responses, "This (my/your) x," a quick movement of your hand toward the possessor immediately after the child signs "This. . . ." (in response to the question "Whose x is this?") is a good visual prompt.

III. AFFIRMATIONS AND DENIALS: "YES" AND "NO."
Finally, teach the child to affirm or deny the truth of a proposition. We suggest beginning with affirmation since it is easier for the child to learn.

A. "Yes." You present an object, x, whose name the child knows very well, sign and say "Is this a x?" and prompt the child to respond "yes." You fade your prompts as the child learns to sign "yes" on his own. Then you teach him to sign "yes" for a variety of familiar objects in answer to the question "Is this a (familiar object)?"

B. **"No."** You present a familiar object, x, ask "Is this a y?" and prompt the child to sign "no" in response to the question. You fade your prompts as the child learns to sign "no" on his own. Then you teach him to sign "no" for a variety of familiar but incorrectly named objects.

C. **Discrimination between "yes" and "no."** You present blocks of "yes" and "no" trials first. Then, after the child learns to answer correctly during blocked trials, you can randomly order "yes" and "no" trials.

D. **Questions as "yes-no" prompts.** Asking a question related to the name of the object immediately before you ask "Is this a x?" is often a good "yes-no" prompt. For example, if you are asking a "yes-no" question about a ball, you might first ask, "What is this?" After the child signs, "This ball," you can then ask, "Is this a ball?" Such indirect questions help the child learn to compare the name of the object as he signs it with the name you sign as you ask him to affirm or deny your proposition.

E. **Focusing "yes" and "no" on other concepts.** You can focus "yes-no" truth-value questions on any concept the child knows by merely asking the question about that concept. For example, to focus on possessive terms, you might ask, "Is this (Teacher's, Child's, my, your) x?" as you point to your or the child's x; to focus on locations, you might ask, "Is the x (in, on, beside) the y?" By appropriately focusing "yes-no" questions you can teach the child to begin to think abstractly about any concept he knows. However, you should not expect him to master all "yes-no" questions with equal ease. Learning to answer "no" to deny a proposition is typically very difficult for a handicapped child.

16

Abstraction II: Initial Sight-Reading and Number Skills

I. Initial sight reading

II. Initial number skills

After the child is using the request "I want x" spontaneously, she will be ready to begin learning initial sight-reading and number skills. These two skills are crucial because they motivate her to learn new and more complex reading and number skills. Eventually the use of printed words and number concepts may become intrinsically rewarding.

I. **INITIAL SIGHT READING.** Word recognition and comprehension are the first two sight-reading skills to teach the child. We recommend teaching word recognition as a sight-reading skill, not a phonics skill. Sight-reading instruction allows the previously alinguistic child to learn to recognize words easily and to deal with their meanings immediately. For these children, phonics instruction interposes an arbitrary and difficult code between the child and the printed word. (This is not the case for normal children.)

A. **Word recognition.** The concepts the child uses most frequently and spontaneously (in signs, Signed Speech, or speech) are likely to be the ones most intimately related to what she desires and to what intrigues her. Her core reading vocabulary should be drawn from these concepts. It might include food names (cookie, pretzel, apple), drinks (juice, water, milk), toys (book, puzzle, car), people's names (Mommy, Daddy, I), activity labels (tickle, swing, slide), and functional concepts (want, put).

1. *The first sight word.* The first sight word you teach the child should be the name of her favorite object, activity, or person. (In your daily interactions, you will undoubtedly have discovered who or what this is. If you are unsure, you can ask the child's parents.) You print the word (for example, "car") in lower-case block letters (except for the upper-case first letter of a person's name) on a piece of heavy construction paper which is approximately 2" x 4". You show the child the word, say and sign "Read this word," and move your index finger from left to right underneath the printed word as you say and sign it. Prompt the child to sign, say, or simultaneously sign and say the word.

After the child can consistently sign, say, or simultaneously sign and say "car" to the verbal prompt and the sight of the printed word, gradually fade your saying and signing the word. You show the child the printed word, place your index finger underneath the first letter of the word, give the reading command, and wait for the child to begin signing, talking, or signing and talking. Then you move your index finger from left to right underneath the word as the child reads "car." If she does not read "car" after a few seconds, you may prompt the correct response. Possible prompts include vocalizing the first phoneme in the word (verbal prompt), shaping your mouth into the initial part of the word (visual prompt), or signing the initial part of the corresponding sign (visual prompt).

2. *The second sight word.* This word should be the name of another "favorite" object, activity, or person. You print it in block lower-case letters on a piece of heavy construction paper as you did the first and use the same techniques you used to teach the first word.

3. *Discrimination between the first and second sight words.* You present the printed words in random order while saying for each "Read this word." If the child does not respond correctly, you should then reintroduce the necessary prompts.

4. *The third and later sight words.* These should also be the names of "favorite" objects, activities, or people. The sight words "I" and "want" should be included in the child's core reading vocabulary.

B. Word comprehension. It is not enough for the child to learn to recognize and read or sign the printed words for her favorite objects, activities, and people. She must very early also learn that each word she learns to sight read has a meaning. Unlike most normal children, the typical nonverbal child does not automatically associate sight words with their referents. To teach her to comprehend, you can teach her to show you that she knows that a printed word such as "cookie" refers to the class of objects which taste sweet, which she likes to eat, which are brownish, and so forth. Two tasks are particularly good for teaching word comprehension: matching and building personal interest sentences.

　1. *Comprehension through matching.* You can begin teaching the child to comprehend the word through matching, that is, you can teach her to place the printed word she reads on or next to the object, person, or picture to which it refers. For example, if the child has learned to recognize the words "car" and "cookie," you might teach her to place the printed word "car" next to a favorite toy car and the printed word "cookie" next to a favorite cookie.

　　Instruction should follow a progression. First, you teach the child to sight read the single printed word on the table in front of her and to place it next to the single (appropriate) referent on the table. Then you gradually increase the number of possible referents to four. Finally, you have the child choose the word you say and sign from one of two printed words, and then have her place this word next to one, two, three, or four referents.

　　The child may link the sight word to its meaning immediately and match the word to its referent with no difficulty at all. On the other hand, she may have difficulty and need many prompts. With prompting, however, the child who has difficulty can learn to match sight words to their referents (pictures or actual objects).

　2. *The personal interest sentences "I want x."* You teach sentence building, a more complex comprehension task than matching, to help the child further develop her sight-reading skills. Focus on personal interest involves the child in the task and makes sentence building personally meaningful. You should teach the child to build and read the personal interest sentence "I want x" and

to use the sentence to obtain what she wants, then move on to other similar sentences. "I want x" is the first sentence to teach. Since the child uses it spontaneously to express her desires and to get what she wants, she is likely to comprehend it immediately and to enjoy building and reading it.

Let us assume the child can sight read the words "car," "puzzle," "tickle," "cookie," "water," "I," and "want" and can correctly match the words "car," "puzzle," "cookie," and "water" to their referents. You begin instruction by placing the words "I" and "want" in left-to-right ("I want") order on a tray before the child, and near the tray place the words "car," "puzzle," "cookie," "water," and "tickle," along with the child's favorite toy car, favorite puzzle, favorite cookie, and a glass of water. You then ask the child "What do you want?" After she produces the request "I want x" (perhaps "I want car") in signs and/or words, you sign and say, "Make the sentence" and then prompt her to select and place the word "car" on the tray to the right of "I-want." After she does this, you sign and say, "Now read the sentence" and prompt her to point successively to each word with her index finger (moving her finger from left to right under each word) and simultaneously read (say and/or sign) the word to which she is pointing. After she reads the sentence "I-want-car," you should praise her and give her the toy car she asked for by her reading. It is important to provide as many prompts as the child needs to learn this skill.

After the child can read sentences with a preformed "I-want," you can then teach her to build "I-want" on her own. You place the words "I" and "want" on the table in front of the tray with the other words and ask, "What do you want?" After the child says and/or signs, "I want x," you say, "Make the sentence" and prompt her to select and place on the tray the word "I," then the word "want," and then the word for the requested object. Next you say, "Read the sentence," and after she reads it correctly as she moves her index finger from left to right under each word, praise her and grant her request.

3. *Other personal interest sentences.* Using a format similar to that described above, you can teach the child to build any personal interest sentences she signs and/or

says. Suppose, for example, that the child is interested in possession and uses possessive descriptions spontaneously. You might ask her, "Whose candy is this?" as you point to her mother's candy. After she answers, "This Mama candy," you would say, "Make the sentence" and teach her to select "This," "Mama," and "candy" from the words near the tray and arrange them on the tray in proper order. You would then say, "Read the sentence," require her to read "This Mama candy," and reward her at this point by allowing her to request her mother's candy.

II. **INITIAL NUMBER SKILLS.** The content of beginning number instruction for a previously alinguistic child, as well as the manner in which instruction is executed, will depend on the language level of the child at the beginning of instruction. The child who uses words can be taught the beginning number skills normally included in a TMR (Trainable Mentally Retarded) curriculum through verbal instruction. The minimally verbal child who still signs as he talks, or only signs, is more limited, however, and will probably not be able to learn through verbal instruction alone. He will probably need the teacher to sign as well as talk. More importantly, however, the minimally verbal or signs-only child will require intensive instruction on three important number skills prior to TMR level instruction: matching the number signs one to four to the corresponding quantity of objects; forming requests with the number signs "one" to "four," such as "I want two chip"; and saying the number word with the number sign (if he talks as he signs). Now we will outline the instructional procedures for teaching these important beginning number skills to minimally verbal children.

A. **Matching number signs to quantities.** Direct the child to match the number signs "one" to "four" to the corresponding number of objects. This will give him a beginning understanding of the relationship between number sign and quantity.
   1. *"One."* Teach the child to sign "one" when you ask, "How many?" and point to the one object (such as a favorite food or toy) on the table near him. To begin, place an object (such as a corn chip) on the table, and say and sign "How many?" Then prompt the child to touch the object (corn chip) lightly with his index finger and point his finger upward to form the sign "one." Say

"one" as you prompt him into and through the "one" sign. You can fade your prompts gradually until the only remaining prompt for the "one" sign is the child's own index finger on the object. You can then teach him to sign "one" to a wide variety of single objects.

2. *"Two."* Place two objects, for example, two chips, on the table next to him and ask "How many?" Prompt the child to lightly touch the two chips with his index and middle fingers (one finger on each chip) and then to form the sign "two" by pointing the two fingers upward. His two fingers touching the two objects is a "natural" referent prompt for "two," just as his one finger touching one object was for "one." You should say "two" as you prompt the child through the sign "two."

3. *Discrimination between "one" and "two."* You can teach the child to discriminate between "one" and "two" by randomly placing one or two objects on the table and asking the child to number them. Use prompts if necessary, then gradually fade them.

4. *"Three" and "four."* The sign "three" is formed by pointing the thumb, index finger, and middle finger upwards; "four," by pointing four fingers upwards with the thumb against the front of the palm. Initially, you should teach the child to use the "natural" referent prompt, that is, to touch each of the objects with the tip of one finger. This will help him see the relationship between the number sign, the number of fingers, and the number of objects. At first, you should keep objects close enough together so the child can touch each object with a finger at the same time. Then you may spread the objects apart and allow him to touch them sequentially.

5. *"(Number) x."* Next you can teach the child to lengthen his response to "(Number) x." For example, you might ask, "How many cookies?" and teach him to sign "two cookie" or ask, "How many blocks?" and teach him to sign "Four block." You may initially use manual prompts, then gradually fade them; be sure to say the corresponding words as he signs.

6. *An important point.* Any time the child spontaneously and correctly produces a number sign or a number sign followed by the object name, you should reward him warmly for using a number concept, even if you have not specifically asked, "How many?"

B. **The number request.** It is important to teach the child to use number signs to request objects: this will foster his spontaneous use of number concepts. After he learns to respond to the question "How many x's?" with "(Number) x," you can teach him to use the number request "I want (number) x." You place one to four highly desired objects, for example, small cookies, on the table near him and ask, "How many cookies?" After he responds, "Two cookie," you ask, "How many cookies do you want?" and prompt him to sign "I want two cookie." You should say the words as he signs and then reward him with the two small cookies. Use a variety of desired objects for this task. Should the child sign "I want (number) x" on his own during the lesson or during another part of the school day, you should reward him immediately and warmly. Teaching the child to use numbers in requests will increase his interest in and motivation for learning new and more complex number skills.

C. **Saying and signing "one" through "four."** It is important to teach the child to say the number word as he produces the number sign so he will tie his number concepts to spoken language. To do this, combine the instructional methods outlined in this chapter with those discussed in Chapters 7 and 8. In this way you will help the child develop and expand his number vocabulary.

Classroom Management

The Classroom Management component of the Signed Speech Program presents a Signed Speech approach to issues in instruction and classroom organization that every teacher of nonverbal children faces. Chapter 17 discusses instruction in eye contact and sitting still, suppression of problem behaviors, and use of activity labels. Chapter 18 discusses the daily classroom schedule, data collection and interpretation, and staff and parent training. When the teacher handles difficulties related to these issues well, the classroom runs more smoothly and the children learn more easily.

17

Classroom Management I: Eye Contact, Sitting Still, Problem Behaviors, and Activity Labels

I. Eye contact

II. Sitting still

III. Problem behaviors

IV. Special issues in punishment

V. Activity labels

The Signed Speech Program fosters spontaneous language in nonverbal children but cannot by itself maintain a classroom. Teachers who used Signed Speech techniques must therefore know about classroom management. In this chapter, we consider four important classroom management topics: eye contact, sitting still, the suppression of problem behaviors, and activity labels. In the next chapter, Classroom Management II, we consider classroom schedules, data collection, and staff and parent training.

I. EYE CONTACT. The time a child spends learning language skills is a time of social contact between him and his teacher, that is, of joint attention to the same task and of reciprocal responsiveness. Eye contact is an important component of this social contact and, therefore, demands the same careful attention as do language skills.

A. Eye contact as a component of communication. Appropriate

eye contact is a component of normal communicative inter-action that the typical nonverbal child does not usually master on his own. Nevertheless, it need not be taught prior to the initiation of language instruction. Eye contact is a component of communication, not a prerequisite to it. Therefore, it is best for the teacher to foster eye contact during regular language lessons, not prior to them, and not with special eye contact lessons. We present three reasons for this statement.

1. *Language primacy.* The primary focus of language instruction is language, not eye contact. If the teacher focuses most of his effort on language instruction and fosters eye contact as a secondary skill while he teaches, the child will likewise treat language as primary.

2. *Language without eye contact.* Eye contact between child and teacher is not a necessary component of language use. A child can often sign for a desired object or imitate a sound without looking directly at his teacher: he can use his peripheral vision to see and sign for an object, and he can usually use his hearing ability alone to imitate a sound. If the child feels he must make eye contact prior to communicating, he will find spontaneous communication more difficult.

3. *Eye contact taught over time.* Eye contact is best taught over time along with language. If so fostered, it will maintain better, generalize further, and be more appropriately integrated with a greater number of language skills and situations than if taught prior to language instruction.

B. **Teaching eye contact.** You should treat eye contact as a component of sign language and verbal imitation skills. Begin with reinforcement of eye contact, then move to control by command, and finish with the child's communication about and control of your eye contact.

1. *Reinforce eye contact.* During sign language and verbal imitation lessons, the child will occasionally look you in the eye. You should reinforce these direct glances with a signed and spoken "Good looking" and physical affection, and occasionally with food or another desired object. (Food and other desired objects sometimes distract the child from continued eye contact.) You can make eye contact easier for the child by seating him on a chair

taller than yours so that your eyes and his are at about the same level. Children find it easier to make eye contact when they do not need to raise their heads to do so and when adults do not loom intimidatingly above them. You can also make eye contact more compelling by riveting the child with your eyes when he glances at you, that is, by looking directly into his eyes. Like normal children, nonverbal children find very direct eye contact harder to avoid than a passing glance.

An important point to remember as you teach is that you need not reward the child for every direct glance. You will probably be the child's teacher for at least a year. Therefore, you can afford to reward him for eye contact on a partial reinforcement schedule which will take hold gradually and not coerce him into looking at you continuously. You do not want the child to learn to look at you continuously, but only to maintain a level of eye contact that facilitates communication. Even though you do not reward the child for every glance, however, when you do reward him, you should be as warm and affectionate as you can: if he likes you he will look at you.

2. *Control eye contact by command.* The signed and spoken commands "Pay-attention" and "Look-at-me" are compelling orders. The sign "Pay-attention" is formed by placing your flat hands palms-in against the child's temples and then moving them toward your temples. Your moving hands act like blinders as you sign "Pay-attention": they keep out distracting visual information and guide the child's gaze toward you. The sign "Look-at-me" is formed by placing a forefinger-middle-finger-Vee against the child's face, one finger just below each of his eyes, fingernails on the child's face, and then drawing the Vee from below the child's eyes toward your eyes.

Sign and say "Pay-attention" or "Look-at-me" only when the child's looking away interferes with language instruction, and reward him with praise and affection for obeying your commands. (Only infrequently reward with food or other desired objects.) You will occasionally need to turn his head toward you with a nonsigning hand as you sign and say, "Pay-attention" and, "Look-at-me," especially early in instruction. As you continue to give, enforce, and reward gaze commands, however, and as you reinforce spontaneous gazes directed toward you, the child will come to obey your gaze commands easily and look at you spontaneously more frequently.

After the child learns to look at you on command, you may begin teaching him to look at objects on command. Sign "Look-at-the" as you signed "Look-at-me" but, instead of moving your Vee toward your face, move it toward the object before you sign the object label. You should give the command only when the child's not looking at the object interferes with his discrimination of it from other objects. You may need to enforce the command early in training by physically turning the child's head toward the object or by waving or holding it in front of the child's eyes. Over time, however, the child will learn to obey you and this kind of enforcement will become unnecessary.

3. *Use the child's communication about, and control of, your eye contact.* Some nonverbal children who sign learn on their own to tap their teachers' faces to gain attention for their signs. To teach a child who taps for attention to sign "Look-at-me" instead, mold his facial taps into the "Look-at-me" sign (or a reasonable approximation) and respond to them as if they were commands. Do not mold the child through the sign before he taps (or begins to sign "Look-at-me" on his own).

Other nonverbal children do not spontaneously learn to tap the teacher's face for attention. Teach the child who does not tap on his own to sign "Look-at-me" after he learns to obey the command "Look-at-me." His receptive knowledge of the sign will help him master it expressively. Use structured waiting to teach the sign. When the child wants an object and begins to request it in sign, deliberately turn away from him. Then, while you are turned away, put his hand to your face, shape it through the "Look-at-me" sign (as you say "Look-at-me"), turn back to the child, and allow him to sign for what he wanted. To fade your prompts, frustrate the child first into executing the final movement of the "Look-at-me" Vee on his own; then into positioning his Vee below your eyes and moving it on his own; and, last, into forming, positioning and moving the Vee on his own, that is, into producing the entire sign on his own.

II. **SITTING STILL.** You need not teach the typical child under 10-years-old to sit still before you start teaching her signs and sounds. First, to hold the child still enough for instruction, you probably will merely need to hold her knees between yours as she sits facing you. (For the child who does not respond to this procedure, not sitting still should be treated as a problem behavior and dealt with as we describe later.) Second, sitting still, like eye contact, is a component of communication rather than a prerequisite, so it is best fostered during language instruction rather than separately. The reasons are similar to those for not treating eye contact as a prerequisite. Language, not sitting still, is the primary focus of language instruction, and overstressing sitting still could teach the child otherwise. Also, if the child learns that she need not always sit still to sign and talk she will use her language more freely.

Moving around is likely to interfere with language instruction early in training and whenever new material is introduced. At these times, when the child must pay close attention, sitting still will help her learn. Teach sitting still much as you taught eye contact.

A. **Hold the child still.** Hold her between your knees when her squirming or trying to walk away interferes with language instruction. This will allow you to continue teaching and will tell her that during language lessons you expect her to sit still enough to communicate.

B. **Reinforce sitting still.** Reinforce the child occasionally with a signed and spoken "Good sitting" and affection. As you will be the child's teacher for many months, you need not reward her every time she sits still, but can reward her at convenient times and allow appropriate sitting to develop gradually. Gradual training makes sitting still tranquil rather than tense and better fosters the development of spontaneous language.

C. **Control sitting still by command.** You can teach the child to obey the signed and spoken command "Sit still" by saying "Sit still" and then holding her still with your knees. The child will learn to obey your command in anticipation, that is, before you have to squeeze her between your knees. (To teach her to obey the related command "Sit down," you can use the same procedure: say "Sit down" and the pull her down into her seat.)

D. **Allow occasional wandering.** After the child learns to sit still on command, you should occasionally allow her to wander around the room and sign for what she wants when she is not sitting facing you. This will teach her that she need not always sit still to sign (or otherwise communicate), and will make her less resistant to obeying other commands.

III. **PROBLEM BEHAVIORS.** Many children engage in problem behaviors that interfere with learning. These range from minor annoyances such as repetitive squinting, to more interfering behaviors such as continual tapping (on tables, chairs, and other surfaces), to severely disruptive and harmful self-destructive behaviors such as head-banging. When such behaviors interfere with instruction, especially language instruction, they must be suppressed. It is important, however, to suppress the behavior and not the child. Also, it is crucial to follow the policy guidelines of the school or institution in which you work.

There are seven basic techniques for suppressing problem behaviors. For the purpose of this discussion, these techniques are discussed under the categories of application of punishing consequences, goal appropriation, commands, ignoring, overcorrection, time-out, and corporal punishment.

A. **Application of punishing consequences.** Any event that decreases the frequency of the behavior it follows serves as a punishing consequence. Restraint, in the form of holding the child tightly still in one position on your lap with his legs between yours and his arms crossed on his chest, is a punishing event when it decreases a problem behavior. Pushing and holding the child's head down between his knees as he sits in front of you in his chair can also be a punishing event. Likewise, a flick of your middle finger, or a spray of water in the face with an atomizer, are punishers. Administer punishing events as consequences for problem behaviors to suppress the behaviors. Punishment is an effective negative consequence for self-stimulatory behaviors (such as hand-posturing, hand-watching, object-twirling, and tapping) and for tantrums. You can increase your control over problem behaviors by using a variety of punishments and by administering them in a thoroughgoing fashion on an intermittent schedule.

1. *Use a variety of punishments.* If you use only one form of punishment, the child will learn to anticipate it (on the basis of the subtle cues you emit unwittingly before you administer it) and will develop manipulative tactics to try to avoid it. If you use a variety, anticipation will be less likely, and the unpredictability of punishment will increase its effectiveness in decreasing problem behaviors. Therefore, you should randomly vary the punishments you administer as consequences for self-stimulation and tantrums.

2. *Be thoroughgoing in applying punishment.* Punishment is most effective when it is immediate, unwavering, and, where possible, immediately ignored. When punishment is immediate the child learns exactly what behaviors have led to it; when it is unwavering he learns that his teacher is serious; and when it is followed by ignoring, he learns that his teacher is not guilty about punishing him. (Many teachers out of guilt show a child affection shortly after punishment and so partially undo suppression.) We mentioned physical restraint, a head between the knees, a spray in the face, and a flick as usually effective punishments. Sprays and flicks are easy to administer quickly and decisively. Restraining a child and holding his head between his knees may not be; therefore, it is especially important not to remove restraint or allow the child to lift his head until he is still and quiet.

3. *Apply punishment on an intermittent schedule.* Contrary to widespread belief, punishments for problem behaviors administered on an intermittent schedule are more effective than those administered after each occurrence. There are three reasons for this.

   a. *Unpredictability*—This is more discomforting to the child; it makes preparation and partial avoidance of punishment less possible.

   b. *Generalization*—The child has difficulty discriminating occasions when he will be punished for problem behaviors from occasions when he will not. This facilitates the generalization of suppression to many settings and many problem behaviors. When the child cannot tell whether or not he will be punished for problem behaviors he is less likely to risk emitting them.

   c. *Impossibility of constant vigilance*—Teachers and

parents who believe that they must punish every instance of a problem behavior to suppress it effectively inadvertently establish impossible goals for themselves. First of all, the unpredictability and pervasiveness of the child's problem behaviors makes it impossible to punish every instance. Second, even when the most effective punishment procedures are used, problem behaviors do not completely disappear. Therefore, do not try to punish every instance of a problem behavior. If you punish in a thoroughgoing fashion the majority of instances that interfere with instruction (and only those), you will find that the problem behavior decreases in frequency.

4. *Use restraint for tantrums.* Hold the child's legs between yours, cross his arms uncomfortably, and, if possible, force his head between his knees as soon as he begins to throw a tantrum. Loosen your grip when the tantrum begins to fade and tighten it again when it returns. After it is completely gone, let the child sit still and relax and reward him with praise (signed and spoken) and affection.

5. *Use a variety of punishments for self-stimulation.* Flicking, hand-holding, spraying with an atomizer, and other minor, irritating punishments are effective tools for reducing the level of self-stimulation. Remember when you use these techniques, however, that you will probably not be able to eliminate self-stimulation completely and will, therefore, do best to ignore minor episodes that do not interfere with instruction.

B. **Goal appropriation.** This is a method for reducing the frequency of problem behaviors by removing the sense of control the behaviors generate. Nonverbal children work to maintain control over themselves, their physical environment, and the people in it just as do normal children: they show competence motivation. Because of their low skill levels, however, they often use problem behaviors which are easy for them to execute voluntarily to express their competence. Goal appropriation frustrates this expression of competence by usurping its goal. (It is similar to negative practice but does not aim at immediately satiating the child on the problem behavior.) In using this technique, the teacher forces the child over and over again to achieve his goal of executing the problem behavior, thus preventing him from achieving it voluntarily. It is important to have the child engage in the behavior more often or for a longer period of time than he would on his own. Some examples will help explain.

1. *Squinting.* The child probably squints to shut out visual stimulation and to annoy the people around him, and his effectiveness probably gives him a sense of control and power. You can force him to achieve his goals by holding your hand over his eyes when he squints. We have found that squinters do not like us to hold our hands over their eyes when they squint, that they attempt to remove our hands after we cover their eyes, that they open their eyes when we remove our hands, and that over time they stop squinting as much.

2. *Leaning sideways in a seat.* To remove the child's control of this behavior, you might push him farther in the direction he leans and hold him in that position for some time. We have found that leaners do not like to be held down, that they sit up when we stop holding them down, and that over time they stop leaning so much.

3. *Stuffing objects into the mouth.* To appropriate the goal of the child who stuffs, you might put several more objects into his mouth after he puts in one and hold his mouth shut over the objects for a while. We have found that stuffers do not like us to execute and control their stuffing and that they do not stuff nearly as frequently after we begin to do so.

4. *Yelling.* Sometimes a child yells too often. To correct him, you might yell in his ear as soon as he starts to yell. This treatment effectively combines removal of control with punishment.

5. *Hitting.* Suppose a child hits you. You might take his offending hand and strike your knee with it. This will hurt him a little (but not you) and will remove his control over hitting.

6. *Wiggling lips.* To control this behavior, you might decide to move his lips up, down, and sideways with your hands.

7. *Dribbling food.* If a child lets his food dribble out of his mouth when he need not, you might then open his mouth when it is full and rub its contents on his face.

8. *Pants stuffing.* Suppose a child stuffs toys in his pants. You might decide to discourage him by adding big un-

comfortable objects to his collection.

You should remember as you appropriate goals that you will be the child's teacher for a long while. Therefore, you need not appropriate the goal after every offense but only after offenses that interfere with instruction. When you do appropriate, however, you should be sure to carry your efforts through to a thorough conclusion. To increase your effectiveness, employ punishment along with goal appropriation in a mixed and unpredictable fashion.

C. **Command-control.** At the same time as you administer punishments and appropriate goals, you would do well to begin to bring problem behaviors under command-control so that you can say and sign, "No hitting," "Sit up," or "Stop screaming" and have the child obey. You can generate command-control for yourself by giving commands before punishment. Give the command to cease before you punish a problem behavior, and if the child ceases, reward him with praise such as "Good sitting" or "Good looking" and affection. Follow unobeyed commands with punishment. The child will first begin decreasing the magnitude and intensity of the problem behavior after your command in anticipation of punishment, then learn to cease engaging in the problem behavior. You begin decreasing the magnitude and intensity of your punishment as the child learns to cease on command. Do not expect perfect command-control, however, and do be ready to reintroduce punishment if the frequency of a problem behavior increases.

D. **Ignoring small problem behaviors.** Feel free to ignore, that is, let pass without negative consequence, small-scale problem behaviors such as minor finger twiddling that do not interfere with instruction. The effects of your negative pressures on large-scale problem behaviors that do interfere with instruction will eventually generalize to small-scale behaviors. In addition, by letting small-scale annoyances pass, you will deprive the child of opportunities to gain attention for problem behaviors.

E. **Overcorrection.** Technically, overcorrection refers to forcing the child to execute the correct response many times strenuously and in an uncomfortable fashion immediately after an error. In the case of problem behaviors, however, the correct response is merely absence of the problem behavior and, as such, is hard to force. Nevertheless, forcing the child to execute strenuously some uncomfortable arm and hand movement after a problem behavior can be effective in reducing its frequency. Repetitive, strenuous movements which are tiring, uncomfortable, and not under the child's control do act as a punishment.

F. **Corporal punishment.** Nonverbal children sometimes engage in problem behaviors that could endanger their own welfare, such as running out into the street where there are moving vehicles or running uncaringly behind moving swings on the playground. Punish the child for such behaviors corporally, that is, with a stiff jerk on the arm which harshly removes the child from the dangerous situation and a hard swat on the buttocks. Like 1- and 2-year-olds, nonverbal children often lack the foresight necessary for understanding potential as opposed to immediate dangers, and are best kept from entering the dangerous situations by fear. For this reason corporal punishment is more effective for dealing with entry into dangerous situations than other forms of punishment or goal appropriation. (Of course, you should try to establish command-control over entry into dangerous situations just as you try to establish command-control over other problem behaviors.) The situation-specificity of your corporal punishment will help the child differentiate between entry into dangerous situations and other problem behaviors. In addition, the corporal punishment will teach the child that when he engages in the same sorts of foolish activities as a normal child, he will be treated as a normal child.

G. **Time-out.** Time-out is a negative consequence (or punishment) for problem behaviors that consists of placing the child in isolation for a specified period of time and is probably the technique most often used for suppressing problem behaviors. We do not recommend its use, despite its popularity. Our reasons follow.
1. *Time-out promotes avoidance of people.* The nonverbal child put in time-out for problem behaviors learns over the long run that problem behaviors are good ways of avoiding people and communication, even as he learns

over the short run not to engage in them. Because explicit communication with other people is so difficult and sometimes aversive for the nonverbal child, he needs to learn that he cannot avoid people and communication. Punishments other than time-out keep the child near people and people near the child. Punishment, goal appropriation, and other negative procedures maintain contact between the nonverbal child and his teachers, and do not teach the child to try to avoid people and communication as time-out does.

2. *Time-out prevents working through problem behaviors.* Often it is possible to continue language instruction while a child is engaging in a problem behavior. You (the teacher) can cease instruction to punish the child for a problem behavior, reintroduce instruction when he stops executing the behavior, punish him again when he recommences, reintroduce instruction when he stops, and so forth. Working through problem behaviors during instruction is a good way of teaching the child that he cannot use problem behaviors to avoid communication, and a good way of helping him channel the energies that motivate problem behaviors into communication. Time-out does not net you these advantages.

We do not mean to imply, however, that there are no troublesome situations for which time-out is a useful punishment. When you work with an older child (11-years-old or more) who is so strong that you cannot easily control him physically, you should use time-out as a negative consequence for problem behaviors.

H. **Use several techniques.** We have discussed seven techniques for suppressing problem behaviors. We suggest that you use more than one of the seven techniques in an unpredictable fashion with each of the problem behaviors you encounter. The variety and unpredictability of your punishments will increase the potency of each punishment and make anticipation of and preparation for punishment difficult. We find goal appropriation and another punishment a particularly effective combination.

IV. **SPECIAL ISSUES IN PUNISHMENT.** We have discussed techniques for dealing with problem behaviors and issues related to the use of punishment. Now we consider self-destructive behavior, running away, and the relationship between punishment and communication. These topics demand individual discussion.

A. **Self-destructive behaviors.** Some nonverbal children engage in self-destructive behaviors such as head-banging and wrist- and shoulder-biting. These behaviors can in time interfere with brain function (head-banging) and normal grasping and manipulatory behavior (wrist- and shoulder-biting), and may lead to infection. They should therefore be eliminated. The first aversive technique to try with self-destructive behavior consists of a combination of severe overcorrection and severe goal appropriation. If the application of this combination of techniques does not eliminate the self-destructive behavior or very substantially reduce its frequency, however, more powerful measures may be needed. Contact an experienced professional to help you deal with severe self-destructive behaviors.

B. **Running away.** Some nonverbal children run away from adults, school, and social interactions whenever they are left alone on an open playground, on the street, or in a room with an open door. Such children need to be taught not to run away, for running away could involve entry into dangerous situations. However, controlling a child who is beyond your reach is not easy. The best way to deal with this problem is therefore to teach the child to stay close to you and to obey your signed and spoken commands to return when you allow him to roam a bit, not to punish him after the fact.

   1. *Staying close.* To teach the child to stay close to you, hold his hand as you walk with him through the halls, on the playground, in stores, to parks, or on the sidewalk. Hold his hand firmly at first, then more and more gently, until you are barely touching it. Then let go of his hand on occasion and only jerk him back roughly when he starts to leave. All the while, praise and show him affection for staying close to you, especially when your hand is not touching his. Work toward command-control over his tendency to leave. Teach him to obey the signed and spoken commands "No running," "Give me your hand," "Hold my hand," "Stay here," "Stay with me," and "Come back." Start with one command and after the child learns to obey it, introduce new ones.

2. *Returning.* Next, gradually allow the child to go farther and farther away from you on his own, first two arm lengths, then three, then four, and so forth, before you call him back. Increase the distance between you and the child very slowly as you teach the child to return: the power of signed and spoken commands grows slowly and seldom becomes as strong as a clasping hand or a rough jerk back.

After the child learns to return on command from a distance of three to four arm lengths, the best technique to use to teach him to stay near you and obey your commands to return is the indirect one of pacing off the child's territory with him many times. This means walking with the child through the areas he normally traverses, staying within arm's reach of him but not in physical contact. The child will be more likely to obey your long distance commands after you have patrolled his territory with him.

C. **Punishment and communication.** The relationship between punishment for problem behaviors and the acquisition of communication skills is complex. As a teacher, you punish problem behaviors primarily to create more time for instruction. The child's reactions to punishment, however, are more complicated than your reasons for employing it. Punishment can either interfere with the child's exercise of communication skills or promote a child-teacher relationship that fosters communication.

1. *Punishment as interference with communication.* The use of language is a frustrating and difficult problem for the nonverbal child. The difficulty of the problem for the nonverbal child may be viewed as analogous to the difficulty a normal adult would have if he were faced with the problem of solving a complex system of simultaneous equations without pencil and paper. In both cases, even low levels of fear and anxiety could completely disrupt the information processing necessary for adequate problem solving. Clearly, then, any punishment that causes fear and anxiety to be associated with the nonverbal child's language skills can interfere with his communication. We therefore suggest that you follow three guidelines to avoid punishment which interferes with communication.

a. *Do not punish signed, signed and spoken, or spoken language errors*—Nonverbal children often make language errors that frustrate their teachers. Especially frustrating are those all too frequent occasions when a child who has used a given language concept or skill correctly many, many times seems suddenly not to understand it at all and makes error after error after error. In such instances, you may be tempted to punish the child for his perseverative communication errors (for example, for repeatedly signing "peach" to the sight of an apple). If you punish the child for his language errors, you may succeed in forcing him to respond correctly. However, you will also connect fear and anxiety to his language skills and, over time, lower his potential level of communicative competence. Complicated communications which demand the integration of many component language skills will be very difficult for the child who fears using those skills. Therefore, you should correct but not punish communication errors.

b. *Speak in a gentle tone*—All of us have had the experience of being asked an apparently innocuous question in a harsh (hostile, demanding, or sarcastic) tone of voice, and of finding ourselves unable to answer. The same holds true for nonverbal children, only more so. To a nonverbal child a harsh tone of voice can both disrupt the immediate communication and condition fear and anxiety to communication skills. Over time, it can have harmful effects almost equal to those of more obvious punishments. Therefore, vary your tone of voice in interesting ways but do not speak harshly.

c. *Do not fault yourself*—Every teacher at times becomes more angry and punishes more harshly than he intends to. Do not fault yourself for minor excesses. The child needs to know that you are human and, therefore, fallible. Further, your appropriate punishments will be more effective if you are able to show anger occasionally as you administer them.

2. *Punishment which promotes the child-teacher relationship.* You will probably find the child more responsive and accurate immediately after you punish him for engaging in a problem behavior. Part of his good perfor-

mance flows from fear of further punishment. Appropriate punishment for problem behaviors, however, also strengthens the positive emotional relations between the teacher and the child by specifying behavior limits and giving the child a sense of security.

V. **ACTIVITY LABELS.** Activity labels are more powerful program aids than they at first appear. They help the nonverbal child deal with the frustration of not understanding and the inability to communicate that arise during transitions between activities. For example, the child may want to change activities but be unable to express her desire, or she may not understand the change to a new activity that, from her point of view, her teacher forces on her unreasonably at an unexpected time. Again, she may want but be unable to signal her desire to begin an activity when she arrives at an activity center, or she may want but be unable to express her satisfaction at completing an activity by telling her teacher that she has finished. All these potentially frustrating and tantrum-provoking difficulties can be at least partially overcome by using signed and spoken labels at transition points between activities. What follows is a sample list of activity labels.

"Signing time."
"Talking time."
"Play time; Time to go play."
"Lunch time; Time to eat lunch."
"Time to go outside."
"Time to go home."
"Time to work."
"Potty time."
"Puzzle time; Time to play with puzzles."
"Drawing time."
"Dressing time."
"Nap time."
"Talking time is finished. Time to go play."
"Play time finished. Time to work. Talking time."
"Work time finished. Time to go outside and play."

The child will show you that she understands the labels by beginning to make the transition to the appropriate activity after you say and sign the label, and she may even occasionally spontaneously sign an activity label that she has learned. Note that you will naturally use activity labels not only at transition points but also as you reward the child. For example, when you say and sign phrases such as "Good signing," "Good talking," "Good eating," and "Good playing," you are using activity labels.

A. **Teaching activity labels.** You can begin teaching the child to use activity labels herself as soon as she can make reference statements. Mold her through labels in response to your activity questions; then, as she begins to anticipate the answers to the questions, you can fade your assistance. After she learns to answer several activity questions she will probably begin using activity labels spontaneously as requests. An activity label instructional sequence might run as follows:

Teacher: "What time is it?"

Child: "Play time." (Molded or prompted.)

Teacher: "What time is it?"

Child: "Play time."

Do not ask and have the child answer an activity question more than four times at a transition point between activities; excessive repetitions drag out the transition period and make your questions meaningless.

You will probably find that after the child understands and can answer several activity questions, you will be able to use activity labels to reduce her occasional frustration near the ends of lessons by telling her what activity is next. For example, if the child expects her talking lesson to end 5 minutes before it is really due to terminate, you can probably reduce her frustration and help her calm herself by saying and signing "It's talking time."

After the child can answer several activity questions, you can begin teaching her to use the signed and spoken concept "finished" in activity labels at the ends of lessons and tasks, as in "Talking time finished" and "Puzzle finished." Then you can teach her to combine activity labels.

Teacher: "What time is it?"

Child: "Signing time finished. Time go outside."

B. **The child's spontaneous use of activity labels.** The child will probably use activity labels spontaneously in both appropriate and manipulative ways.

   1. *Appropriate activity labels.* The child might, for example, sign and say, "Talking time" at the beginning of a verbal imitation lesson to ask you whether or not the activity about to begin will be a talking lesson or to tell you that she knows it will be. In response to her presumed question or comment, you could sign and say, "Yes, it is talking time." Or the child might, for example, sign and say, "Talking time finished" or "Play time," or both, at the end of a verbal imitation lesson—either to ask whether or not talking time is over and play time is about to begin, or to convince you of this. In response, you could answer, "Yes, talking time is finished, it's time to play." Alternatively, if she guessed wrong, you could sign and say, "Later, not now," or "No, later." "Later" is a particularly good answer in such instances because as the child learns the meaning of "later" she will also learn to delay gratification. She will learn that a signed and spoken "later" means that her temporal judgment was incorrect and that she is to sit down and continue working at the activity at hand. If you are lucky and the child is bright, she may even learn how to use the concept "later" to control you, using it as a manipulative activity label.

   2. *Manipulative activity labels.* Manipulative activity labels are those the child uses to convince you to switch from an undesired to a desired activity. The child signs the label for a new activity (such as "Play time") in the middle of an ongoing one (such as "Talking time"). We suggest that you respond playfully to manipulative activity labels, most often correcting the child's error but occasionally giving in and agreeing to switch to the new activity he proposes. Manipulative language is language used for new purposes and is indicative of spontaneity, internalization, and voluntary control.

18

Classroom Management II: Daily Schedule, Data Collection, and Staff and Parent Training

I. Daily schedule: Language lessons

II. Daily schedule: Nonlanguage lessons

III. Data collection

IV. Staff and parent training

When each child is treated as an individual, with his own unique needs, it is almost impossible for a teacher to perform well without good classroom organization. Daily scheduling helps the teacher use her time efficiently; data collection systems assist in keeping track of each child's progress; and well-trained staff and parents aid instruction by providing further communication experiences for the children and sharing information about the children's behavior. This chapter provides suggestions for utilizing these three components—scheduling, data collection, and staff and parent training—in the Signed Speech Program classroom.

I. DAILY SCHEDULE: LANGUAGE LESSONS. As you prepare the children's daily schedule, arrange for them to be involved in language lessons during the majority of the school day. Between each of the language lessons schedule short lessons to teach important nonlanguage skills. Transitions from lesson to lesson can be facilitated by the use of activity labels, as was described in Chapter 17.

A. **Length of lessons.** To provide the children with concentrated language instruction and to maximize their acquisition of language, schedule 30- to 45-minute language lessons. A 30- to 45-minute lesson is short enough not to overtax a child's interest and attention span and long enough for the presentation of an adequate number of instructional trials, particularly when instruction is provided in a small group setting.

B. **Content of lessons.** During the initial stages of language instruction, when the child is learning to sign spontaneously and imitate speech, you should spend half of the language lessons on sign instruction and half on verbal imitation. Later, when the child begins learning to verbalize simultaneously as he signs, you can devote a third to Signed Speech instruction, and a third to verbal imitation training. After the child learns to produce spontaneous Signed Speech, all of your sign language instruction will become Signed Speech instruction. The child's verbal articulation will still require improvement, however, so spend half of the lessons on Signed Speech instruction and half on verbal articulation. Schedule instruction in initial sight-reading and number skills during Signed Speech lessons (or verbal language lessons, for children who have faded their signs from Signed Speech) and continue verbal articulation training.

C. **Group language instruction.** If the child-staff ratio in the classroom does not allow for one-to-one instruction throughout the daily classroom activities, provide language instruction in a small group.
   1. *Group size.* A language group of two severely handicapped students is ideal; four is maximum.
   2. *Group members.* Assign children to language groups according to language skill levels, for example, children learning to sign requests and imitate initial sounds in one group, and those learning to identify people and to generate Signed Speech in another group. Another factor to consider as you form language groups besides language skill levels is the children's behavior problems. A group with two or more children who manifest severe behavior problems is extremely difficult to teach and manage, so you may decide to assign each of the children with behavior problems to a different group.

3. *Staff-group assignments.* Two possible approaches to making staff-group assignments are to give each staff member the responsibility for all language lessons with one group or to give each staff member the responsibility for one type of language lesson (sign lessons, speech lessons, and so forth) with more than one group. Each type of staff-group assignment has advantages which the other does not have; you yourself will need to determine which type is most appropriate for the children in your classroom. For example, if it seems important that each staff member be intimately familiar with all the abilities and deficiencies of a small number of children, and also have a detailed understanding of how best to teach skills to those children, you would probably assign each staff member to instruct the same group throughout the day. If, on the other hand, it seems important that each staff member be proficient at teaching a particular language skill to all of the children who need such instruction, and also have a detailed understanding of how best to teach that skill to diverse populations, you would probably assign each staff member to teach one language skill to more than one group. Of course, you might also decide to combine these approaches. You might assign each staff member to one group at the outset of the language program, at a point when detailed knowledge of each child's specific learning characteristics as he begins to acquire language is important. Then you might later assign each staff member to teach one particular language skill to more than one group, after detailed information about the learning characteristics of each child has been amassed and shared among all staff members, and when a staff member's refinement of teaching techniques specific to a language skill would be advantageous to the children learning that language skill. However you decide to make staff-group assignments, a periodic informal assessment of their effectiveness is essential.

4. *Group management procedures.* Children in the group will differ in terms of the prompts which effectively facilitate the acquisition of particular language skills and the types of positive and negative feedback which increase or decrease the occurrence of particular responses. Therefore, you will need to provide the major

proportion of your language instruction to each child in the group individually, one after the other, rather than to all children in the group at the same time. To provide individual instruction in the small group setting, you will need to provide individual language trials when you focus on a child and appropriate feedback when you are not focusing on him.

a. *Language trials*—Give the child who learns slowly a large number of consecutive language trials (ten to fifteen) when it is his turn and provide the other children with toys or other materials to play with while they wait. Provide the child who learns quickly with a small number of language trials (five or fewer). While focusing on this child, require the other children to wait quietly for their turns.

b. *Feedback*—When the child awaiting his turn for language instruction is playing or waiting appropriately, give him positive feedback (praise, positive physical contact, or food). Giving positive feedback to the child who is playing or waiting as you focus language instruction on another child is critical to the maintenance of group order. Pace yourself to give the child whom you are directly teaching quick positive feedback so that while he is occupied with the reward you have given him, you can provide the other children with some positive feedback.

II. **DAILY SCHEDULE: NONLANGUAGE LESSONS.** The classroom schedule will probably include instruction in the following nonlanguage skills: self-help (toileting, hand-washing, putting on and taking off coats, and so forth); independent and social play (supervised free play, intrusive and cooperative play activities, group games); fine motor skills (simple art activities and activities involving manipulative toys); gross motor skills; "normalization" activities (lunch with the elementary school students in the school cafeteria); music; physical education; and "Hi time" and "Bye time" at the start and close of the children's day, respectively. Again, transitions from lesson to lesson will be easier if activity labels are used (see Chapter 17).

As you teach nonlanguage skills, integrate them with language concepts and utterances which the children have learned or are learning. Language can be linked to all activities in which the children are involved throughout the school day.

These linkages will help the child generalize language skills to situations and settings outside the language lesson itself and will also promote creative use of language. Different nonlanguage activities will stimulate different types of spontaneous language; certain activities apparently arouse the social motives appropriate to certain types of spontaneous language. Here are some activities which have been found to foster spontaneous use of the functions of Expression of Desires, Reference, Person Concepts, Inquiry, and Abstraction. Make these activities (or ones like them) an integral part of each child's day.

A. **Expression of Desires.**
   1. *Intrusive play activities.* Ask the child if he would like an intrusive play activity, for example, a swing, a tickle, or a chase. This will stimulate him to produce other requests.
   2. *Playful refusal.* Offer objects playfully which the child is likely to refuse, letting him know by your facial expression and tone of voice that you are playing. You might say, for example, "Do you want this x? . . . No! Well, then maybe you want this x?" This tells the child spontaneous choice is valued.
   3. *Multi-toy requests.* After the child learns two toy signs (such as "block" and "truck") or more, playfully present the two toys together (pile blocks onto the carrier of the truck) and prompt the child to request both at once. This will stimulate the spontaneous production of longer requests such as, "(Child) want block truck."
   4. *Nonlanguage lessons.* Include physical education, music, and art in your weekly schedule. If the child enjoys these activities, he will eventually learn to request them spontaneously.

B. **Reference.**
   1. *Toy naming.* As the child plays with a toy during free play, you can ask, "What is this?" Also, name and describe the toy in other ways as the child plays with it.
   2. *Descriptive statements.* Throughout the day, you should use a variety of descriptive statements to label and describe aspects of the environment and encourage the child to do the same.
   3. *Object hiding.* During Reference lessons, place the object to be named in a box, close the box, then show the

closed box to the child and ask "What's in the box?" To
further arouse the child's curiosity, you can shake the
box or open the lid quickly, let the child look in, and then
close it again. You should attempt to elicit from the
child the name of the object he sees or hears.

4. *Nonlanguage lessons.* Include physical education,
music, and art in your weekly schedule and encourage
the child to label these activities.

5. *Imaginative play.*

   a. *Toys*—You can use blocks to build pretend versions
   of a variety of the child's favorite objects: cookies,
   cakes, hamburgers, and so forth. Play with the make-
   believe objects with the child and encourage him to
   use them in an imaginative fashion. In addition, you
   can name the objects and inquire about their names.

   b. *Body parts*—If the child is able to play somewhat im-
   aginatively, you can use your body parts to "make"
   certain of his favorite toys and ask "What is this?"
   For example, make an airplane out of your hand.

C. **Person Concepts.**

1. *Group games.* Games such as "A-rig-a-jig-jig," "Sally
Saucer," and "Blue Bird" call attention to and foster
the use of people's names. The children focus attention
on and name their peers as they choose partners for
these games.

2. *Missing-person game.* One teacher and one child leave
the group and the remaining children are encouraged by
the remaining teachers to guess who is missing. The
teachers ask, "Who is not here?" After the names of the
missing child and teacher have been guessed, the entire
group calls each of the missing people back to the group.

3. *Songs.* Children's songs can be taught which require exaggeration and which focus on emotions such as happiness and sadness. These include "Baby Bumble Bee"
and "Three Black Buzzards."

4. *Intrusive and cooperative play activities.* Certain play
activities focus on names.

   a. *"Monster"*—The teacher says and signs, "Here
   comes the monster, the monster is going to get
   (Child)."

   b. *Rocking boat*—The teacher chooses a child to ride on
   one side of the boat and encourages him to name the

child whom he wants to join him on the other side.

  c. *Puppet kisses*—The teacher gives the child a hand puppet and encourages him to give each of his peers a kiss with the puppet, requiring that he name each child he wants to kiss.

  d. *Two-adult swings*—Two adults give the child a two-adult swing: one adult holds his feet and the other holds his arms as they both swing him. Before receiving a swing, however, the child is required to name the adults he wants to give the swing.

  e. *Ball-throwing*—As the child throws the ball successively to each of his peers, who are sitting in chairs, the teacher requires him to name the peer to whom he is throwing the ball. Also, he teaches the child to give the command "Throw the ball" to a peer.

5. *Pantomime.* The teacher encourages the child to engage in actions, such as ball-throwing, eating, and so forth, which he engages in daily, but without using the objects necessary for the actions. Pantomime allows the child to use his imagination as he focuses on familiar actions.

6. *Classroom routines.* Certain daily routines call attention to Person Concepts.

  a. *Coat storage*—The child is taught to deposit and retrieve his coat and other belongings (lunch box, swimming bag) in a particular area of the room at the beginning and end of the school day. He will probably begin using possessive terms to describe which belongings are his and, if his name is posted near his belongings, may learn to read his name.

  b. *Chair movement*—During transitions between activities, you should encourage the children to move their chairs from the old activity to the appropriate spots in the room for the new activity. The children will eventually learn teachers' names if you tell them to "Take your chair to (Teacher)'s work area."

  c. *"Hello time"*—During "Hello time," you may include the following language activities.

    (i) The long "Hello, hello, hello. How do you do?" (sung and/or signed by each child to each peer and teacher)

    (ii) The greeting "Hi, (Person)" (signed and/or spoken by each child to each peer and teacher)

(iii) "Who is here today?"—The teacher asks, "Who is here today?" Each child names the children and teachers present in his group, using "(Person)" or "(Person) here."

(iv) "Who is not here?"—The teacher asks, "Who is not here?" The child names the children and teachers not present in his group, using "(Person)" or "(Person) not here." This is a difficult task for most children.

(v) "What did you eat?"—The instructor asks, "What did you eat for breakfast (lunch)?" and teaches the child to answer appropriately.

D. Inquiry.

1. *Object hiding.* See discussion under Reference activities.

2. *Missing-person game.* See discussion under Person Concepts.

3. *Person hiding.* During the intrusive play lesson, cover a child with a blanket or large towel and ask questions such as "Who is not here?" and "Where is (Child)?" to elicit guessing and naming.

E. Abstraction.

1. *Hand-raising.* During various lessons and activities you can ask, "Who wants a turn?" and teach the child to raise his hand to indicate his desire to be chosen. Some children may eventually begin signing and/or saying "me" as they raise their hands.

2. *Reading.* Use large storybooks to tell familiar stories such as "The Three Bears," and teach the child to match an appropriate printed word to each page of the storybook.

3. *Number skills.* During a large group activity, count the students in the group in a very exaggerated and enthusiastic fashion and encourage each child to do the same.

III. DATA COLLECTION. To determine when a child has mastered particular signs, Signed Speech, purely verbal concepts and utterances, and sounds and sound clusters, you should be sure to collect two kinds of data: (1) daily recordings of the child's performance on specific language tasks (in terms of accuracy and prompts needed) and (2) recordings of the child's spontaneous, creative use of the language he learns.

A. **Daily performance.** To document the child's daily performance on language tasks, use the Daily Lesson Record and the Performance Record.
   1. *Daily Lesson Record.* On the Daily Lesson Record, record information about the quality of the child's performance on the specific skills taught during the daily language lessons to determine when the child reaches the criterion performance level in terms of accuracy. Figure 1 presents the Daily Lesson Record. Blanks should be filled as shown here.

> Child: Child's name
>
> Skill Area: Signs, verbal imitation, Signed Speech, verbal language, or articulation
>
> Skill: Specific skill being taught, such as "Bob want x"
>
> Time Period: Time of day

     a. *Data codes*—Data codes go in the spaces below Days of Instruction. Use the following codes to evaluate the child's performance on a particular skill:

> R = Response: the child produced a correct response without assistance.
>
> A = Approximation: the child produced an approximation to the correct response without assistance.
>
> PP = Partially Prompted: the child was given some assistance in producing the correct response (in the form of prompts or cues).
>
> P = Prompted: the child was given total assistance in producing the correct response (complete molding, a complete modeled sign).

     b. *Procedure for coding*—Code performance on a particular skill during and/or after the lesson. On the basis of all trials on a given skill throughout the day, indicate the child's performance: If on all trials the child's performance was the same (all responses were

Figure 1 Daily Lesson Record

Child: _____

Skill Area: _____

Time Period: _____ To _____

SKILL	Days of Instruction														
	M	T	W	TH	F	M	T	W	TH	F	M	T	W	TH	F

spontaneous, or prompted, or whatever), write only one code in the appropriate space, thus:

| R | | A | | PP | | P |

If the child's performance varied (on some trials responses were prompted; on some, partially prompted; and so forth), write more than one code in the appropriate space, thus:

| PP/R | | P/PP/A | | P/A |

2. *Performance Record.* On the Performance Record, record the date the child masters the skills taught during language lessons. Consider a child to have mastered a skill to criterion accuracy after he produces only the appropriate response without assistance or approximations to the appropriate response without assistance during 9 out of 10 consecutive days. The last of the 10 consecutive days is designated as the date of mastery. The data on the Daily Lesson Record provide you with mastery dates. Figure 2 presents the Performance Record. Blanks are to be filled as follows.

Child: Child's name

Skill Area: Signs, verbal imitation, Signed Speech, verbal language, or articulation

Skill: Specific skill being taught, such as "Bob want x"

Date Started: Date when instruction on the skill was initiated

Date Mastered: Date when the child attained the criterion accuracy level, as recorded on the Daily Lesson Record

Description: A brief account describing the specific way the child manually produces the signed or Signed Speech utterance, or the way he produces the sound, syllable, or word.

B. **Spontaneous language.** To describe and document the

Figure 2 Performance Record

Child: _____

Skill Area: _____

Skill	Date Started	Date Mastered	Description

child's spontaneous use of language, that is, what he does with language beyond what he is specifically taught, you can use the Spontaneous Utterance Record and the Classroom Observation Form.

1. *Spontaneous Utterance Record.* A spontaneous utterance is either one the child produces on his own in the absence of any question or prompt, or a newly generated (novel form) utterance in response to a question. Figure 3 presents the Spontaneous Utterance Record. The use of the Contexts column and the data codes for the Mode, Type, and Intended Listener columns are specified here.

Context: Brief description of the situation in which the utterance was produced

Mode:
   S = Signs
   SS = Signed Speech (simultaneous signs and words)
   W = Words

Type:
   T = Taught concept/utterance
   G = Generalized concept/utterance: a learned concept/utterance used with a new meaning or in a new situation
   U = Untaught concept: a concept incidentally learned
   I = Insertion: placement of a concept into an utterance without prior instruction
   NG = Newly generated utterance: a novel, never-before-produced utterance form

Intended Listener:
   S = Self
   P = Peer
   A = Adult

2. *Classroom Observation Form.* Use the Classroom Observation Form periodically throughout the school year (four observations per year) to assess the child's generalization of spontaneous language to a semistructured play situation in the classroom. Before the observation, confine a small group of children (two to four) and one teacher to a limited area of the classroom

Figure 3 Spontaneous Utterance Record

Child: _____

Date	Utterance	Context	Mode	Type	Intended Listener

and place a variety of desired objects in the area where the children can see them but cannot reach them. Being confined with out-of-reach desired objects stimulates the children to make requests and statements. During the observation, record in numbered order each utterance each child produces, and code each of these utterances with regard to Mode, Type, Intended Listener, and Appropriateness of Language. Figure 4 presents the Classroom Observation Form. The use of the various categories within Mode, Type, Intended Listener, and Appropriateness of Language is explained in detail here.

Mode:

Gesture—A motion produced by the child in a communicative fashion that is not a manual sign. Some typical gestures are pointing to an object, and nodding or shaking the head.

Manipulation—The child's act of putting another person's hand(s) or body through some action which would help satisfy the child's desire. For example, the child might push an adult's hand toward a toy on a shelf which he is unable to reach.

Vocalization—A vocalization produced by the child in a communicative fashion which is not a word or word approximation.

Signs

Signed Speech

Words

Type:

Initiation—Any utterance or communicative action that is not the child's reply to another person's utterance.

Response—A reply by the child to an utterance produced by another person (peer or adult).

Intended Listener:

Adult—One of the adults in the room: teacher, teaching assistant, parent, special observer.

Figure 4   Classroom Observation Form

Child:_____Page:_____of _____

Date:_____Time:_____to _____

Observer:_____

Context: _____

	Mode						Type		Intended Listener			Appropriateness of Language		
# Utterance	Gesture	Manipulation	Vocalization	Signs	Signed Speech	Words	Initiation	Response	Adult	Peer	Self	Appropriate	Inappropriate	Questionable

Peer—One of the child's classmates.

Self—Child himself; egocentric communication.

Appropriateness of Language:

Appropriate—The communication produced by the child is meaningful in the context.

Inappropriate—The communication produced by the child is clearly meaningless in the context: echolalia, perseveration, or self-stimulatory language.

Questionable—The meaning of the communication produced by the child is unclear in the context.

IV. **STAFF AND PARENT TRAINING.** Two important components of training for staff and parents working with nonverbal children are sign language instruction and information sharing.

A. **Sign language instruction.** It is extremely important that the staff and the parents know sign language. We suggest beginning with regularly scheduled workshops. Teach the signs which the children are learning or will learn (including the children's approximations to the signs), and also the signs and sign utterances which you use regularly with the children. In Figures 5 and 6, we present the initial sign repertoire (single signs and utterances) we teach and the sign utterances we frequently use with them. We teach all of these to the staff and the parents. (The signs are described in the Sign Glossary, Chapter 19.)

B. **Information sharing.** At staff meetings and meetings with the children's parents, we share and exchange information about each child's progress in the Signed Speech Program, what language concepts and skills the child has learned, and how he uses his language creatively. We also discuss the further facilitation of the child's spontaneous language, in the classroom by teachers and at home by parents (and siblings).

Figure 5   Initial Signs

Foods/Drinks	Activities	Toys
apple	art	ball
banana	chase	block
candy	down	boat
cereal	game	book
cheese	help	bubbles
chip	lunch	camera
cookie	P.E.	car
juice	ride	doll
milk	slide	drum
nut	swing	guitar
orange	tickle	music
popcorn	up	puppet
pretzel		puzzle
raisin	Body Parts	telephone
water	ear	
yogurt	eye	Clothing
	hair	coat
Emotions	hand	dress
angry	lap	hat
happy	mouth	pants
hurt	nose	shirt
sad		shoe
tired	Numbers	sock
	1	
	2	Times
	3	again
	4	later
	5	time

Figure 5 Initial Signs

Function Terms	*Actions*	*Inquiries*
Bye-bye	ask	beside
do	come	here
Hi	cry	how
is	drink	in
it	eat	off
no	find	on
not	finish	under
potty (toilet)	get	what
stop	give	where
this	go	who
want	hug	whose
yes	jump	
	kiss	*Names/Pronouns*
Objects	laugh	Daddy
box	Look-at-me	I
bus	Pay-attention	me
chair	play	Mommy
cup	put	my
picture	run	you
table	say	your
tree	sign	
	sit	*Places*
Animals	stand	area
cat	take	home
dog	talk	house
horse	touch	school
	turn	outside
	wait	
	walk	
	work	

Figure 6   Initial Signed Utterances

General Utterances
Good _____ .
Sign and say _____ .
Look-at-me.
Pay-attention.
Come here.
Sit down.
Stand up.
Wait *for* me.*
Stop _____ .
It is _____ time.
It is time to _____ .
_____ time is finished.
Take *the* _____ .
Get *the* _____ .
Put on your _____ .
Take off your _____ .

Requests
What do you want?
Do you want _____ ?

References
What is this?
Talk *to* me *about* this.

Person Concepts
Who is this?
Touch (Person)
Give (Person) *the* x.
Touch (Person)'s x.
Whose x is this?
Whose x do you want?
What is (Person) doing?
How is (Person)?

Inquiries
Touch *the* x.
Find *the* x.
Where is *the* x?
Put (object A) (location) (object B).

Abstractions
Is this *a(n)* x?
Who is here?
Who is not here?
What time is it? (playtime, etc.)

*Italicized words are not included in the Sign Glossary. Typically, these words are spoken but not signed by the teacher during initial language instruction.

19

Sign Glossary

On the following pages, you will find a sign glossary of the manual alphabet and 150 signs. The glossary contains most of the initial signs you will use with the nonverbal children in your classroom as you implement the Signed Speech Program. You may use it as a helpful reference as you take your first sign language classes and as you teach the children signs.

The majority of the signs pictured were selected from the two sign language dictionaries most widely used with nonverbal children, according to a national survey by Fristoe and Lloyd (1978): *Signing Exact English* (Gustason, Pfetzing, & Zawalkow, 1980), and *The Signed English Dictionary: For Preschool and Elementary Levels* (Bornstein, Hamilton, Saulnier, & Roy, 1975). Where different versions of a sign are pictured in the two sign dictionaries, we selected the sign which we have found easiest for nonverbal children to produce. In some cases, a sign as we use it with nonverbal children was not pictured in either dictionary. These signs are indicated with an asterisk (*). For these signs, we have either drawn our version of the sign or have altered a similar sign pictured in one of the dictionaries.

You will find as you use the signs with nonverbal children that you may need to simplify the sign. For example, the "cookie" sign pictured in this glossary is the adult version of the sign "cookie." For purposes of instruction, you may decide to teach the child a simplified version (as described in Chapter 3).

REFERENCES

Bornstein, H., Hamilton, L. B., Saulnier, K. L., and Roy, H. L. (Eds.). *The Signed English dictionary: For preschool and elementary levels.* Washington, DC: Gallaudet College Press, 1975.

Fristoe, M. and Lloyd, L. L. A survey of the use of non-speech systems with the severely communication impaired. *Mental Retardation*, April 1978, 99-103.

Gustason, G., Pfetzing, D., and Zawalkow, E. *Signing exact English.* Rossmoor, CA: Modern Signs Press, 1980.

SIGN CREDITS

These signs were taken from Bornstein, H., Hamilton, L. B., Saulnier, K. L., and Roy, H. L. (Eds.). *The Signed English dictionary: For preschool and elementary levels.* Washington DC: Gallaudet College Press, 1975:

again	Daddy	Mommy	puzzle	tired
angry	down	not	right	turn
banana	eat	outside	slide	up
beside	finish	play	swing	water
camera	give	pretzel	table	who
come	go	puppet	take	whose
cookie	many	put	telephone	work
				yes

These signs were taken from Gustason, G., Pfetzing, D., and Zawalkow, E. *Signing exact English.* Rossmoor, CA: Modern Signs Press, 1980:

the alphabet	coat	here	milk	sign
numbers	cry	hi	mouth	sit
apple	cup	home	music	sock
area	do	horse	my	stand
art	dog	house	nose	stop
ask	doll	how	nut	talk
ball	dress	hug	off	tickle
block	drink	hurt	on	time
boat	drum	I	orange	touch
book	ear	in	pants	tree
box	eye	is	picture	under
bubble	find	it	potty	very
bus	game	juice	quicker	wait
candy	get	jump	raisin	walk
car	good	kiss	ride	want
cat	guitar	lap	run	what
cereal	hair	later	sad	where
chair	hand	laugh	say	yogurt
chase	happy	louder	school	you
cheese	hat	lunch	shirt	your
chip	help	me	shoe	

THE ALPHABET

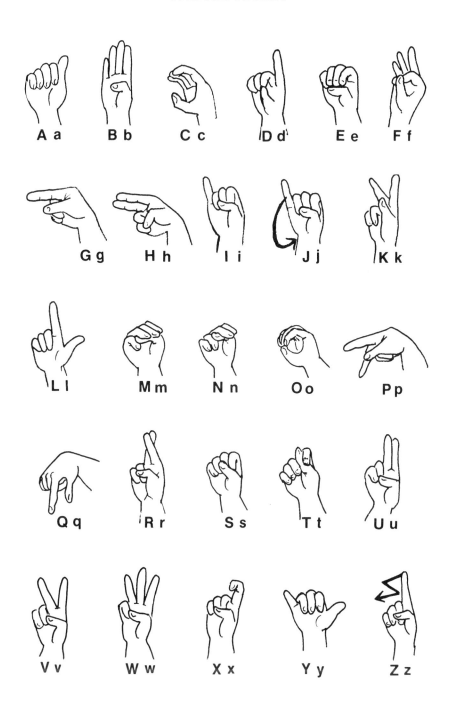

AGAIN
Open B left hand palm up, tips out. Bent B right hand palm up. Arc to left and place tips in left palm.

ANGRY
Claw shape both hands palms in, tips facing. Place on chest and draw up to shoulders in forceful manner.

APPLE
X twists against corner of mouth.

AREA
A-thumbs touch, circle in toward chest, touch again.

ART
I-fingertip draws wavy line on palm.

ASK
Palms of open hands come together and arc toward body.

BALL
Claw-hands form ball-shape.

BANANA
Hold left index finger up. Go through motions of peeling a banana with tips of right flat O.

BESIDE
B shape both hands tips out, left palm right, right palm left. Place right B on left then move off to right ending with palms opposite.

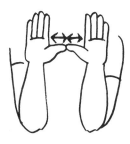

BLOCK
Thumb-tips, palms out, tap.

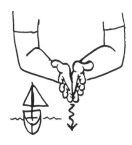

BOAT
Flat hands joined at little finger side, move forward in wavy up-and-down motion.

BOOK
Palm-to-palm hand open, palms up.

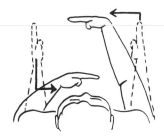

BOX
B-hands make a box.

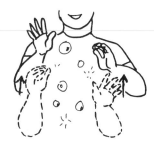

BUBBLE
O-hands rise, alternately opening several times with a flicking motion.

BUS
Left B, palm-right, in front of right B, palm-left; right moves back.

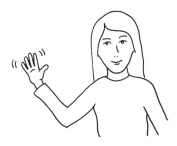

BYE-BYE*
Wave dominant hand.

CAMERA
Mime holding camera in front of face and clicking shutter.

CANDY
Index finger on cheek, twist hand.

CAR
Right C behind left C; right moves
backwards.

CAT
9-hand draws out whiskers; repeat.

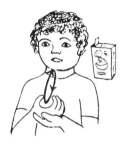

CEREAL
C-hand ladles up to mouth from
left hand.

CHAIR
2 fingers "sit" on thumb of left C.

CHASE
Right extended-A behind left extended A; both move forward and
left; right hand circles slightly.

CHEESE
Right heel on left heel mashes and
twists slightly.

CHIP
Right C arcs down and up, hitting side of left index with thumb.

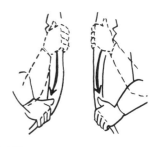

COAT
A-hand thumbs slide down lapels.

COME
One shape both hands knuckles up, tips out. Bring tips up and back toward chest.

COOKIE
Open B left hand palm up, tips out. C shape right hand palm down. Place tips of right C in left palm and twist as if cutting out cookies.

CRY
Drag index fingers alternately, move down cheeks, marking tear-tracks.

CUP
X is set on palm, as if holding a cup handle.

DADDY
Five shape right hand palm left, tips up. Tap forehead with thumb twice.

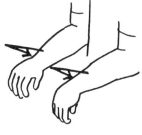

DO
Palm-down C-hands move side-to-side.

DOG
Fingers of D-hand snap several times (to call a dog).

DOLL
Right X-finger brushes off tip of nose.

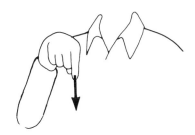

DOWN
Point index finger down.

DRESS
Thumbs of palm-in 5-hands brush down chest twice.

DRINK
Thumb on chin, drink from C.

DRUM
Both A-hands drum alternately.

EAR
Point to ear.

EAT
Place tips of right flat O on lips.
Repeat several times.

EYE
Point to eye.

FIND
F-hand pulls up past palm of left
hand.

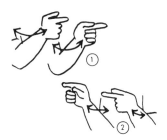

FINISH
Five shape both hands palms in.
Turn suddenly so that palms and
tips face out.

GAME
G-hands, one palm-out, one palm-
in, swing back and forth, pivoting
at wrists.

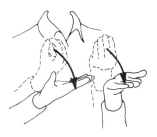

GET
Right open hand above left, draw
toward body, closing to S-hands.

GIVE
O shape both hands, palms up, left
a little ahead of right. Move out
opening fingers.

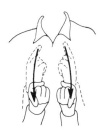

GO
One shape both hands knuckles in.
Point fingers out ending with
knuckles up.

GOOD
Palm-in fingers on chin drop to
palm of left hand.

GUITAR
Hold and strum on invisible guitar.

HAIR
Hold hair with 9-hand.

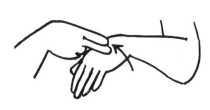

HAND
H-finger draws across back of left hand.

HAPPY
Open hand brushes middle of chest upward; repeat.

HAT
Pat head.

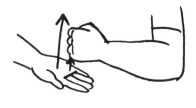

HELP
Palm lifts bottom of left S.

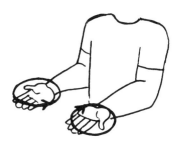

HERE
Palm-up hands circle horizontally in opposite directions.

HI
(**HELLO** in *Signing Exact English*)
Flat hand, fingertips at forehead, moves forwards slightly right.

HOME
Flat-O fingertips on chin then flat palm on cheek.

HORSE
Thumb on temple, flap H-fingers.

HOUSE
Flat palms outline roof and sides.

HOW
Backs of palm-down bent hands touching, roll hands from inward to outward.

HUG
Hug self with H's.

HURT
Palm-in index fingers jerk toward each other; repeat.

I
Palm-left I-hand touches chest.

IN
Fingertips of right flat-O enter left O.

IS
I on chin moves straight forward.

IT
Tip of I touches palm of left hand.

JUICE
Thumb-side of Y cuts down back of S.

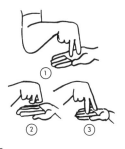

JUMP
V-fingertips on left palm, jump up with bent fingers and down again.

KISS
Fingertips of palm-in hand touch below lips and on cheek.

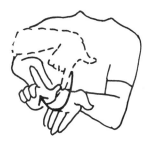

LAP
L arcs forward twice, knuckles hitting left palm; repeat.

LATER
(**LATE** in *Signing Exact English*)
Thumbtip of palm-out L on left palm, twist to palm down.

LAUGH
Index fingers of L's brush up and outward at corners of mouth several times.

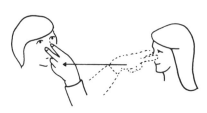

LOOK-AT-ME*
Move your dominant V hand from your student's eyes to your own eyes.

LOUDER
(**LOUD** in *Signing Exact English*)
Right index at ear opens to 5 and shakes down to right.

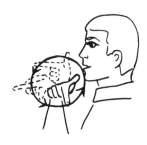

LUNCH
Thumb of L circles in and up near mouth.

MANY
O shape both hands tips up. Snap open quickly into five shapes palms up.

ME
Index points to and touches chest.

MILK
C to S-hand squeezes in a milking motion.

MOMMY
Five shape right hand palm left,
tips up. Tap chin with thumb
twice.

MOUTH
Index circles mouth once.

MUSIC
Fingertips pointing toward left
palm, flat hand arcs side-to-side
behind palm.

MY
Flat hand palm on chest.

NO*
S shape right hand. Move from
side to side in front of chest.

NOSE
Point to nose.

NOT
A shape right hand knuckles left, thumb extended. Place thumb under chin and move out.

NUT
Thumb flips out from under teeth.

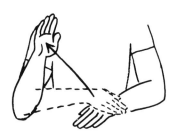

OFF
Right palm on back of left hand; lift off.

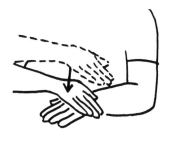

ON
Right palm touches back of left hand.

ORANGE
S squeezes in front of chin; repeat.

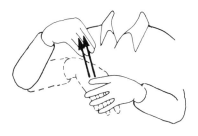

OUTSIDE
C shape left hand palm right. Place tips of right flat O in left C and draw out. Repeat.

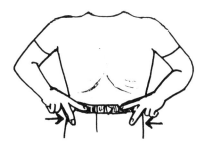

PANTS
P's tap at waist twice.

PAY-ATTENTION*
Move your parallel palms from the student's temples to your own temples.

P.E.*
Fingerspell the letters, P.E.

PICTURE
C moves from side of eye to palm of left hand.

PLAY
Y shape both hands palms in. Twist back and forth.

POPCORN*
Twist hand inward and out near chin.

POTTY (or TOILET)
(TOILET in *Signing Exact English*)
Palm-out T shakes.

PRETZEL
X shape both hands left palm in, right palm down. Hook X's together.

PUPPET
A shape both hands palms down. Move up and down alternately as if pulling strings.

PUT
Flat O shape both hands palms down. Move forward and down.

PUZZLE
A shape both hands thumbs down. Make motion of fitting together.

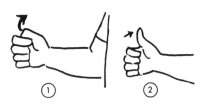

QUICKER
(QUICK in *Signing Exact English*)
Thumb inside right fist, snaps out.

RAISIN
R hops down back of S-hand.

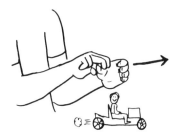

RIDE
First two fingers sit on thumb of horizontal palm-right C-hand; both move forward.

RIGHT (CORRECT)
One shape both hands, left palm right, right palm left, tips out. Place right hand on top of left hand.

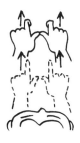

RUN
Palm-down L-thumbtips touch; hands move forward, index fingers flicking in and out rapidly.

SAD
Open hands pull down in front of face.

SAY
Index circles up and outward near mouth.

SCHOOL
Clap hands.

SHIRT
Palm-out S-hands on chest, arc inward, downward.

SHOE
S-hands bump together; repeat.

SIGN
Palm-out indexes circle alternately and vertically (sign language).

SIT
Right U sits 2 fingers on left palm-down U.

SLIDE
B shape right hand palm down held at shoulder. Bring down in sweeping movement (i.e., sliding board).

SOCK
S hits forward along side of palm-
down left index finger.

STAND
V-fingertips stand on left palm.

STOP
Side of right flat hand strikes left
flat palm.

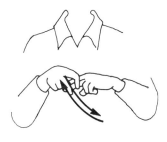

SWING
Hook right V over left H and
swing back and forth.

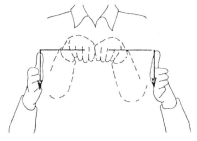

TABLE
Open B shape both hands palms
down, tips out, index fingers
touching. Draw apart and bring
down palms facing, thumbs up.

TAKE
Five shape right hand palm down,
fingers slightly curved. Draw up
quickly ending in fist.

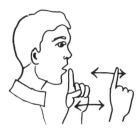

TALK
Index fingers move alternately to
and from lips.

TELEPHONE
Y shape right hand. Place thumb
on ear and little finger on mouth.

THIS*
Point to referent with index finger.

TICKLE
Bent index finger tickles near side.

TIME
X-index finger taps wrist.

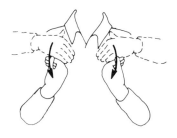

TIRED
Bent open B shapes both hands
palms in. Place tips just under
shoulders and let hands droop
slightly.

TOUCH
Middle finger of right hand touches back of left hand.

TREE
Elbow on back of left hand, shake 5.

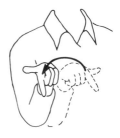

TURN
L shape right hand palm down. Turn so that palm faces up.

UNDER
Right A slides under left palm.

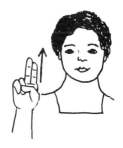

UP
Point index finger up.

VERY
Middle fingertips of V's touch and then arc apart.

WAIT
Palm-up right hand behind palm-up left, all fingers fluttering.

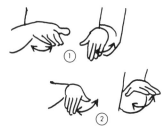

WALK
Wrists stationary, hands flip alternately.

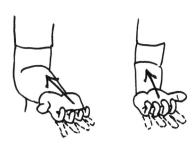

WANT
Palms-up 5's pull back to claws toward body.

WATER
Tap lips twice with index finger of right W.

WHAT
Index fingertip brushes down across left fingers.

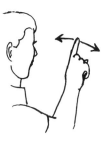

WHERE
Palm-out index shakes sideways.

WHO
Circle right index finger around mouth clockwise.

WHOSE
Circle right index finger around mouth and form right S.

WORK
S shape both hands palms down. Hit back of left S with right S.

YES
S shape right hand. Shake up and down.

YOGURT
Palm-up Y circles from left palm to mouth.

YOU
Index points at person addressed.

YOUR
Flat palm moves toward person
addressed.

One (1)   **Two** (2)

Three (3)   **Four** (4)   **Five** (5)

About the Authors

Photo by Danna Wilner

Benson Schaeffer is a Research Psychologist at the Neurological Sciences Center, Good Samaritan Hospital and Medical Center, Portland, Oregon, and an Associate Professor of Psychology in the Department of Psychology, University of Oregon, Eugene, Oregon. He received his doctorate in psychology from the University of California at Los Angeles in 1967 and has worked with handicapped children (autistic, mentally retarded, cerebral palsied, aphasic, and developmentally delayed) since 1963. During that time he has also served as an educational consultant to a wide variety of programs. The central focus of his clinical efforts and research is language instruction for the handicapped. Presently he is also studying the effects of a handicapped child on family structure, and is developing guidance procedures to deal with the family problems the handicapped child can sometimes create.

Arlene Musil is a teacher, writer, and consultant in the Beaverton Public Schools, Beaverton, Oregon. She received her master's degree in special education from the University of Oregon in 1975 and has had eight-and-a-half years of experience teaching severely to moderately language-handicapped children. The primary focus of her efforts is language instruction, with a strong secondary interest in the training and supervision of teachers, paraprofessionals, and parents.

George Kollinzas is a consultant, teacher, and writer in the Beaverton Public Schools, Beaverton, Oregon. He received his master's degree in special education from the University of Oregon in 1975 and has had eight-and-a-half years of experience teaching profoundly to severely handicapped children. The two focal points of his efforts are the training and supervision of teachers, paraprofessionals, and parents, and language instruction.